TWO-WHEEL

Manchester to Cape T

CW01662207

TWO-WHEEL TREK

Manchester to Cape Town – by bicycle

Neil Clough

ARROW

With thanks to my parents for the laborious hours spent in carefully typing the manscrupit and patient correction of speeling misstaks.

Arrow Books Limited
17-21 Conway Street, London W1P 5HL

An imprint of the Hutchinson Publishing Group

London Melbourne Sydney Auckland
Johannesburg and agencies throughout
the world

First published in Great Britain 1983

© Neil Clough 1983

This book is sold subject to the condition that it shall not, by way of trade or otherwise, be lent, resold, hired out, or otherwise circulated without the publisher's prior consent in any form of binding or cover other than that in which it is published and without a similar condition including this condition being imposed on the subsequent purchaser.

Set in Linotron Baskerville by
Book Economy Services, Crawley, Sussex

Made and printed in Great Britain
by The Anchor Press Ltd
Tiptree, Essex

ISBN 0 09 930820 7

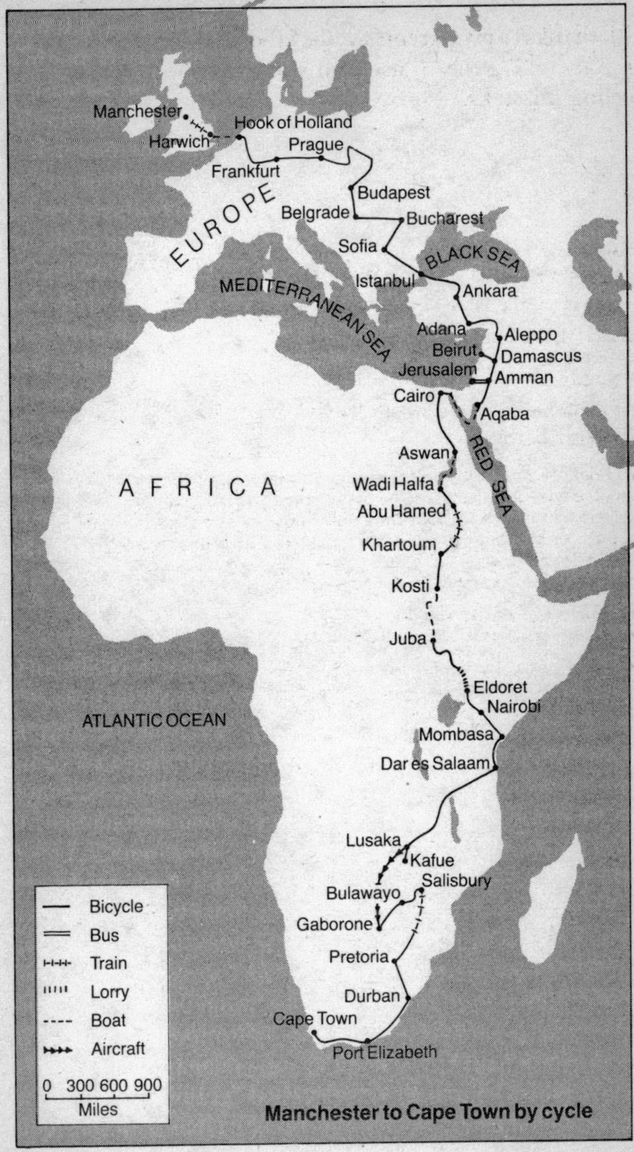

Manchester to Cape Town by cycle

1

I saw the first of the pack even before I had finished erecting the tent. A large mongrel loped across the hillside, moving silently, as if with purpose. Seconds later it had vanished over the crest of the hill, leaving me wondering whether, in the murky twilight, it had ever existed, or if it was merely the shadows of a Turkish evening playing tricks with my imagination. I soon knew! As I returned to my nightly task of attempting to push slender aluminium tent pegs into rock-hard ground, a distant barking echoed eerily around the barren slopes of the surrounding hills. As the barking faded into an anguished howl I straightened up and looked around. Straining my eyes into the gloom I thought I could make out an occasional low form some distance away, then it seemed to be rocks that I was looking at, and then again the shapes seemed to move as if they were coming closer, steadily but furtively.

There was no alternative place to go. Ankara was still some miles distant and here, on this barren moorland, if the wild dogs chose to attack I would have no other protection than the thin nylon walls of my lightweight tent and no other weapons than a sheath-knife and a bicycle pump. There would be no human help. The last people I had seen had been two soldiers who had been passing nearby as I was setting down the bike and unrolling the tent. They had approached waving excitedly, obviously trying to tell me not to camp there, before shrugging their shoulders and hurrying away in the direction of the main Istanbul-Ankara road, leaving me alone again in the gathering darkness. Now, as I prepared my evening meal of bread, apples, nuts and raisins, a chill feeling of isolation caused me to reflect how I had chosen to come alone, to set out on a bicycle to travel through Europe and the Middle East, on to the southern tip of the African Continent and the Cape of Good Hope. As night closed in around me, the mournful howls from the surrounding hills increased and, while I ate my food, I was aware of low shapes moving stealthily through the darkness, not coming close enough to be seen clearly, but present none the less. They seemed to be all around me and I moved into the tent in the forlorn hope that they would lose interest and go away. As I drifted into an uneasy sleep, I could sense that they were waiting for total darkness to give them complete control of the situation.

I had never really ridden a bicycle before. I'd fallen off one fairly often, usually because the longest bicycle journeys I made were evening trips down to the local pub in my Lancashire home town.

On the return leg of the journey I would often find that the road wasn't in quite the same place as it had been before or that my centre of gravity wasn't quite so easy to adjust to. On occasions I'd been known to wake up, some hours after leaving the pub, to find that I had been slumbering peacefully in the wet grass beside the roadside, the bicycle, having apparently had a softer landing, lying on top of me.

So it was that when, in early 1978, I announced my decision to cycle from England to the Cape of Good Hope, my friends sadly shook their heads and muttered, 'He'll never make it to South Africa' or 'He'll never get across the English Channel' or even 'He'll never get past the George and Dragon.'

Certainly the odds in favour of my successfully completing a ten thousand mile pedal to the Cape were not an attractive proposition, even to the most reckless gambler. Yet such expressions of mock-derision were not unfamiliar to me. I had heard similar cries five years earlier when, having recently left Teachers Training College and being due to spend the next forty years or more of my life teaching in a primary school, I had left England with Jeff, a former college acquaintance, to drive around Africa. We had left with high hopes, a battered old diesel-engined Land Rover, and the intention of driving until our limited supply of money ran out at which point we agreed that we would worry about what to do next. As we had sailed across the English Channel in the summer of 1973 we did not realize that instead of just several months and a few different countries, three years, sixty thousand miles of driving and fifty-one countries lay between ourselves and our next view of Dover's white cliffs. Nor was I aware that, before completing the journey in the Land Rover, I would be planning to cross Africa again, this time on a bicycle.

The idea first came to me in a deserted Watutsi village one evening in August 1975. Jeff and I had entered Burundi earlier that day in our Land Rover, and were sitting in the quietness of the African night beneath our Tilley lamp, fifty miles from the Burundi capital, Bujumbura. I suppose that a deserted African village almost on the shores of Lake Tanganyika and within a few miles of Ujiji, the Tanzanian village where Henry Norton Stanley had ventured to presume the identity of Dr Livingstone, was as unlikely a place as any to conceive the idea of travelling from England to the Cape of Good Hope by bicycle. I don't even know why the village was deserted. At any rate, beside the Land Rover, among the empty mud huts, I began to consider the idea.

It was an idea that, at the time, I soon put to one side. Heading northwards with a crossing of central Africa and then a drive up the West African coast to think about, Jeff and I had enough to occupy our time, and it was not until early 1978, eighteen months after we had driven our Land Rover back to the north of England and when I was once more firmly ensconced as a teacher, that I began to think about crossing Africa again, this time on only half the number of wheels. So, as in August 1978, I stood on a main street of Rotterdam on my first day of cycling on the Continent, inspecting a flat tyre and trying to recall in which direction I should turn the nuts to remove the wheel, I wondered if the idea was such a good one. The next day, the second of the journey, I again found myself with a puncture. 'Perhaps it's usual in cycling to have a puncture every day,' I thought to myself, and I must have turned visibly pale as I calculated the number of patches that I would be likely to need during the next twelve months. To watch the experienced bicycle owner repair a puncture is to witness a work of art as fingers dance nimbly around the wheel rim. But to a hamfisted non-cyclist such as myself the repairing of a punctured inner tube was, and still remains, a major surgical operation. When removing the tyre do you begin next to the valve or at the opposite side to it? Do you in fact remove the tyre or merely lever one side over the rim of the wheel? When your fingers become trapped between the edge of the tyre and the rim of the wheel do you painfully wrench them out or do you make an embarrassed call to a passer-by to extract you? Do you apply the patch to the tube when the glue is wet, dry or tacky? By how much should you inflate the inner-tube before returning it to the wheel? What have you done wrong when fingers, tyre-levers, and even a three-foot crow bar will not prise the last six inches of tyre back on to the wheel? And when, having replaced the wheel on the bike and being reduced to a near nervous breakdown, you finally inflate the tyre and it promptly goes down again, does it mean that you failed to patch the hole correctly, the cause of the puncture is still in the tyre, you trapped the inner-tube when wrenching the last bit of tyre on or that you had two holes not one in the inner tube in the first place?

In the five months between the final decision to set out on two wheels to the Cape of Good Hope and actually setting off I had devoted as much time as possible to attempting to learn at least a little about the workings of a bicycle. First I had to be sure that it was physically possible for someone who had never previously ridden a bicycle further than his local, and of no more (probably considerably less) than average physical fitness, to disappear at one end of the journey and hope to emerge still reasonably sane ten thousand miles further on. It was concerning this point that I had my first piece of luck. I didn't know any cyclist whose advice I could ask, so I visited a bicycle shop in Preston and asked for the address of a local cycling club and the name of its secretary. I had a number to choose from, and opted for a Derek Hughes of Preston Cycling Touring Club. My letter to him was not easy to write (how do you explain to someone that you have never ridden a bicycle very far before but that now you would like to cycle to Capetown?), but back came an uncompromising reply saying that you can cycle to the moon if you set your mind to it and that, if I was determined to go ahead, I had better cycle round to his house so that we could discuss the matter in more detail.

Cycling to Derek's house hadn't been quite what I'd had in mind. My bicycle was in the garden shed and hadn't seen service since before my days driving the Land Rover in Africa. It was about as fit for pedalling as a combine harvester. 'It's twenty miles,' I objected over the telephone.

'How far is Capetown?'

'But it might be raining.'

'It might be raining in Capetown!'

'But I've never cycled so far.'

'Then it's time you did!'

Twenty miles there and twenty miles back again all in the same night seemed to me to be a qualification for the Guinness Book of Records. It was 0·004 of the distance to Capetown and I argued with myself that I ought to be saving energy not expending it unnecessarily, reasoning that if the process was too painful I would only be causing myself discouragement. But I knew that I had to start sometime. The sooner I rid myself of the initial aches and pains the better, I decided, not realizing that it would be eight months before the initial aches and pains would even begin to dispel. So, saddle-sore and weary, I arrived at the house of Derek Hughes on a freezing March night in 1978.

'Sit down,' said Derek.

'No thanks. I think I'll stand,' I replied, and so we began to build, piece by piece, the bicycle on which I was to cycle to the Cape of Good Hope.

Derek didn't really know what he was letting himself in for when he took on the job of coaching me in the art of bicycle maintenance. Teaching me anything mechanical is like trying to teach a sheep to produce piglets.

August 1978. Belgium. Three days out from England. Miles cycled, one hundred and thirty. Miles yet to cycle, nine thousand eight hundred and seventy approximately. Strange, unbicycle-like sounds were occurring with each revolution of the wheel. I had listened carefully to ensure that the grinding noises were coming from the bicycle and not from my legs. Satisfied that the noise was emanating from the gear block on the rear wheel I proceeded to unearth my tool kit from one of the loaded panniers and attempted to dismantle the block. By my standards I was coping with considerable efficiency, much to the delight of a small group of Belgian passers-by who had accumulated to observe this roadside spectacle. Only one lock-nut stood between me and a successful dismantling of the gear assembly in the way that Derek had shown me so many times over back in Preston. The lock-nut, however, refused to budge as I attempted to unscrew it, despite persistent tapping with my hammer on a centre-punch.

The Belgian onlookers whispered unintelligible phrases to one another as the beats of the hammer increased, but still the lock-nut refused to unscrew. My lack of skill with mechanical objects is surpassed only by my lack of patience when they refuse to do as they should and I was soon muttering curses and delivering frenzied blows with what was fortunately only a very small hammer, but still the lock-nut refused to unscrew. 'You are trying to turn it the wrong way,' observed a helpful Belgian onlooker, in more perfect Queen's English than I could have spoken myself. 'Which way should I be turning it?' I asked helplessly. 'The opposite way to that which you are trying to do,' replied the helpful one. A change of tactic revealed that the self-appointed adviser was indeed correct. I had been trying to unscrew a left-hand thread by turning it anti-clockwise. 'How far are you hoping to cycle?' asked the smirking Belgian, as he watched me clumsily reassemble the block after finding that the mysterious noises had been caused not by a fault in the freewheel device but simply by mud trapped between the mudguard and the rear wheel. 'South Africa,' I answered without much conviction. 'You are crazy! You are mad!' he informed me, and I mounted the heavily loaded bicycle and wobbled away, wondering if he was right again.

Like any sportsmen who take their pastime seriously, cyclists see themselves as missionaries sent down into the World from that great bicycle-shed in the sky to convert the pagan to their cause. Rumour that someone (a heathen non-cyclist in fact) intended to cycle to the bottom of Africa spread rapidly through Preston and cyclists were soon slotting like spokes in a hub into Derek Hughes' tiny kitchen. Heated discussions took place between the experts as to the types of equipment that should be used to build up my bicycle. Tempers frayed and fingers wagged and if I tried to interrupt and express an opinion I would receive looks that implied that I was merely the driver in the enterprise and that I should leave the thinking to the backroom boys. Terms that I had never heard before rolled fluently from tongues; should the bike frame have Nervex lugs and Campag. ends, should the cranks be cottered and the spokes double-butted, should the brakes be cantilever or calliper, and what should be the derailleur capacity? They may as well have been talking in Portuguese for all the understanding I had of the phrases. I began to realize that there is more to a bicycle than a frame, two wheels and two pedals and when the debates became too technical or too heated I would switch my mind to the numerous other details. Many of my plans for the route that I hoped to cover on the bicycle took shape while my cycling advisers were engaged in fierce discussion. My intention was not only to reach the Cape of Good Hope but also to see as much as possible on the way. I decided against cycling from my home in Manchester to the Channel Ferry embarkation point at Harwich. To do that might involve embarrassing incidents such as developing trouble in the bottom bracket or headset around Leicester. Imagined conversations with interested spectators – 'How far are you going? Birmingham?' 'No, just to Capetown.' – persuaded me that the best policy would be to take the train to Harwich. Once on the Continent it would at least seem that I had made some progress, even if I hadn't.

I had considered cycling along the Baltic Coast of East Germany and Poland into Russia but both the German Democratic Republic and the Soviet Union made the extent of their welcome for me clear with the statement that 'we have no facilities for cyclists in our country'. That was unfortunate because it meant that instead of cycling a relatively flat first thousand miles, I would be broken in the hard way on the slopes of the Ardennes in southern Belgium.

Poland being the only one of the Eastern European

Communist Bloc countries that I had not visited during the earlier expedition, I decided on a diversion northwards from Czechoslovakia into southern Poland (more mountains), back to Czechoslovakia (again more mountains) and through Hungary into Rumania (still more mountains – the Carpathians each time). It didn't look too far in the atlas and, from a comfortable fireside armchair I calculated that by the time I had continued through Yugoslavia and Bulgaria into Turkey, I should be well and truly cycling fit. In fact, when I finally reached Istanbul I was too exhausted to know whether I was cycling fit or not! But it never looks so bad in the atlas and from my armchair mountains were crossed with the stroke of a pen as my imagination led me across Syria and into Lebanon. The higher I go the more downhill there will be I cheerfully decided.

Trying to obtain information on sailing from Lebanon to Egypt was a classic case of banging one's head on the proverbial brick wall. I must have contacted every single company that does not run ships between these two countries. It seemed that, for all the chance I had of crossing with my bicycle from the Middle East to Egypt for a price that I could afford, I may as well have stood with bike pump in hand on the shores of the Red Sea and commanded the waters to part while I pedalled across. It became evident that the only place that I would obtain positive information on a passage from Lebanon to Africa was in Beirut. So I eventually set on one side the matter of crossing from the Middle East to Egypt, feeling that it would turn out all right.

I had considered the possibility of sailing up the River Nile through Egypt and Sudan to Uganda, feeling that if such a thing was possible, it would be rather a pleasant break from cycling. If I found it to be impossible I was sure I would be able to find some means of transporting myself and the bicycle across the one and a half thousand miles of sand and dirt track in Sudan, despite the fact that the first two hundred and twenty miles in the north of the country is the empty waste of the Nubian Desert and contacts in Khartoum had gloatingly assured me, 'You will never cross that with a bicycle!' Running my finger southwards across the map of Africa I found that if I blinked slowly at the right moment, by the time my eyes opened and refocused, my finger had magically reappeared across the desert and was well on the way towards Kenya. 'Once I've crossed the Sudan,' I consoled myself, 'I'll only have another four thousand miles to pedal.' I was reasonably happy that a few days in Nairobi would rehabilitate me enough to cycle the two thousand five hundred miles through Tanzania and Zambia to Rhodesia where I had arranged to spend four months working, between May and August of 1979, in order to earn the return air fare home (somehow I had the impression that having cycled so far I would have little desire to pedal back to England), before continuing my bicycle journey into South Africa and on to the Cape itself.

As I sailed across the Channel to the Hook of Holland in August 1978 I knew that many of the cyclists in Preston had done all that they could to encourage me, many of the embassies of the countries that I hoped to visit had done all that they could to discourage me, and that now I was on my own. Construction of the bicycle had taken longer than planned, due partly to my hamfisted attempt to fit the front gear changer during which I sheared off the fixing bolt. A new bolt had to be specially ordered and the building process was finally completed in Derek Hughes' kitchen on the night before I was due to leave. The weeks of cycling practice that I had planned in order to build up my leg muscles before setting out on the journey were never fitted in, last minute packing had to be done in such a rush that I almost missed the train to Harwich. But, after five months of preparation the journey was under way, the bicycle sagging beneath the weight of bags loaded with all manner of equipment from tent and sleeping bag to fruit cakes from misguided but well-meaning aunties. The bicycle looked a far cry from the condition in which it would be six months hence. The frame was newly painted in green and white, the colours of the Rhodesian flag – the result of a rash claim in the pub one night that I would not only cycle through Africa but would do so on a bicycle painted in the colours of the flag of what was then Africa's number 1 enemy.

As I cycled for my first time on to foreign soil, still half hoping that I might wake up and find that it was all a dream, I experienced the familiar feeling inside which I had known when setting out by Land Rover five years earlier: the knowledge that each day now would bring problems or pleasures that could never have been foreseen. Whatever happened, though, one thing was certain: I could never allow myself to return to England without having first reached the Cape of Good Hope.

2

'The prevailing wind blowing across Europe is a westerly,' I remembered teaching to classes of children only a few weeks before, when I had anticipated days of carefree cycling all the way to Turkey with a breeze at my back. As I struggled across the plains of Holland and Belgium into a fierce headwind, I made mental apologies to my former pupils for misinforming them. I soon learned the first law of cycling: the direction from which the wind is blowing is *always* opposite to the direction in which one is cycling.

Belgium, according to the books that I had read, is completely flat. There seemed to have been some volcanic activity since the books were published. As I crossed into Luxembourg the wind dropped and the hills rose. It was to become a familiar pattern: cycling in mountains and longing for an expanse of flat road but, as soon as the hills gave way to plains, inevitably finding a wind howling across the flat surface into my face. Riding a bicycle laden with equipment was now a completely different proposition to the spin down to the local pub on a fine summer's evening. As my leg muscles strained to the unfamiliar task of pedalling the loaded bicycle up the slopes of the Ardennes, I contemplated the advice of friends before I left England. 'When you are cycling up hills, keep your brakes on. That prevents you from rolling back down!' had been one helpful suggestion. 'Turn the saddle of the bicycle round so that you are looking over the back of the bike,' was another. 'You'll think that you are going downhill then!' But, as I crossed first the Ardennes and, later, the Carpathians of Eastern Europe and the Taurus Mountains of Turkey, I learned that there was no easy way. The only method of crossing any mountain range on a bicycle loaded with tent, sleeping bag, clothes, food and water, tools and spare parts was to select one of the lowest of the bicycle's ten gears, put my head down, and keep pedalling for as long as necessary. So low was the range of gears, so steep some of the escarpments, and consequently so slow was progress up such hills, that locals would often walk up a slope alongside me as I rode. While sweat streamed from me, they chatted to me, curious as to why I had chosen a bicycle in preference to a more conventional form of transport. On such occasions, I also wondered!

German Federal Republic. Six days out from England. Miles cycled two hundred and seventy-five. Miles yet to cycle nine thousand seven hundred and twenty-five approximately. Calling upon my recently acquired bicycle maintenance prowess I attempted to adjust the front brakes. I should have known better and left well alone. After more than two hours tightening nuts and slackening bolts, I found that I had achieved a situation where the front brake, instead of functioning badly, no longer functioned at all. I fumed at myself, I cursed at the spanners, and I shouted at the bicycle. I pushed it over on to the ground, stood it up, then pushed it over again. I tried that tactic several times accompanied by a stream of insults directed at the bike, but still the front brake would not work. I stopped, wiped my oily hands on my shorts, and laughed. Before I left England a doctor had jokingly advised me that I should not worry if I discovered that I was talking to myself, nor should I really be concerned if I found that I was talking to the bicycle. It was if I heard the bicycle talking to me that I should start to worry! I had to laugh as I recalled the advice. Most people talk to themselves but I had already passed the first and moved on to the second of the doctor's three stages, and I still hadn't been out of England a week!

The Autobahns of West Germany are a great asset to cyclists. Comparatively straight and flat they enable the cyclist to put his head down, ignore everything and keep turning his legs. The miles passed as I pedalled rhythmically. Somewhere outside my dreamlike state I was vaguely aware of blaring car horns as Opels, B.M.W.'s and Mercedes swept past me at up to ten times the speed at which I was laboriously pedalling. It was only when I sat resting at a service station, however, that I became aware of the strange side-glances shot at me from numerous directions and the noticeable lack of other cyclists. I began to realize that, like the British motorways, when Autobahns are constructed they are not done so with cyclists as a prime consideration. Returning to the Autobahn I cycled along awaiting the inevitable, which eventually came when I was stopped by a police car and escorted back to the world of hills and bends which awaits those using more mundane forms of transport.

'The road ahead is quite flat. There are no hills,' I was constantly assured in rich Bavarian tones as I made my way towards the border with Czechoslovakia. 'I know; I have made the journey myself, many times, by motor car.' And, as I sweated up each hill, to see, from the top, another hill ahead, then another, and another, I felt relieved that the road had been described as flat. I would have hated to have had to have cycled along one defined as hilly!

By the time I reached the Czech border I had covered nearly six hundred miles in ten days and felt satisfied with my progress. I was feeling reasonably fit which quite surprised me. I had expected a lot of stiffness and saddle-soreness during the first thousand miles, but was experiencing very little discomfort. True, I seemed to have discovered the remedy for those sleepless nights that I had spent shortly before leaving England, when I had lain awake for countless hours mentally checking every detail of preparation for the journey. An average of sixty miles pedalling a heavy bicycle each day ensured that dropping off to sleep now presented no problem. The only difficulty was in getting up each morning, which was when it was noticeable that the legs were not particularly anxious to respond. Otherwise, my confidence was growing with each mile covered, though it was unfortunate that, in my enthusiastic desire to cycle as far as possible each day, I did not stop for a moment to consider that it was exactly as the cycling experts had warned me: having never cycled seriously before, if I tried to ride all day every day at first, the effects would eventually catch up with me. It was like a novice runner setting out to run a marathon at a fast sprint and feeling confident after the first mile that he is going to complete the distance in record time.

I felt rather out of place waiting to cross the border into Czechoslovakia sitting astride a bicycle in the midst of a queue of cars. The Customs and Immigration Officials looked at me in a rather odd sort of way as if unsure what a Capitalist was doing without an engine in front of him, but waved me through the barriers. I cycled into the shadow of the watch-towers and between two rows of high, barbed-wire-topped mesh fencing which gives the impression that emigration from Czechoslovakia is not encouraged. To people of the West who carry a passport as a right, it seems strange to think of the ordinary people of the six East European 'Satellite' states who may travel only within those six states except with special permission. As one Czech citizen had sarcastically remarked to me on my previous visit to his country, 'We can travel anywhere in the world, as long as we do not leave the Socialist Bloc!'

The Communist Bloc of Eastern Europe holds, for many people, visions of subversion, oppression, espionage, terrorism, and political intrigue; but those who consider it necessary to cycle through such countries with gun in one hand and bicycle pump in the other have a mistaken impression. Having visited all of these countries of Eastern Europe, none of these states would appeal to me to live in. Both the people and the towns seem to compete with each other for drabness and lack of life. Yet, while the people could not be termed friendly, neither are they unfriendly. They simply prefer to pretend that the tourist from the West is not really there at all and just ignore him. It satisfied me, however, that I could leave the bicycle for hours unattended and unlocked, in a town centre, and return to find it untouched. I would not be willing to risk that in Western Europe!

It was with great physical and mental effort that I pitched my tent on my first night in Czechoslovakia. Physical because, for the first time since I began the journey, every muscle ached and every joint felt like a rusty door hinge. Mental, because it was tempting to just lie down by the roadside and go to sleep. I calculated my distance from Prague to be fifty-three miles and I was determined to be there as early as possible the following day in order to visit the Passport Office to obtain the visa which I would require in order to re-enter Czechoslovakia after I had visited Poland.

The following morning I awoke with the feeling that someone had entered the tent during the night and stolen my legs. I lifted my head and felt reassured to see the bulge of my feet at the bottom of my sleeping bag since the feeling from my legs indicated that they had dissolved. I shakily arose and loaded the bicycle, then made my way back to the road. Once I began cycling my legs quickly returned to normal and I decided to prove to myself that the shakiness had been merely a passing phase by setting a cracking pace to Prague. It was a cool, cloudy morning, ideal for cycling, and with the wind, for once, negligible. Little more than four hours later, well before midday, I was in the centre of Prague. The shakiness had passed.

The Czech capital which, with its rich architectural

heritage is one of the finest cities in Europe, lies at the heart of the Continent. Like most cities of the world, it seems, it is claimed that Prague is built on seven hills, though there appear to be considerably more when one visits the city on a bicycle.

At the Passport Office in Prague I was informed that it was not possible for them to issue a Czech tourist visa to me in Czechoslovakia. I could obtain a Czech visa in Poland if I cared to cycle the thousand miles to Warsaw and back, 'In fact you may obtain a tourist visa for Czechoslovakia in almost any country of the world,' I was proudly told by the official. 'Then I can have a tourist visa?' I asked. 'You may obtain a tourist visa for Czechoslovakia in almost any country of the world except Czechoslovakia,' the official corrected himself, and I felt that something didn't quite make sense. Though I was prepared to divert northwards and spend a few extra days cycling in order to visit Poland, I had no intention of travelling almost five hundred extra miles to Warsaw just to obtain a visa to re-enter Czechoslovakia. However, the official then informed me that though he could not issue me with a tourist visa which would cover a stay of several days in Czechoslovakia, I would be able to obtain a twenty-four hour transit visa at the border between Poland and Czechoslovakia when I came to re-enter the country. I was far from convinced that once I re-entered Czechoslovakia from Poland I would be able to cover the ninety miles to the Hungarian border in one day, but I worked on the principle that I would worry about that once I had been readmitted to Czechoslovakia. Satisfied on this point I left Prague and headed north towards Poland. By the time I pitched camp that evening the shakes had returned to my legs and I crawled into my sleeping bag wondering if a bicycle ride to the southern tip of Africa was not sufficient without engaging in unnecessary diversions northwards.

The summer of 1978, throughout Europe, was notable

as being the worst summer since 1977. The morning of the day after my visit to Prague I awoke to the sound of rain beating on the tent. I felt awful. My legs felt like unset jellies and the rest of my body did not feel too healthy either. I peered at my watch, desperately hoping that it would tell me that it was only about 5 am and that I could go back to sleep. It was 9 am I had slept for more than twelve hours and felt that I could comfortably sleep for twelve more. The scene through the tent doorway was not encouraging with mist hanging over the pine trees and a cold wind blowing. Nevertheless I was encouraged by the fact that on the previous day, despite the delay in Prague, I had cycled my highest mileage to date, eighty-three miles. I reluctantly determined to cover at least seventy more miles that day.

As the days passed, cycling seemed to require ever-increasing effort and the weather deteriorated constantly, but I made my first crossing of the Carpathian Mountains into Poland. On the relief map that I studied before leaving England I had found that, by pressing my thumb on to the plastic lumps marked 'Carpathians', I was able to flatten out the mountains to insignificant little mounds. Though it made me feel happier when planning the journey, it was of no help when I reached the mountain range that forms the eastward continuation of the Alps.

At the Polish frontier the Immigration Officer copied down details from my passport and then, under 'method of transport', wrote 'Rower'. Since he spoke English as fluently as I speak Polish we had some difficulty in communication, but eventually I was able to grasp that 'Rower', pronounced 'Rov-air', is Polish for bicycle, and, having for some time been looking for a suitable name for the bike decided that 'Rover' seemed appropriate. So the bicycle became 'Rover', though that was only one of many names that I called it during the journey.

In Poland the weather grew even worse. Wearing both the shirts that I carried, woollen pullover, nylon anorak, shorts and shoes, and with one of my two pairs of socks on my hands in an attempt to give my fingers enough warmth to grip the handlebars, I alternately poured with sweat as I cycled up steep slopes then shivered uncontrollably as I rode down the other side. As darkness fell each night, I would set up the saturated tent which it was impossible to dry and crawl, cold and tired, into my sleeping bag which seemed to be the only place that offered any warmth. Within minutes I would be asleep, and stay that way for up to fifteen hours.

My diversion into Poland took me to Wroclaw but as I turned south-east towards Krakow, even the fact that I was now cycling across flat land did little to ease my aches and pains. I still had not realized that I would not rid myself of tiredness by cycling harder, and I pushed myself more, determined to 'cycle off' all feelings of exhaustion. I pedalled the one hundred and fifty miles to Krakow in a day and a half, furious at the feeling of weakness in my legs. At a camp site on the outskirts of the city I erected a wet tent and climbed, shivering, into my sleeping bag.

September 1978. Krakow, Poland. Three weeks out from England. Miles cycled, one thousand two hundred. Miles yet to cycle, eight thousand eight hundred approximately. It is not an encouraging sign when one is trying to ride a bicycle to South Africa but is unable to lift one's legs over the crossbar. That was the position in which I now found myself as I forced myself from my sleeping bag at midday on my first day in Krakow. Cycling all day, every day had eventually caught up with me, as it had been sure to do. For the next four days I stayed at the camp site, leaving the bicycle by the tent during the day and walking like an old man around the city which few people outside Poland had even heard of until, four weeks later, Cardinal Karol Wojtyla, Archbishop of Krakow, became Pope John Paul II.

Despite the complete break from cycling my legs refused to strengthen beyond the resilience of a partially set jelly and each day it seemed that I would not have the energy to cycle down a hill let alone up one. On the fifth day I decided that I could not remain in Krakow indefinitely and that I would be better cycling even just ten miles a day rather than none at all. With the incentive of the unpleasant alternative of a large bill for camping fees if I left the site through the main gate, I was able to pass the first test of my recovery by summoning the strength to lift the bicycle over the fence at the rear of the camp site from where I pedalled slowly away, back towards Czechoslovakia.

During the course of the next few days my legs gradually regained their strength. I was more careful now to use the low gears when climbing hills or pedalling against the wind, contrary to my previous policy of simply pressing harder on the pedals when the going became more difficult.

The weather as I climbed the slopes of the Carpathians for the second time was no kinder than it had been for most of my stay in the country and soon my tent, sleeping bag and all my clothes were damp and clammy. When I re-entered Czechoslovakia and signed a travellers' cheque in order to cash it, my hand was so cold that my signature bore not the slightest resemblance to the original one. The bank clerk, quite understandably, refused to accept the signature as genuine, and indicated that I should sign it again on the back. I did so, with a signature that looked even less like the original than the previous one. Fortunately, stationed at this outpost in the Carpathians, the clerk must have had certain sympathies with my condition, and accepted the cheque.

The twenty-four hours allowed by my transit visa was sufficient to see me through Czechoslovakia and into Hungary. As I moved south, the weather improved, the days becoming warmer and drier, and though the nights were cool I was now able to put on dry clothes again.

The flat plains of Hungary were a welcome relief from the mountains and my cycling fitness increased each day.

I was still careful to take regular roadside breaks but at night my sleep was more natural now, ten hours of deep, restful sleep from which I would wake feeling refreshed and ready to continue cycling. My back ached less now from bending over the handlebars each day and though, when I walked, my legs seemed as though they preferred to move in a circular motion, muscles had developed. Saddle-soreness, one of my greatest worries before leaving England, was now less of a problem too, though I still had to take care how I sat down on the roadside or I would find that I would arise with great alacrity.

It was interesting to cycle along roads which I had previously driven along in the Land Rover. Camping beside a small river in Hungary brought back memories when I realized that it was the River Tisza, the tributary of the Danube which, for part of its course, marks the boundary between Rumania and the Soviet Union and which I had last stood beside five years earlier near the Rumanian village of Sighetu Marmatiei and across which I had swum to pay a visit to Russia. It had been on a Sunday that we had driven past the tall wooden look-out tower at the entrance to Sighetu Marmatiei. As in all Rumanian villages on a Sunday, the people were out in the streets in either their best clothes or in national dress and, having nothing much on in the way of entertainment, they were wandering around the streets with their friends or just sitting and talking. Wanting a close look at Russia, we drove out of the village, past another of the watch-towers manned by its guards with their high-powered binoculars, and stopped again outside the village, obscured by trees from the watchers in their tower. After a walk of about a mile through fields of tall maize we came across a broken-down barbed-wire fence and, just behind it, the deep, fast-flowing river, and we were able to take our photographs of the Soviet Union. It irritated me, however, that there should be laws denying people a right to cross from one country into another and I decided that it was time to go swimming. Knowing that the penalty could be severe if I was caught crossing the frontier by people who would not look upon such an act as a mere bit of fun, I checked that we were out of sight of the watch-towers, the tops of which were fortunately shrouded in mist, and stripped off and plunged into the river. No Olympic standard swimmer, I was soon in trouble in the current and was seeing visions of being washed ashore in Sighetu Marmatiei, when I found myself in an eddy and a moment later had my wish of standing in the Soviet Union. Not only was I without a visa, I was also without clothes! From there I had to return to Rumania and, after another battle with the river, I surfaced some way down stream from where Jeff was standing. It was as I made my way back towards him up the river bank that I froze. I realized that the low mist had cleared and we were in the uninterrupted view of one of the watch-towers. We could have given Roger Bannister a head start on the mile run back to the Land Rover and still have beaten him comfortably.

From Hungary I cycled into Rumania to make my third and final crossing of the Carpathians, meeting again with some of the most friendly of Europe's inhabitants, and then into Yugoslavia where, after sampling the rocky dirt roads that in places are the only alternative to the Autobahn, I decided to try my luck again on the smooth tarmac of the main highway to Bulgaria. I managed a good mileage before a short, red-faced Yugoslav police officer leapt almost suicidally into the road in front of me. With no front brake it took the force of both feet on the road to bring me skidding to a stop inches before him, whereupon I made innocent noises to suggest that I had no idea why he had stopped me. The more surprised I looked, the more enraged he became, placing his by now crimson face a full six inches from mine and bellowing Slavonic phrases at me. When he unbuttoned his holster and waved his gun at me I decided that the issue was not really worth being shot over and beat a hasty retreat to the dirt tracks.

September 1978. Sofia, Bulgaria. Six weeks out from England. Miles cycled, two thousand. Miles yet to cycle, eight thousand approximately. I had tried to adjust the position of the saddle to give a more comfortable ride but, as usual with my adjustments, at some point I had unscrewed the wrong nut. Pieces of saddle and saddle bracket fell everywhere. After two hours of trying to replace all the pieces in the right places I gave up, gave the bicycle another kick, refitted the parts that were willing to be refitted and dropped the remainder into a pannier. I never did find out where those pieces were meant to fit but, for the remainder of the journey, the saddle was liable to make peculiar noises and twist unexpectedly into odd positions.

The chaste female has to be rather careful in Bulgaria since the firm shake of the head which may mean disappointment to a persuasive male, could present her with unexpected problems. In Bulgaria a nod of the head means 'no'; shaking the head means 'yes'. It takes a while to adjust to. My torch battery had become flat and I needed a new one of a certain type. I joined the inevitable queue in the inevitably sparsely stocked shops of Sofia looking for the correct kind of battery. Eventually, at one shop, the assistant nodded her head vigorously and I waited for her to fetch the battery. She went on to serve the next customer. I asked again, and again she nodded, so I continued to wait patiently. After a while I tried once more, receiving a nodding head accompanied by a stony glare from which I realized that I was not going to obtain the battery at that shop. Some days later on the road between Sofia and Istanbul I was looking for a place to pitch my tent one evening. An old shepherd approached me and, after contorting himself into various positions in efforts to show his humility while at the same time shaking my hand with the enthusiasm of the prodigal son's father welcoming his returning offspring, he led me to a tiny hut which contained a bed and, by pointing and miming, asked if I would like to sleep there. The prospect of a change from erecting the tent and from sleeping on the ground appealed and I nodded my head in agreement to his invitation. The old man's face fell and I quickly altered my action to shaking my head, whereupon his broad smile reappeared. Later, when he returned and offered me some fruit, I had to think carefully before moving my head correctly. It seems so unnatural to shake for 'yes' and nod for 'no' that I am surprised the Bulgarians remember to do it that way! I was never sure whether the Bulgarians were unaware that other cultures do the opposite to them and so expected me to do the same as them, or whether they realized that their head signals were different and so made allowances and assumed that a foreigner would follow his own traditional method and do the opposite to what they did. Eventually I settled on a kind of non-committal, diagonal motion of my head which could be interpreted either way.

By the time I reached Turkey my daily mileage had risen into the seventies and eighties. I had settled into a routine of packing equipment in the mornings, preparing meals, shopping for supplies, and the other time-consuming chores which, each day, severely reduced the amount of time available for cycling. I entered Turkey with the bicycle laden with several dozen large apples from Bulgarian orchards, having decided that in a Peoples' State they must be Peoples' Apples, and so helped myself. For the next few days apples seemed to be everywhere, in the panniers, in the tent, in my sleeping bag, but it was pleasant to ride steadily along in the warm sunshine eating some of the most delicious apples I have ever tasted.

In the last days of September, as I neared Istanbul, I noticed that the fields across which I had been looking as I rode, ended in a blue line and I felt a surge of triumph as I realized that I was looking at the Mediterranean Sea. In terms of adjusting to cycling, the most difficult section of the journey was behind me and even if I had known that, in every other sense, what I had come through was a holiday compared to what was to come, I could not have cared as, the following day, I rode into Istanbul. At last I felt that I was getting somewhere.

3

Before leaving England, my plan to cycle through Turkey had met with cries of dismay from all kinds of interested parties. Gripping stories were related to me with spine-chilling intensity, of travellers through Turkey who had been robbed of everything they possessed. One unlucky victim had apparently been attacked by bandits and relieved of all his possessions including his clothes. His assailants had left him by the roadside wearing only his underpants, and the story went that he considered himself fortunate to have been left even with those.

'The inhabitants of the mountains are the worst,' I was told. 'They stretch a rope across the road, then hide behind the rocks. When the rope forces you to stop, they jump out on you. They do that if you're in a car. On a bicycle . . . !' Grotesque shudders left me with visions of myself cycling between a network of ropes that had been interwoven across the road while swarthy Turks, daggers between their teeth, leered at me in anticipation from the cover of nearby boulders. So many stories were told to me, and so detailed were the descriptions, that I became convinced that at some point in Turkey I was sure to have the bicycle and all my equipment stolen. I had even thought, at one stage of the planning, of filling the frame of the bicycle with petrol and keeping a box of matches convenient in the saddlebag, so that if anyone tried to forcibly take the bike away from me I could at least have the satisfaction of destroying it. Thoughts of riding beneath a hot sun on a home-made petrol bomb, however, soon discouraged that idea, and I eventually had to accept the risk of a robbery in the mountains of Turkey as an occupational hazard.

While I could do little to prevent robbery by a hostile group, I realized from my previous experience in Africa, that the main threat to one's possessions is liable to come from the snatch-thief. Since leaving the Communist Bloc and entering Turkey I knew that, for the remainder of the journey, throughout the Middle East and Africa, I could never afford to take my eyes from the bicycle for a moment without first carefully considering the chances of theft. The panniers and bags on the bicycle were secured to the carriers only by straps which could easily be cut with a knife so, from the streets of Istanbul, I collected pieces of wire which I used to fasten the bags securely to the carriers which were bolted to the bicycle frame. With the small mole wrench that I carried in my tool bag I could easily break the wire if I needed to remove the bags but with bare hands it would be almost impossible for a prospective thief to separate them from the bicycle. As a further precaution I carried an eight-foot-long piece of thick wire cable, looped at each end, which, whenever I left the bicycle unattended, I wrapped around the frame, wheels, bags, and an immovable object, before padlocking together the two ends. The initiative of supposedly simple people should never be underestimated and a careful check made on the object to which the bike is secured, or it is possible to return and find that not only have the bicycle, padlock and chain all vanished, but so has the 'immovable' object.

The need for the traveller to be constantly aware of the problem of security, whether his possessions be a Land Rover or only a rucksack, cannot be over-emphasized. The assortment of wire, chains and padlocks with which I was laden would have been admired by the Ghost of Jacob Marley, but I preferred to carry the extra weight and keep the bicycle, rather than have less luggage and perhaps no bicycle. My biggest problem concerning theft had been what to do with the bicycle at night. It would have been impossible to fit it into the tent, and I knew that there would not always be a convenient tree outside the tent to which I could lock it. The problem was solved by a friend who created one of my most valuable pieces of equipment by converting a simple torch alarm into a burglar alarm. The alarm, no bigger than a cigarette packet, was powered by penlite torch batteries and contained a siren. It was altered so that two pieces of wire came from the alarm and at night I would attach these two wires to the bicycle to form a circuit. With the two wires leading from the bicycle into the tent, I would place the alarm next to where I was sleeping. If the bicycle was moved at all the wires would be disturbed, the circuit broken, and the alarm would emit its piercing screech. From entering Turkey I set the alarm almost every night that I camped, until it was broken in Zambia when the authorities there decided that it was actually a short-wave radio which I used to send messages to their enemy in Rhodesia.

The youth hostel in Istanbul was an ideal place to stay. With the bicycle securely locked away in a store-room, I was able to rediscover leg muscles that I had forgotten existed after six weeks of movement almost entirely by pedalling. Istanbul represented a remarkable change from the Communist Bloc, a contrast in every way. The freedom of speech, political demonstrations, religious fervour, abundance of seemingly every commodity imaginable, the colours, noise, and the extrovert natures of the people all contributed to form a different world, and to explain the Turkish distrust of anything Russian.

A week in Istanbul was long enough. Accommodation was costing nearly one pound each night. In my tent it cost nothing. And there were too many tasty but expensive delicacies on sale in the city that were out of the way of temptation when I was on the road. It had been my intention to give the bicycle a thorough cleaning in Istanbul, taking it apart piece by piece, and reassembling it with all the parts spotless and lubricated. Somehow, though, the opportunity never seemed to arise. If I went to the storeroom in which the bike was kept to begin work, the room would be locked and the caretaker had gone out with the key. Besides, there seemed little point in cleaning the bike when it would soon be dirty again and I knew that if I dismantled any mechanical parts not even the will of Allah would fit them together again in the correct order. And anyway, what was the point of cleaning the bicycle when it was sure to be stolen by bandits somewhere in the mountains of Central Turkey? Having, with the unwitting help of the caretaker, suitably convinced myself that it would not be practical to clean the bike, after another frustrating and unsuccessful attempt to make the front brakes work I settled for a squirt of oil here and there and the promise that I would definitely give Rover a good clean when I reached Cairo.

The break from cycling had been welcome and I awoke on the morning of the day that I was due to cross the Bosphorus with that indescribable sensation of excitement and freedom, that seems to grip deep down in the stomach, a feeling heightened by the awareness that I would soon be in Asia. I had planned to cycle across the Bogazici Koprusu, the modern suspension bridge which is one of the longest in the world, into Asiatic Turkey, but was told that pedestrians and cyclists are now prohibited from crossing the Bosphorus by means of the bridge and that I must take the ferry. The official reason was that so many pedestrians and cyclists had committed suicide by jumping from the bridge, two hundred feet to the water below. That seemed to be a polite way of saying that, in the turmoil of Turkish politics, it was more difficult for individuals to deposit explosive packages on the bridge if they were in vehicles than if they were walking or cycling.

The ferry was of the drive-on, drive-off variety, accommodating half a dozen vehicles and scores of passengers. The stern end acted as a tail-gate which could be lowered to allow access, raised to form the back of the boat, then lowered again to allow disembarkation at the opposite bank. The ferry had finished taking on board its next passengers as I pedalled towards it and was being cast off. The motor which raised the gangplank had been started and the heavy chains on each side of the boat had just begun to lift the stern. Not wishing to have to sit and wait for the ferry to make its journey and then return, and urged on by the excited passengers on board the boat, I rode to the end of the jetty and hurriedly lifted the heavy bicycle the four feet into the air necessary to place it on to the rising stern of the ferry. The weight was greater than I had anticipated and I was only able to place the front section of the bicycle on to the boat as it began to move away from the quayside. For a moment the bike hung there, balanced on the slowly rising stern of the boat, before some of the passengers hurried forward and dragged it on board. Anxious not to have the bicycle arriving in Asia while I remained stranded in Europe, I made a despairing leap at the back of the boat and, while I repeated the bicycle's momentary feat of balancing above the waters of the Bosphorus, the helpful Turks again reached forward and I slid down the inside of the stern where I landed in a heap on top of the bike, resolving as I picked myself up that the next time I appeared to be missing a ferry I would sit and wait patiently for the next one.

In Europe I had been plagued by friendly motorists. So many of them would give a pip on the car horn as they passed me. The next car would do the same, and the next and the next, until, as I heard a car behind, I would feel myself tensed waiting for the inevitable pip. If I waved cheerily they would pip again in reply to my wave, if I ignored them they would think that I hadn't heard and pip a second time, and if, as often happened, my patience became exhausted and I replied to their pip with unorthodox gestures and a torrent of abuse, they would think that I was being friendly in my curious British way and would pip again. I looked forward to the secluded roads of Turkey where, even if there were ropes stretched across the road and bandits hiding behind rocks, at least I would not be irritated by car horns. My dream of a quiet Turkish road, however, did not materialize in the main Istanbul to Ankara highway and I was nearly swept from the bike as the first juggernaut swept past, loaded to capacity with Western European exports for the oil-rich markets of the Gulf. I was still being carried along by the back-draught when the displaced air from a lorry travelling at full speed in the opposite direction caught me up. The two air-currents caused me to sway wildly on the bicycle and a horn blared from behind several times louder than the gentle pips of the cars in Europe, as another TIR lorry tore past me, its driver clearly intent on reaching his destination in the shortest possible time.

The buffeting air currents continued throughout the day. My throat was parched from the constant haze of exhaust fumes and my ears were ringing from the roar of the heavy diesel engines and the blast of horns. The road was just wide enough for two lanes of heavy lorries, one in each direction. If there was a lull in the traffic from behind me, vehicles travelling towards me would use the opportunity to overtake, and several times I heard blaring horns ahead and looked up to see a lorry bearing down on me and occupying the whole of my lane. On such occasions it was apparent why the name Juggernaut means 'Lord of the World', and it was equally clear that it would be of little benefit to resolutely stand my ground waving a copy of the Highway Code. I took the wisest way, if not the boldest, and rode off the road and if that meant riding over a drop of perhaps two feet, it was preferable to examining a lorry's sump plug at close quarters. The rule was straightforward enough: the smaller vehicle gave way to the larger and he who broke the rule would suffer the gravest consequences. I soon learned that, when I saw a cow wander into the road a little way ahead of me. A huge TIR lorry swept past me, its horn blaring a warning to the cow which was presumably either very deaf or very stubborn. Seconds later it was very dead and pieces of prime Turkish topside littered the road.

Late in the afternoon, after a tiring uphill section, a police road block loomed at the foot of the hill ahead and as I gathered speed on the rewarding run down I muttered exasperated requests for providence to intervene and not cause me to be stopped. Between ferries and lorries I had had rather a harrowing day for the first day back in the saddle. I was hot, dusty and tired and the last thing that I wanted was for the absurd questions and passport check that a police road block would be sure to bring if I was stopped. Providence was obviously not in the mood to do me any favours, and as I sped towards the police signs, a uniformed officer stepped into the road in front of me, his hand raised. I applied the back brake to slow me down, the front brake out of optimism, and dropped both feet to the tarmac, but I was still doing at least ten miles an hour when I hit him. He was built like a bull and must have weighed over two hundred pounds and he barely flinched as he caught hold of the handlebars and I came to a dead stop. I waited for an enraged outburst, but instead he bellowed with laughter and roared at me, 'Cay! Turkish Cay!' He led me into a nearby building where beneath an overhead fan we drank glasses of hot, sweet Turkish tea with his fellow officers. Half an hour later I was back on the road feeling a different person. The cool of the office had refreshed me, the sweet tea given me new energy, and the amiable attitude of the Turkish police, none of whom could speak English, had revitalized me. In a day of cycling, late afternoon was usually my low point. Often beneath a hot sun, with my legs tiring, the saddle feeling hard and faced with still more miles to cover before stopping for the night, it was invariably the hardest time of the day. I often remembered that Turkish police check and wished that I could have been stopped by them in mid-afternoon every day.

The following day, I decided that in order to alleviate the problems of sadistic lorry drivers and carbon monoxide poisoning, I would divert to the Black Sea Coast from where I could continue cycling in the direction of Ankara, the Turkish capital, at the same time enjoying the benefits of the beaches. Life for the next few days became more relaxing as I camped on the coast, swam in the Black Sea and, considerably less pleasant, fed the mosquitoes which descended on me in multitudes. Traffic almost disappeared. So, in places, did the road, as I followed tracks between villages. In some places the road was a mere sand track and I had to push the bicycle. 'Good practice for the Sudan,' I comforted myself, not realizing what an accurate prediction that would prove to be. It was during these days that I became more familiar with the people of Turkey, who were not hiding behind rocks with knives at the ready but stepping forward to shake hands and talk. Numerous times they would step out in front of the bicycle to offer me fruit, and, in the villages, whenever I stopped to ask a direction I would be invited into the local tea-house to drink Cay with the men of the village. To talk of travelling to South Africa, or any other part of Africa, to these village people was a waste of time, so I would simply say that I was cycling to Ankara. Even this brought strangled gasps from their throats and calls for more Cay to be served. If pressed for more information I would go as far as to say that I was cycling on from Ankara to Adana, the town in the south of the country through which I would pass before reaching the Syrian border, and this was sure to bring even stranger sounds and still more Cay. In Turkey, where food in a roadside restaurant was quite cheap, I would occasionally make a change from preparing my own meal on my primus stove and eat in a village.

On several occasions I was joined by Turks who would insist on paying for my meal. Could these really be the 'bandits' who were sure to steal all that I possessed, I wondered?

The time came to turn back inland where I rejoined the main Istanbul-Ankara trunk road. This meant not only resumption of the lorries with their fumes and multi-tone blaring horns, but that I was now approaching Ankara and entering the interior of the country. And the interior of Turkey meant mountains. It also meant wild dogs!

October 1978. Turkey. Two months out from England. Miles cycled, two and a half thousand. Miles yet to cycle, seven and a half thousand approximately. I had been asleep for about two hours when the dogs came. Dumb creatures they may have been but they knew how to attack. I had learned to sleep lightly, always with one ear cocked for a sound outside which may have been anyone approaching the bicycle, but the dogs surrounded the tent without disturbing me. Suddenly from all around, as if on a given signal, they began to bark, a hoarse, unnatural bark, maniacal in its sound. I came awake immediately. There was total darkness. Outside the tent the barking became louder, more hysterical. I considered my alternatives. If I went outside the tent and tried to scare the dogs away it seemed unlikely that they would stand around waiting to be petted or scamper playfully into the night. I didn't know exactly how many there were, but the noise and the angles from which it was coming suggested that, unless they had mastered the art of ventriloquism, there were more than one or two, and I was aware that any of them could be rabid. If they came at me, especially in darkness, they were likely to come off the best, and once they were on top they would be unlikely to withdraw before they had bitten quite a few pieces out of me. My only hope was to stay crouched inside the tent with my only weapon, a large sheath-knife, at the ready. I hoped that if I remained silent the dogs would go away but they seemed to have other ideas. As the barking continued, a scratching on the outside of the tent told me that they were pawing at the flysheet. The scratching intensified. Then they began to throw themselves on to the tent. I considered jabbing the knife through the tent at the moment a dog hit it, but this would only serve their purpose in that it would open up a hole in the nylon. The rear tent pole lurched inwards and I realized that the back guy-line must have snapped. It seemed only a matter of time before the tent collapsed on top of me leaving me completely helpless. Suddenly I realized that the barking had lessened and, as I listened, I realized that the dogs were leaving. Soon there was complete silence again and I cautiously put my head out of the tent door. I could see no sign of them, but that did not mean that they were not waiting in the night some yards away. I wondered if they had gone permanently or if they had merely withdrawn to gather reinforcements, returning later with more of the pack. I could not risk dismantling the tent to leave in case they returned in the darkness while I was doing it, leaving me without protection, so I organized my defences as best I could, tying extra guy-lines on to the tent and placing the bike at right-angles to a tree so that if I was forced to leave the tent I could back up against the tree and the bicycle, with my knife, and only be attacked from one side. Then I returned to the tent and lay wondering which would come first, the dawn or the dogs.

I awakened in the first grey light and looked outside the tent; no dogs. Quickly I moved out of the tent and began to take it down. A hundred yards away a large black mongrel appeared, then another dog then another. The tent was down and the bicycle packed in record time but, before I left, I counted twenty dogs all watching me with interest and gradually moving closer as their numbers increased. I didn't wait to count the total number in the pack, but slowly pushed the bicycle away in the direction of the main road.

Ankara, like most cities, held little to interest me and before long I was back on the road, heading south-east towards Syria and, before that, the Taurus Mountains, the great mountain range of southern Turkey that runs parallel to the Mediterranean Sea. I was on a plateau now and the road was somewhat flatter. The difficulty with heavy lorries had decreased since Ankara, but it was still a problem especially if there was a strong cross-wind blowing. One minute the wind was blowing from the side and I had to lean into it to make allowance. Then I was being thrust forward as a Juggernaut swept past; then another side wind, then a surge of head wind as a lorry came from the opposite direction. It required continuous concentration to avoid straying towards the middle of the road.

Not all the lorries were troublesome. Many drivers would screech to a halt ahead of me, wait until I caught up, and then almost beg me to take a lift with them. When I refused, they would often shrug their shoulders and give me a glass of Cay or some fruit. A stop for a chat was always welcome, even if we were unable to communicate in a common language. For a few minutes we would be travellers, joined in friendship by a mutual fleeting need of company, and, as we separated and the lorry drove past me, blaring its horn and flashing its lights, we would both feel refreshed by the break in the journey and the companionship. I was frequently passed by lorries bearing the familiar GB plate and I regretted as they sped by not having thought to affix a GB sticker to the rear of the bicycle before leaving England. Sometimes I would come across them at the roadside, parked for safety in a convoy of three of four lorries, and brewing coffee. Then I would stop to hear English spoken naturally again and to hear recent news of England which they had usually left only a few days before. One British TIR driver overtook me, then pulled to a stop and jumped from his cab to greet me. 'How did you know I'm English?' I asked. 'Only an Englishman would be crazy enough to be out here alone, on a bicycle!' he replied.

The days in Turkey were hot and sunny, far from ideal conditions for cycling up mountain passes, but it was mid-October and the nights were very cold. My sleeping bag was nearly twenty years old and most of the inside had long since disintegrated. It was ideal to keep me cool on hot African nights, but in the mountains of Turkey it was about as much use as a cotton sheet. Fortunately, it was the harvest time in Turkey and I was often able to use the tactic that Jeff and I had been grateful for in Ethiopia three years earlier, of sleeping in piles of hay. That had been in the Simien Mountains, at over twelve thousand feet, in the winter time, when the cold was so intense at night that mountain streams ceased to flow as they turned to ice and waterfalls became stalactites. We had been thankful for haystacks then and, in Turkey, I was thankful again as I buried both myself and the bicycle beneath piles of hay and was untroubled by the cold night air.

It was in Turkey that I discovered the advantages of using slow-moving lorries and tractor-drawn trailers as wind-breaks. Cycling close behind a slow vehicle, I would not only be sheltered from a head-wind, but would be drawn along in the back-draught. It was a method of cycling that required a minimum of effort and I covered many easy miles during the journey in this way, in both Asia and Africa. The system did hold disadvantages. It was necessary to cycle at perhaps fifteen or twenty miles an hour, directly behind the vehicle, thus totally obscuring my view of the road ahead. It meant that if the vehicle stopped suddenly, I had to do likewise – and, still with no front brake, the soles of my shoes were becoming rather worn. It also meant that if there was any obstruction in the road I would not see it until it was too late. On one occasion, following a tractor-drawn trailer laden with straw, the vehicle passed straight over a pile of sand – and I passed straight over the handlebars of the bicycle! On another occasion I had spent an hour helping myself to grapes from a vineyard outside Aksaray, which I packed into the front panniers so that I could reach them easily and eat them as I was cycling. Back on the bicycle I was overtaken by a tractor which was pulling a trailer on which were stacked hundreds of bunches of grapes. A group of farm hands sat on the back of the tractor, facing towards the trailer and its contents. As they passed me they shouted to me, urging me to cycle faster. I increased my speed and tucked in close behind the trailer. For some minutes I kept my eyes on the road beneath the trailer and pedalled slowly as I was drawn along by the displaced air. Suddenly an object hurtled past my right ear, then another and, as I looked up, a bunch of grapes caught me full in the chest. The farm hands were using me for a good-natured target practice and were rolling on the trailer clutching their sides with laughter at their joke. Ducking the next missile, I reached into one of my front panniers, withdrew one of the bunches of grapes that I had picked earlier, and returned the fire. The enemy, caught off their guard, were taken by surprise, but the difficulty of throwing while cycling, and my limited supply of ammunition, put me at too great a disadvantage, and I was soon forced to reduce my speed until the tractor had drawn well ahead and I was out of range.

South of the town of Aksaray, the extinct volcano of Hasan Dargi rose up over ten thousand feet, like a great gatepost to the formidable Taurus Mountains and ahead, stretched across the horizon, was the uneven line of the Taurus Range where the road again ascended to over five thousand feet. Turkey is a country of beautiful scenery, but I had learned by now that beautiful scenery invariably meant mountains to cycle across and, though it was not quite logical, there always appeared to be twice as much uphill as downhill. I had begun to dread the downhill stretches as much as the uphill ones since, in cycling terms, what comes down must go back up! Often the road seemed like a spiral staircase going round and round and up and up. The sun would blaze down and the sweat roll from me, running from my face and down my chest and back, soaking my black cotton shorts and leaving white salty streaks which gave them the appearance of having been made from the skin of a rather mangy zebra. A trail of sweat droplets would glisten on the tarmac, stretching back the way I had come. Then, when it seemed I would ascend for ever, the road fell away, dropping down through the Cilician Gates, the narrow gorge just wide enough for the road and a fast flowing river. Another long, steep climb followed, the road winding to the summit, before a welcome drop down to the plains of the Mediterranean coast. The Taurus Mountains were behind me.

The scenery had changed now, from the fertile valleys and rocky mountains to a dry, dusty landscape where only desert plants could grow. The sun seemed to have moved much closer and the nights were no longer cold. The people too had changed. Seeming to possess a wilder character, they would be liable to jump out from the roadside in front of the bike, shouting and waving in uncontrollable excitement at the sight of a westerner travelling by bicycle. Their hospitality was no less than it had been further north, however, and, on the occasions that I accepted the offer from villagers of a place to sleep at nights, I was taken into their homes, where I found their simple desire to please almost overwhelming as they nearly fell over each other in their rush to fetch and carry.

In south-east Turkey I left the village of Tarsus and cycled towards the Syrian capital of Damascus, realizing that I would be following in the tracks of St Paul two thousand years earlier except that Paul had more sense than to handicap himself with a bicycle. Through Antakya, the former city of Antioch, once rated the third city in the world behind Rome and Alexandria, and on to the Turkish border. I had spent a month in Turkey and cycled almost a thousand miles. The people had, on the whole, been a pleasure to meet. No-one had jumped out at me from behind a rock or tangled up the bicycle in a web of ropes stretched across the road. But I was now coming into the true Arab lands, and the hair-raising stories that I had been told about the Turks were as a child's nursery rhymes compared to the flesh-creeping warning that I had received in England of life among the Arabs.

4

Damascus. Claimed to be the oldest city in constant habitation in the world. On his way there Alexander the Great would have commanded his carriage bearers to march harder, Saladin would have spurred his horse to greater efforts, Lawrence of Arabia would have whispered encouraging words of Oxfordian Arabic into his camel's ear. I could only drop down yet another gear and cycle on into the gale that howled towards me across the desolate plains. The discomfort was doubled because, with no Syrian money until I reached a bank in the first large town of Hama, I had only raisins brought from Turkey, to eat for the first two days. Water was more of a problem too than it had been anywhere else during the journey so far. Previously garages had been convenient sources of fresh water but outside the main towns of Syria petrol stations were few and far between, and obtaining water meant diverting to one of the villages set back from the main road. There the loaded bicycle would sink into the sandy tracks as I attempted to push it amongst the mud-brick houses and, while the Moslem women veiled their faces and raced for cover, the men sat and stared, and the children darted forward to cluster around me and the bicycle. Leaving a village I would usually be escorted by children riding solid Chinese-made bicycles, sometimes packed four or five on a bike and, in their excitement, they would weave in and out around me, narrowly avoiding collisions with one another.

The bicycle had attracted a great deal of curiosity in Turkey, but that was nothing compared with the attention that it received in Syria. Anywhere I stopped groups of curious onlookers would appear as if drawn by a magnet. In the town of Homs, a hundred miles before Damascus, it was almost impossible to force the bicycle through the crowd, who had gathered to ask me repeatedly if it was really possible to travel by bicycle all the way from there to Damascus.

Leaving Homs at midday, the wind increased again. Cycling beneath a hot sun causes one to sweat like a leaking tap and in the desert and semi-desert countries, even on a windless day, the body quickly becomes caked in layers of dirt which stick as if you are sweating super-glue. On the plains of Syria I remembered how I had muttered constant streams of obscenities while pedalling up the mountains of Europe and Turkey, but at least the mountain ranges had had the decency to provide generous quantities of running water by way of regular streams. The Syrian landscape was as undulating as the Lords cricket pitch after the heavy roller has been applied, with nowhere for streams to run from and nowhere for streams to run to, which is perhaps fortunate because there are no streams to run. As the dust swept across the plains it accumulated on my body until I looked like a newly opened pack of sandpaper. Working presumably on the geographical principle of erosion, streams of sweat would wash channels in the layers of dirt, until exposed skin quickly became covered again by the next swirl of dust.

Two windswept hours after leaving Homs, during which I battled in lowest gear long a completely flat road and covered an estimated four miles, I retired for the day, fastening down the tent with rocks and muttering dire threats against the forces of Nature who were causing the wind to blow in precisely the wrong direction. During the night I was awoken by the burglar alarm, its harsh note penetrating the darkness and drowning the flapping noise of the tent's fly-sheet. I was out of the tent in a second, yelling the first words to come into my head at the top of my voice. Anything to create suden noise and, in the darkness, confuse whoever had touched the bicycle. There was no-one to be seen. The wind howled mournfully around the boulders in whose shelter I had erected the tent. Shadows jumped among the surrounding rocks but were caused merely by clouds scudding beneath the faded moonlight. I walked between the rocks alert for any sign of intruders, but it was only as I returned to the tent that I realized that the alarm must have been set off, not by prowling Arabs, but by the wind disturbing one of the alarm's wires attached to the bicycle, causing the circuit to be broken.

I awoke the following morning to find that the wind had not abated in the least, nor had my threats of the previous night caused Mother Nature to have second thoughts as to its direction. Three hours' hard toil brought me to a village with a school close to the road. I filled my water bottles at the school while the teachers made tea, and we sat for an hour discussing the Christian and Islamic religions. My theories must have pleased someone in higher places for, as we talked, clouds came over and after a shower of rain I suddenly noticed that something outside was different. Swirls of dust were moving in the opposite direction to that in which they had been doing before the rain. The wind was now blowing not from the south but from the north, towards Damascus. I broke off my discussion with the school teachers rather abruptly and left the school at several times the speed at which I had arrived.

In Damascus I was accommodated by a Syrian businessman in a flat which had been standing empty for some time, but where I was able to have the luxury of a cold shower. The flat had been taken over by a large family of mice who provided me with great sport as I tried to reduce their numbers. They avenged their dead relatives, however, by chewing their way into one of my panniers and devouring most of my remaining packets of dehydrated food.

The lost food would soon be replaced according to my planned itinerary, however. From Damascus I had decided, before leaving England, to cycle to Beirut, from where I hoped to take a boat down the Mediterranean to Egypt. Lebanon was an important destination, for not only did I hope to sail from there, but I had made arrangements with a Lebanese acquaintance in England, to collect various items which I had sent out with him to his Beirut home. Spare parts for the bicycle, new shoes, vitamin and anti-malaria tablets and dehydrated food for my crossing of the Nubian Desert in Sudan, were all awaiting my arrival in Beirut. I also planned to collect some more tyres and inner tubes from the Middle East agency of the British rubber company who were supplying me with tyres during the journey. But this was late October 1978 and war in Beirut was in full swing as the Palestinians supported by the Syrian 'peace-keeping' army battled with the Lebanese Right Wing backed by the Israelis.

The Lebanese had stopped issuing tourist visas when the fighting broke out, but I had obtained mine before leaving England. With pleas not to go to Lebanon ringing in my ears, I cycled from Damascus on the road to Beirut. The two cities are only seventy miles apart, but they are separated by two lofty mountain ranges. Damascus is situated at the foot of the range of mountains, Jebel esh Sharqui. The road rises to almost five thousand feet, drops steeply into the Beqa'a Valley where it crosses the Litani River then rises even more steeply, again to nearly five thousand feet, to cross the Jebel Liban before dropping once again, and still more sharply, to Beirut at sea level. I left Syria and rode up a narrow pass, spectacular rock formations to each side, and the occasional traffic being mainly Syrian army vehicles. Then I dropped down towards the Lebanese border post which the Syrian immigration authorities had assured me that I would not be allowed to pass through. Saying that I was intending to visit a good friend in Beirut, I entered without difficulty. I cycled through the outskirts of Zahle, the capital of the Beqa'a Valley, the largest Christian town in the Middle East, more recently made famous as the site of Russian-made, Syrian-installed, SAM 6 missiles. For several miles the road was flat and there were villages and crowds of people. The area was richly cultivated and fruit of all sizes and colours was on sale at the roadside markets – not surprisingly, for the Valley of the Litani River is so fertile that it was once the granary of the Roman Empire in the East. Ahead loomed the second range of mountains and then the road began to climb.

If the climb across the Jebel Liban did not rate as the most difficult of the journey, it certainly deserved to be classed as one of the most difficult and I consoled myself that I only had to cross it once.

It was a climb of more than three hours from the Beqa'a Valley to the top of the Jebel Liban, punctuated by occasional stops at Syrian Army checkpoints where my panniers were thoroughly searched each time lest I be an Israeli agent who was employing a new method of supplying arms to the Christian Militia. I could not help thinking that the Syrians must have considered the Israelis to be very short of Mirages if they needed to promote attacks by bicycle. Each time I was waved on after the soldiers, who were usually very friendly, had satisfied themselves that my panniers were not stuffed with rockets and that I did not have Uzi machine pistols inside my rolled up sleeping bag.

As I crossed the mountain range I was rewarded for my efforts by a breathtaking sight. All around were mountain peaks, some covered by snow. Above was a cloudless sky. Beyond, and far below, was the glistening blue of the

Mediterranean Sea, and through a 'V'-shaped break in the hills, the pure white buildings of Beirut nestled between the mountains and the sea. It was the most tranquil sight imaginable. It was impossible that a war could be taking place in that serene area of white that was Beirut. As I rode down the mountainside I caught regular distant views, between the rocks and pine trees, of the city. Behind it, the sun was reflected from the waters of the Mediterranean. There could be no war here.

It was late afternoon as I cycled into the outskirts of the city. Cars were driving along the road and people walking in the streets. I could have been riding into Ankara or Damascus, and I began to consider how best to find the residence of the Lebanese with whom I was to stay while in Beirut. In my mind, as I cycled along, I pondered the recent news reports that I had heard of the fighting in Lebanon. Most bulletins reported that the heaviest fighting was taking place in the eastern sector of Beirut. Feeling thankful that I would be well away from there, I imagined a map of Lebanon and tried to work out from which direction I would be entering the city. If Turkey lay to the north of Lebanon, then Beirut lay to the west of Damascus, in which case I must by cycling into Beirut from – the east! I suddenly realized that all was not as it should be. While I had been cycling along, lost in thought, the scenery had undergone drastic changes. The traffic, which had been passing me regularly only minutes before, had completely disappeared. The streets, which had been full of people only a few miles back up the road, were now totally deserted. So deeply involved in my thoughts had I been, that I had not noticed that all traffic had apparently turned off the road to by-pass this area of the city. I allowed the bicycle to roll to a stop and examined my surroundings. There was an utter silence that was eerie. Buildings on each side were pock-marked by bullet-holes, some sections had crumbled to the ground as a result of being hit by larger missiles, windows were shattered, empty cartridge cases littered the street. Here and there were cars, abandoned, burned out, the empty shells riddled with bullet-holes.

I dismounted from the bike and picked up an empty cartridge case. Nearby I heard whistles and shouts and I looked towards an empty warehouse yard, from where a group of soldiers were calling to me. I pushed the bicycle across towards them. As I approached I noticed a large gun protruding from a pile of sandbags, and I felt thankful that I hadn't just ignored the soldiers and tried to ride away. They were all Syrian and regarded me more with bewilderment than suspicion as they led me into the warehouse where they examined Rover with interest. One of them, a teacher of English serving his two years of National Service in the Syrian Army, understandably asked me a few questions as to how I came to be riding a bicycle in a war-zone. He was very courteous, but slipped in an occasional half-statement, half-question at intervals such as, 'but I think you have been to Beirut many times before?' It was during our conversation that I first noticed the background noise, which must have been going on for some time, of single-shot and automatic rifle fire, some of it not far away.

After prolonged discussion and attempts to persuade me to return to Damascus, the soldiers decided that if I was determined to go to Beirut I could not continue in the direction in which I had been heading since, though the road was normally the main route into the city centre, no traffic was able to use it because it was blocked by the 'enemy Christians'. I thought it better not to become involved in a debate on the subject of religious creeds, and was told that I would have to return the way that I had come for half a mile, turn south, then circle around the trouble spots to the west until I reached the coast from where I could move into Beirut centre.

I shook hands all round with the group of soldiers and then returned the way I had come. The theory of retracing my steps was very simple. In practice it was less straightforward. Shooting broke out some way ahead of me and I had to turn south earlier than I had intended. Guided by the sound of gunfire ahead I turned back west and soon came to another army checkpoint where they insisted that I return to Damascus. I agreed to do so, rode away, then turned back towards Beirut. After a couple of more turnings at road junctions I was completely lost. There was no-one to ask, evening was closing in, and I had soon discovered that trying to move in the opposite direction to the sound of the shooting was not always practical since the surrounding buildings caused the sounds to echo so that it was impossible to tell exactly where they came from. A further turn into a side street and, as I rode between a number of burned-out cars, I found myself in a cul-de-sac. High buildings rose on each side, ideal sniping positions, and I was not really looking forward to returning the way that I had come in case someone in one of those buildings, knowing that I had entered a cul-de-sac, was waiting for my return.

I was considering the alternatives of engaging a low gear and cycling out of the cul-de-sac with a burst of speed or of exiting at a slow, dignified pace which would look much less incriminating when the problem was solved for me. I heard a shout and, looking in the direction from which it had come, saw what appeared to be simply a hand waving to me from behind a pile of sandbags. I had no real desire to waste time by going through another army 'Pit-Your-Wits' session of questions and answers, so I waved back and then looked away. The shouting increased and the hand was raised to reveal that it was attached to an arm. A moment later a head cautiously appeared from behind the sandbags and since I needed advice on directions, but feeling that the drama was being rather overdone, I put the bike down on the ground and ambled across to the barricade. A soldier lay on his side behind the sandbags, motioning urgently for me to get down. It seemed that he was on guard duty for a group of twelve soldiers who were inside a building, drinking a substance that looked suspiciously like alcohol. They were very much on edge and extremely nervous and, for a few moments, I had an unpleasant feeling that I had involuntarily joined the opposition Christian Falangists. However, one of the soldiers in broken English identified the group as members of the Syrian Army and, after I had explained how I came to be in the battle zone, they radioed to another base. I was informed that it was not safe for me to cycle around that sector of the city (as the gunfire continued to increase outside the building, I was rapidly drawing the same conclusion). They said they would lead me to their major who was in another building a mile away. The only problem was which of the soldiers was going to take me across a mile of exposed ground. Though I did not understand any of the Arabic in which the soldiers were holding their discussion, twelve pairs of eyes turned towards the soldier who had first waved to me and it was obvious that the message was, 'you brought him in, you're the best one to take him out!' Equally apparent was that the chosen one did not feel such a position to be an honour. A heated exchange of Arabic expressions filled the room, during which the number of stripes that soldier wore on his sleeve seemed irrelevant. Finally, democracy won through, my friend losing the vote by twelve to one. With a look in my direction which would have shrivelled the best Christian Militia man in his tracks, the soldier indicated that I should follow him back to the entrance to the building. Flattening himself against a pillar, he surveyed the street from end to end. Then, crouching low, he set off in a zig-zag run to the next building. It was all right for the soldier, he wasn't pushing a bicycle! It must have been a strange sight for any snipers observing the street from nearby buildings as an enemy Syrian soldier flashed from cover to cover, stooping and crouching, Kalashnikov automatic rifle at the ready, followed at a more sedate speed by a European pushing a bicycle and primarily concerned with not ripping his tyres on the broken glass which littered the streets. At last we reached the major's headquarters and, after a few questions, the major ordered tea and fruit for me. It was while eating an orange and talking to the officer that memories of the Jebel Liban were brought abruptly back to me. Why had I come to Beirut? he asked, and I explained that I intended to sail from there to Egypt. 'But you cannot sail from Beirut to Egypt,' he replied in surprise. I smiled to myself behind a handful of orange and thought that the major may know a bit about fighting but, for a prominent member of a race of trading people, he was not so hot on geography. Pausing from eating I was about to point out that the strategic placing of both Beirut and Alexandria ensured that boats would pass regularly between the two cities and that all I had to do was to cycle round to the port, when the major continued 'You cannot sail from Beirut to Egypt. You cannot sail from Beirut to anywhere. There is only one ship in the port of Beirut.' I opened my mouth to interrupt that one ship would be quite adequate for my needs as long as the sharp end was pointing towards Egypt, but was cut short. 'The only ship in the port of Beirut is resting on the sea bed! It has been sunk!'

The major could not have hit me with a bigger bombshell had he rounded up all the warring factions in Lebanon and put a match to them in front of me. If the only ship in Beirut was sunk then it wasn't the only thing. I was too! If I looked, at that point, as if I might be considering the possibility of a spontaneous nervous breakdown, then anyone who has pedalled between Damascus and Beirut would understand why. Cycling up the Jebel Liban had half-killed me, and that was approaching from the *easy* side. Going back would be even worse. That was assuming that I could even get back to the foot of the Jebel Liban and, from the sound of gunfire outside, the prospects of returning the way I had come were clearly not promising. Visions of lying prostrate on a warm deck, soaking up the Mediterranean sun, while a boat rolled lazily on sparkling blue waters as it transported me in ease to Egypt, faded rapidly and I could almost hear my legs groan in dismay.

The major's voice brought me back to reality as I heard him asking me to wait until darkness when a Syrian Army Mercedes Unimog lorry would take me from the Christian sector to the Moslem area of Beirut, where my Lebanese friend worked. This would be the first time that I had put the bicycle on to a vehicle since leaving England and, having already refused dozens of offers of lifts at various points, I was reluctant to take one now. I was satisfied, however, by the thought that I had already reached Beirut and would simply be moving from one part of the city to another. Besides, the major made it quite clear that I had no choice!

When it was dark I boarded the lorry together with six soldiers, and we were driven at break-neck pace across the city to the Moslem area where I was able to find the business address of my Lebanese acquaintance and, although he was abroad at the time, I was able to collect the package which had been brought from England several months previously. I stored the supplies away in my panniers, together with the gift that the Syrian major had given me before leaving – an empty AK 47 cartridge case which he had asked me to carry with me on my travels. I dropped it into the bottom of one of the panniers and forgot all about it. The major could not have known when he gave it to me that, five months later, his gift would come close to causing my execution in Zambia on charges of carrying ammunition for the Rhodesian Army.

November 1978. Beirut. Three months out from England. Miles cycled three and a half thousand. Miles yet to cycle six and a half thousand. Having arrived in Beirut I had only one problem. How to get back to Damascus!

5

My Lebanese acquaintance was a person that I had met only once before leaving England. Though somewhat perplexed as to why I should want to cycle to Lebanon he had offered, in the hospitable way of the Arabs, to carry spare equipment to Lebanon for me and to accommodate me when I arrived there. Although he was away at the time, a business partner had been told to expect a visitor from England. I found on arrival that my friend owned a seventy-five percent share in a large, high-class restaurant, while his colleague held the remaining twenty-five. The partner, obviously expecting the 'visitor from England' to arrive by taxi from the airport wearing full dinner dress, was slightly taken aback when I appeared with the bicycle at the door of his multi-star restaurant in shorts, tee shirt, and caked in dust. He turned rather pale beneath his natural sun-tan and guided me surreptitiously to a quiet corner of the restaurant where the lighting was low. He was less than enthusiastic when I insisted that my bicycle was not to be left out in the street but was to be placed in a part of the restaurant where I could see it and, after watching with obviously growing concern as I devoured all the food that the highly amused waiters placed before me, he directed me with some relief to an upstairs room where the bicycle and I were to be accommodated.

The following morning, the twenty-five percent partner informed me that he had received a telephone call from my Lebanese friend who had told him that I was to be allowed to stay for as long as I liked and to eat what I liked in the restaurant. I didn't like to seem ungrateful, so hurried downstairs to the restaurant for breakfast.

For the next three days I toured Beirut on the bicycle, which, as always, was a good way of meeting people. Moslems, Christians, and the Palestinians who, with no homeland of their own, have become refugees there, were all friendly and polite, which brought home all the more the tragedy of their situation. Crossing from the Moslem to the Christian sector and vice versa was always the most hazardous part of cycling in Beirut. Snipers from both sides were reputed to choose comfortable, shady spots, on these boundaries, just within their own territory, and let off occasional bursts at anyone who looked vaguely like opposition or who they did not particularly like the look of. I became extremely aware of my vulnerability when crossing the boundaries on a bicycle. Once inside the particular sectors, I could cycle around the shell-torn areas, though in the Christian sector where most of the fighting was taking place careful attention had to be paid to the direction of the background gunfire.

The Christian areas around the port and on the hillsides overlooking the city centre were the most badly hit. Apart from the approximate guide-lines of the appalling damage to buildings, it was quite easy to pass from one sector to another without realizing it. In parts, large red crosses hanging from windows of ruined houses and the people wearing silver crosses around their necks defiantly proclaimed Christian areas, but I had to be careful at the road blocks. It was never obvious at first whether a block was controlled by the Syrian Army, Palestinians or Christian Militia. 'Are you for us or against us?' demanded one civilian, pointing his rifle at my chest. 'Oh, I'm for you,' I assured him, without the slightest idea which side he represented.

I would undoubtedly have been turned back at many of

the road blocks had it not been for the address of the agency of the British Tyre Company, from whom I intended to obtain a supply of sponsored tyres. I had written the address on a piece of paper in both English and Arabic, and this seemed to satisfy those manning the road blocks through which I was passing, who then assumed that I was passing through for a legitimate reason. The tyre agency was in the Christian sector of the city and I rode along the streets, carefully picking my way between the rubble and the broken glass and reflecting that the Syrian 'Peace-Keeping Force' seemed to be rather confused as to their intentions. Stopping to ask directions to the agency's address, brought me into regular conversation with the local people, many of whom could speak a little English or French. Most were philosophical about the destruction of their homes, many did not really know exactly who was fighting who, nor why. It took a full day to find the agency who were supposed to supply me with the tyres and it was all a waste of time. The manager wasn't interested in my arrangement with the company's Head Office in England. In fact he wasn't interested in anything. A rocket had made a direct hit on his garage three days earlier, and he had been sitting at his desk at the time. The spare tyres that I was carrying would have to last me until I reached the company's offices in Nairobi.

After three days in Beirut, the twenty-five percent partner hinted that his shares in the restaurant would not be worth a great deal if I stayed much longer so, the following day, I left, with a hand-drawn map from the British Embassy detailing a route to the south of the city, by which I could by-pass the areas of heaviest fighting and rejoin the Damascus road. Either I misread the map, or the embassy official was blessed with a sense of humour, for some time later I found myself at the Beirut International Airport. Rather than return all the way to the city centre and begin all over again I lifted the bike over the broken-down fence of the airport perimeter with the intention of taking a short cut across some of the runways to the coast road at the far side of the airport grounds. Before riding on to the runways I checked carefully that there were no aircraft in sight, then set off towards the distant fence. Up in the sky the sun glinted upon a silver dot. The dot increased in size at an alarming rate, and the markings on the Sabena Jet were uncomfortably clear by the time my rapidly revolving legs had pedalled me clear of the runways.

I camped on the mountainside just outside Beirut that night, and the gunfire that crackled down in the valley was the last that I was to hear until Rhodesia. The following day came the return to Damascus that I had not been looking forward to. The road rose from sea-level so steeply that my calf muscles, even with three and a half thousand miles of pushing down on pedals, ached at times. Some of the hills were so severe that, despite my low gear ratios, I had to dismount and push. It took seven hours to toil up the slopes of the Jebel Liban, and twenty minutes to drop down the other side into the Beqa'a Valley. I then had to begin all over again, climbing for a further three hours to the Syrian border post from where it was downhill again to Damascus.

I could at least congratulate myself on my economical stay in the Lebanon, for my few days there had cost me nothing at all. I had eaten well at the expense of the partnership holdings in the Beirut restaurant, and consequently needed to change none of my travellers' cheques into Lebanese pounds. This was something of a relief since I was now planning to cross the Red Sea from the Jordanian port of Aqaba, sailing to an Egyptian Red Sea port, and I was aware that the price of such a sailing could make a large dent in my financial resources. The fact that I had brought no Lebanese money meant that on the day of my return to Damascus I had only two apples which I could eat to give me some measure of energy to replace that expended in cycling over the mountains. The two apples had come as a result of my noticing a five piasta coin on the ground as I crossed the Beqa'a Valley. Five piastas were roughly equivalent to three-quarters of an English penny but, having just pedalled up the Jebel Liban, anything which could buy even the smallest amount of food was worth picking up. I approached the nearest trader and offered him the five piasta in exchange for a banana. He gave me a look which implied that fruit may be abundant in the Valley but was certainly not that abundant and that five piastas would not even have bought a banana in the days of the Romans. I cycled on a little way thinking that in Turkey or Syria the trader would have given me both the banana and a glass of tea. At the next stall, however, when I tried for an apple, the old trader selected two of his largest apples and gave them to me with a huge toothless grin, refusing to accept my five piastas.

The day after my return to Damascus saw the commencement of a four-day public holiday. In Islamic countries, feast-days seem to occur with monotonous regularity. Though quite often no-one seems too sure what is being celebrated, everything closes down for the duration of the feast. As I had heard that the holiday was also being kept in Jordan, I decided to remain in Damascus for a few more days, rather than be delayed in the far more expensive city of Amman. I left the bicycle in the flat while I spent the days in walking around Damascus, since cycling in the city was rather a strain on the nervous system. The two million population all appeared to be packed together in the main streets and there were no rules for pedestrians or cyclists and not many for motorists. If you wanted to travel by motor vehicle from point A to point B, you took the shortest route, and if that meant driving through a crowded market place or the wrong way down a one-way street, it all seemed to add to the fun of the journey. The most severe form of reprimand that one appeared to receive was a blast on a whistle from a traffic policeman, though that could hardly be heard above the hooting of horns and the continuous uproar of the market traders. It was surprising how tiring I found walking again after several weeks of cycling. Cycling requires different leg muscles and those concerned with walking were clearly out of practice. I resolved that in the future I would walk rather than cycle around the cities I was to visit, in order to exercise muscles which otherwise were being virtually unused.

I visited a Palestinian refugee camp on the outskirts of Damascus. The Palestinian who had invited me led me through a maze of unpaved streets littered with tin cans, car tyres and rubbish, between dilapidated houses with roofs of tiles, corrugated iron or even broken cardboard boxes. Half-starved dogs, ever-hungry goats, scraggy chickens and lean but laughing children seemed to be constantly underfoot. Women peered out from behind their veils. Sometimes, from behind a black cloth, only a blinking eye was visible, sometimes not even that. The men appeared listless, without hope. 'If you have no homeland what do you have?' I was asked. We ate at the home of my guide, he and I, his four sons and some of his neighbours. Cold potatoes, cauliflower, salad, eggs, bread and the inevitable olives, eaten with the hand from communal bowls placed amongst us as we sat on the earth floor.

Before leaving Damascus, I quite accidentally discovered the fault in the bike's front braking system. I had over tightened a nut on the central pivot bolt in West Germany, and that explained why the front brakes had not functioned since. I jubilantly replaced all the four brake blocks with new ones and looked forward to my shoes lasting me a good deal longer than they had been doing, now that I did not need my feet to help me to slow down.

Spending the last of my Syrian money on nuts, raisins, bread, jam and fruit, which I loaded on to the bicycle, I left Damascus and continued along the flat desert plains towards Jordan. The following day I reached the border, the Jordanian side being one of those which most travellers to the underdeveloped world have experienced, where the officials like to emphasize that they have the power and that you are at their command. I had to unpack everything on the bicycle for Customs to show them what I was carrying, and I was then given a piece of paper which I had to show to Immigration. The Immigration Officer refused to examine my passport because my piece of paper had not been stamped by Customs, so I had to return to Customs for the necessary stamp on the paper. This satisfied Immigration and I moved on to the Police. The police officer refused to allow me into the country until my passport was stamped by Immigration, so I had to return to Immigration for the necessary stamp on the passport. All this was done amid queues of squabbling Arabs, and took over two hours.

Cycling towards Amman beneath a blue sky and in a cool breeze was quite pleasant. The countryside was sparsely populated – a landscape of weird rock shapes, low mountain formations, and dry, sandy soil. The four-day public holiday of Syria was a five-day one in Jordan which had acquired a bonus day to celebrate the birthday of King Hussein so when I cycled into the hilly city of Amman, all government buildings were closed. I camped the night on some waste ground on the outskirts of the city, then returned the following morning to try to obtain the necessary permit to travel to Israel.

Before leaving England it had been made clear to me, from Tel Aviv, that no traffic of any kind even a bicycle is allowed to cross the Allenby Bridge border post between Jordan and the Israeli-occupied West Bank. The only exception is the tourist bus which transports visitors across the bridge. Despite official condemnation from Amman of the Israeli occupation of the West Bank, and the fact that the borders between the two countries are supposedly closed, it is easy to cross from one country to the other. Because Jordan claims the West Bank, it is possible to obtain a permit to visit there, since one is still supposedly visiting an occupied part of Jordan. Since the West Bank is at present considered in Tel Aviv to be a part of Israel, it is a straightforward matter to travel from the West Bank into Israel. Provided no Israeli stamp has been entered in the passport as the visitor has crossed to the West Bank, the Jordanians will normally allow him to return into Jordan itself, in theory assuming that he has not been into Israel proper while in practise knowing full well that he has. Since I was unable to cycle into Israel I decided to leave the bike in Amman, hitch-hike into Israel for a few days, then return to Jordan and cycle on to Aqaba.

I had been due to speak about my journey to the Rotary Club of Amman on my arrival there but, due to a confusion in dates, I had arrived a week late. The Rotary Club Secretary was somewhat put out but soon thawed and agreed to look after my bicycle while I crossed to Israel. He also put me in touch with a club member who owned a shipping company and whom I visited next.

The owner of the shipping line went out of his way to be helpful. He ran cargo ships between Aqaba and Egypt, he explained, but had never taken passengers before, especially passengers with bicycles. However, the next boat would leave Aqaba for Egypt in ten days time and if I did not mind sitting on a cargo of oranges for the duration of the voyage, I would be able to join it. For my necessary crossing of the Red Sea to be free and to be so soon, I assured him that I would gladly spend the voyage sitting on a cargo of manure and, with only a few days spare in which to visit Israel before I set off to cycle the two hundred and twenty miles to Aqaba, I hurried off to obtain my permit to cross to the West Bank.

The day was a Thursday. The permit to visit the West Bank would take twenty-four hours to issue, but the next day was Friday, the Moslem Sabbath, and so the issuing office would be closed. I would receive the permit on the Saturday, but that was the Jewish Sabbath and the border would be closed. So I could not cross the Jordan river until the Sunday, and I had to be grateful that there were no Christians involved in the process or I would undoubtedly have been delayed until Monday.

Each night I cycled outside Amman to camp. It was the onset of winter and the nights in Amman were the coldest I spent anywhere on the journey. The temperature dropped below freezing point and, unable to carry heavy clothing on the bicycle, I could do nothing but lie awake for much of each night and shiver.

Leaving the bicycle in Amman I hitchhiked into the Jordan valley and through the wilderness of Samaria and Judea to Jerusalem. On the way we passed a burned-out bus. It had been the victim of a Palestinian bomb attack – a way of marking the first anniversary of the visit of Anwar Sadat to Israel. What had caused the same type of friendly, hospitable people that I had met in Damascus, Beirut and Amman to resort to this? In Jerusalem I searched out the most basic hotel I could find, though, basic as it was, I was still able to obtain a hot shower, the first hot water since Istanbul.

Bethlehem, the Garden of Gethsemene, the Via Dolorosa, the Mount of Olives, the Wailing Wall, the Dome of the Rock. Three days passed in a blur of birth places and burial sites, most places that are mentioned in the Bible and plenty that are not. So little time to see a place with more prophets, Messiahs and religions than I had had flat tyres. Too soon I had to return to Amman to visit the shipping agent.

There had always been the possibility, while I was in Israel, that the Israelis and Jordanians may have had a difference of opinion and closed the border, leaving me stranded in Israel, with Rover still in Jordan. It was with a feeling of relief that I was able to cross the border, return to Amman, and collect the bicycle, this having been the first time in more than three months that it had been out of my sight for a period of more than a few hours.

The boat that was due to sail to Egypt had been delayed but would be arriving in Aqaba in five days' time, I was told in the shipping office. The boat would, appropriately enough, be called the *Aqaba* and a telex would be sent to their company offices in Aqaba to tell them to expect me. As soon as I reached Aqaba I should report to the offices.

There seemed no hurry to set off to Aqaba. If the ship was only due in the port in five days' time and as it still had to unload a cargo, it could be several more days before it left. After another bitterly cold night, even with tent, sleeping bag, survival bag, anorak, and wearing all the other clothes I possessed, I packed a supply of food on to the bicycle and set off for the Red Sea. Once again there was a Palestinian refugee camp through which to ride. It was a depressing sight after comparatively spacious, opulent Amman, made more so by the fact that the Palestinians tend to despise the Jordanians for their compromising attitude towards Israel, despite the fact that Jordan has given a home to more of them than all the other Arab states combined.

Apart from occasional Bedouin tents there was little sign of habitation once I had left Amman. The road was reasonably flat and with a warm sun but a gently cooling breeze the afternoon was perfect for cycling. The rolling landscape seemed to be made of dust, and occasional rocky hills formed strange outlines, some like fortresses others like great beasts. The following day I rode on, passing through an area where sand-flats stretched to each horizon. There, clouds of sand would sweep towards the road in 'dust-devils', conical whirlwinds of flying sand. They whipped across the road, stinging my bare legs below the shorts that I was wearing, before continuing on their way towards the new horizon, twisting and writhing as if possessing minds of their own.

I stopped at a roadside café to fill my water bottles and try to buy bread, and three soldiers insisted that I join them in their meal. It was the exact replica of other meals that I had eaten with Jordanians – bread, olives and a milky cheese. Since I cared neither for olives nor milky cheese and found dry bread alone rather unappetizing, I ate as little as was politely possible before leaving. It would have appeared extravagent to eat with them and then buy my own bread and ride away with it, so I did not buy any bread there but waited until I reached the next café, later in the day. There, exactly the same occurrence took place with different people but with the same choice of food, causing me to think that it must be the only food the people in Jordan eat. Late in the afternoon I again tried to buy bread, stopping in a Bedouin settlement at a small roadside shop, where I was invited to spend the night. Having only cycled forty-six miles that day I would have preferred to cycle for another hour until dark, but the thought of not needing to find a concealed camping place, pitch the tent and organize my own food was too tempting and I accepted the offer. Besides, the sun was going down and it was again turning very cold. The shopkeeper invited a number of his friends from the village, and we joined in a meal of – bread, olives and milky cheese! I had heard about staple diets but this seemed absurd.

Around 10 pm the shopkeeper dragged a mattress into the shop from a storeroom behind and insisted that I sleep on his mattress while he slept on the bare floor. Outside, an icy wind whistled around the sandstone hut, causing me to feel particularly grateful that I was not in my tent. 'The water is turning to ice,' was a quaint expression used to describe the outside temperature and, when I was told that it was the 'beginning of winter', I wondered what the middle of a Jordanian winter would be like! In the morning, before leaving, I was served breakfast, which was a change of diet: bread, olives, and no milky cheese. At lunchtime I ate a vegetable dish in a roadside café, only for the waiter to insist that he would pay for it. During the day, whenever I called into a village for water, I would be given tea to drink. On one occasion the generosity worked in reverse – though not intentionally. I had stopped to eat a portion of one of the pieces of bread that I had at last been able to buy. The bread was of the unleavened variety and shaped rather like a pancake. With it I was eating some of my precious reserves of jam, and had pushed the bicycle away from the road, into the shade of some rocks. A few camels came over the hill followed by a group of women who kept a discreet distance from me, and their children. Finally the owner of the party, a wizened old Arab appeared, and approached me. I had learned by this time that in the Islamic countries if I was eating when an Arab came over, it was good policy to offer him something. No-one had ever yet accepted, and it usually encouraged them to offer something to me! The old nomad either did not realize this rule, or else he had been caught before. I offered him a whole piece of bread, the tin of jam and a knife. In the unlikely event of him accepting the offer, I expected him to do no more than break off a piece of bread and spread a little jam on it, returning the tin, knife and remainder of the bread to me. Instead he grasped all three and set off down the hill after his camels, making grateful Arabic noises. I had to fetch him back, tear off a piece of bread, jam it (conservatively) then give it to him. He seemed no less happy and, pointing down the hill, set off towards his camels for whom he probably thought the jam and bread were intended.

The scenery continued as it had been the previous day and that night, after cycling sixty-seven miles during the day, I camped in the ruins of a rather eerie, abandoned village, the broken-down walls of a house providing shelter from the chill wind. A large moon shone from the clear sky on to the collapsing buildings and I wondered what had caused it to become a ghost village: a water supply that had ceased to exist, or perhaps one of the

Government's less successful attempts to settle the Bedouins, who may have found the call to return to the nomadic life irresistible?

Two days later, after a long downhill ride between spectacular towering cliffs, I reached Aqaba on the day that the *Aqaba* was due to dock. It seemed unreal that now only a handful of cycling miles separated me from Africa. All being well I would be in Egypt in a matter of days. All was not well. On my arrival I visited the offices of the shipping company where the manager of the Aqaba branch made it plain that he did not approve of the company taking a passenger on board one of its freight ships. Without even looking up from his desk he told me that the *Aqaba* had not yet arrived, that it would be at least a week before it did dock, and that it then had to unload its cargo before it sailed again. Still looking at his desk he advised me not to return to the office for several days, and sounded as if he would lose no sleep if I did not return at all.

There is nothing more frustrating to the traveller than to be kept waiting with nothing to do to while away the time, particularly when the wait could be for an indefinite period and is in an area with as high a cost of living as Aqaba. I spent the day in making enquiries among other shipping agents and at the port, but the next boat to Egypt appeared to be the official passenger ferry which was not only expensive but which was not due to leave for more than a month. Finally, to pass the time doing something, I joined the local library where I was able to borrow a book, leaving my passport as security. That evening I selected the most impressive hotel in the town and sat in the lounge performing the usual nocturnal chore of writing my diary of the day's events. Sitting in an armchair beneath electric lights made a pleasant change from writing by candlelight while lying in the tent and it also gave me the opportunity to meet a shipping agent who was drinking at the hotel. He gave me the name of the harbour master at the port and, after camping the night near to the beach, I visited the harbour master the following morning.

I had been advised that I may not be allowed to enter the port area, but the bicycle so fascinated the guards at the gates that one of them rushed away to make tea while the other one signed a permit for me to enter. Once in the port, I was told that the harbour master was out for the morning and that I should return in the afternoon. I did so, receiving another glass of tea at the main gates. The harbour master had not yet returned and I was asked to wait for an hour, until 4 pm. The staff at the Enquiries Office took one look at the bike and set about making glasses of cocoa, and while I drank I resisted the impulse to ask if somebody had broken their teapot. I asked about the *Aqaba* and was told it had already left the port, sailing the previous evening for Suez!

By four o'clock I had forgotten my appointment with the harbour master and had cycled back from the port to the shipping office. The manager jumped as if I had just caught him with his hand in the safe and, without taking his eyes from his desk, announced that the *Aqaba* would be leaving for Suez that same evening. 'If you want to go on it you had better have your passport and health documents here by 5 pm so that we can take you to the port,' he said to his desk, though I assumed that the news was meant for me. There was no point in arguing about why his information had changed so suddenly. I had exactly one hour in which to retrieve my passport from the library, where I had deposited it the previous day as surety on the borrowed book. I rode to the library and there my heart sank. The day was the first day of the Moslem New Year and yet another public holiday. The library was closed and my passport was locked inside. Until I retrieved that I could not even leave the country.

Normally the last people to ask for help from a country of the Third World are the police. Whatever the problem, even if they are willing to help, they are usually too disorganized. The person that you need to see is asleep or all the patrol cars are broken down and, if you were to say that your passport was at the local library, they would be quite liable to arrest you for not being in possession of the document. But in this instance, especially with the language barrier, my chances of finding unaided the person with the key to the library in less than one hour were nil. In the unlikely event of anyone being able to help, it had to be the Royal Police Force of the Hashemite Kingdom of Jordan. It was not an encouraging thought.

I cycled at top speed to the police station where the officer in charge was slumped over his desk fast asleep. I awakened him and tried to instil some sense of urgency into the genial policeman. 'From where you are coming?' he beamed at me and, 'to where you are going?' His face registered disbelief that it was possible for anyone to cycle all the way from Amman to Aqaba, and he and his colleagues had to see the amazing bicycle on which I had travelled more than two hundred miles, to make sure that it did not have a motor. Eventually the officer made a telephone call which he told me was to find out who the librarian was and where he lived. It did not sound very promising and I sat in the cool, whitewashed office waiting for the person to ring back, while the officer in charge resumed his state of hibernation. A few minutes later the telephone rang and, from that point, began a chain of efficiency that would have done credit to the forces of New Scotland Yard. Whoever the officer had previously telephoned was now ringing back with the address of the librarian. A police car had already been summoned and, in the car, with two policemen, I was driven through dusty back streets, between close-packed sandstone houses one of which we stopped outside. The librarian was not there, but we were sent to another house and after touring a number of houses, during which we found a librarian but not the one with the key to the library, we eventually located the correct person on the beach. A dash in the police car to the library, and the librarian ran into the building with the book that I had borrowed, returning moments later with my passport. At 4.50 pm I was back at the police station and re-entered the office of the branch manager of the shipping company at exactly five o'clock.

The manager continued writing as if I had not entered, but told his desk to go straight to the port and someone would meet it at the Passport Office. As the desk didn't move I assumed that the instruction was intended for me and set off back to the port. I arrived at the Passport Office at the same time as the shipping company's agent who had been sent to meet me and he guided me to the Immigration Office. The officer on duty could have been the twin brother of the Immigration Officer who I had encountered as I entered the country, with the same surly expression and attitude of indifference. He took my passport into another office 'to be examined' and then returned to tell me, 'You have money to pay.' Before I had crossed into Israel I had carefully checked my passport to ensure that my Jordanian visa had no expiry date written on it, so that there was no possibility of it expiring while I was in Israel so preventing my return into Jordan. Though the visa was written in Arabic, several Jordanians had checked it and each had told me that it was valid for a full three months. Yet now, at the port, the Immigration Officer showed me the Arabic words for 'one week' written on the visa and insisted that, since I had entered Jordan more than a week ago, I must buy a new visa before I would be allowed to leave the country. It was obvious that he had written the expiry date on to the passport when he had taken it away 'for examination', but it was impossible to prove. It amounted to a bribe. Either I gave him the money for a new visa or I missed the boat. My three years in Africa, passing through dozens of border posts, had educated me in numerous similar attempts at bribery. Experience had taught me that, if you continue to refuse to pay, the Customs or Immigration Officer will realize that he is not going to get rich quick at your expense and you will eventually be allowed to pass through the post. Jeff and I had spent hours in playing waiting games at border posts across Africa, and were irritated by people that we met who preferred to pay the bribe, since we felt that such an attitude simply made life more difficult for the next travellers to arrive at that border post. So, at Aqaba, I refused to pay, reasonably confident that, if I waited patiently and talked in a friendly manner to the official, I would eventually be allowed to leave the country, but determined that I would see the *Aqaba* sail without me rather than give in to the attempted bribe. It was the shipping company's agent who solved the situation by, despite my protests, paying the required money from company funds. Whispering that his firm could not afford to upset Immigration Officials, he ushered me through the barrier to the quayside and on board the *Aqaba.* That night I stood on deck beneath the stars, looking across the bay to the point at which I had pitched the tent the previous night and muttered fervent thanks to all those hands of fate who may have offered a finger towards my unexpected change of fortune. Twenty-four hours previously it had seemed that I might be waiting weeks, enduring an expensive and tedious period of inactivity in Aqaba. Now I was only a few days sail from Africa.

Far from spending the voyage to Suez sitting on a cargo of oranges, or even of manure, the ship's captain provided me with a small cabin, and I was able to eat with the crew – though, as one crew member commented, it was questionable whether the latter was a privilege or punishment. As we sailed down the Gulf of Aqaba I took my last look at the Middle East with some regret. I had left Britain with the impression that the Arabs are dirty, thieving, begging people, but I had found that I could not have done them a greater injustice. The countries of the Middle

East are dirty and full of flies. In the towns litter lies everywhere, while outside the towns dead dogs, goats or camels lie beside the road and rot. But the people themselves take more care to keep clean than many Europeans do. With the understandable exception of the Palestinian refugee camps the standard of living is quite high, with very little absolute poverty. The hospitality of the people, as demanded by their religious code, is almost overwhelming and their generosity had amazed me. I had made the chances of stealing from the bicycle as difficult as possible by always trying to keep at least one eye on the bicycle and by wiring everything on to the frame. But I could never make it burglar-proof, and there had been times when I had been careless and I had realized that an opportunity for thieves had arisen. My impressions, however, of the people of Turkey, Syria, Lebanon, and Jordan, was that not only would the majority of them not steal, but they would do their best to prevent anyone else from stealing. In fact, so far, the only thing that had been stolen from me was a book – and that was before I left England, on the train travelling to London! Even the bicycle had behaved itself surprisingly well so far, all things considered.

With the rugged mountains of the Sinai Peninsula to the right the *Aqaba* turned northwards into the Gulf of Suez. After five nights on board the ship the bicycle was lowered on to the quayside at Suez. Here again I soon ran into difficulties with the Immigration authorities, though this time the fault was mostly mine. I had obtained my visa for Egypt in Damascus. It was written in Arabic and I had assumed that, like most visas, it would be valid for three months from the date of issue. Instead of checking on this I had taken it for granted, but the Immigration Officer at Suez now informed me that the visa had been valid for only one month from the date on which it had been stamped in my passport. Consequently, it had expired five days previously. I would have to buy a new visa. He also informed me that I must change all my foreign currency and travellers' cheques into Egyptian money which I refused to do, knowing that I would almost certainly not be allowed to re-change the money into a convertible currency when I left the country. Unwilling to change more than a small portion of my money and, being unable to read Arabic, suspicious that he might be trying to cheat me concerning the visa, I left the Immigration Office and re-emerged into the port area. A large metal gate stood ajar in front of me and I pushed the bicycle towards it. A uniformed official lounged in a chair beside the gate and asked if I had been through Immigration. 'Yes, I have seen the Immigration Officer,' I replied truthfully, and he waved me through the gate where I found myself immediately caught up in the bustle of the streets of Suez. I knew that having no stamp in my passport to show that I had entered the country legally, I could encounter problems in the eastern parts of Egypt which was still classed as a military zone. However, I decided that I would just hope that my passport was not inspected before I reached Cairo, where the authorities would be accustomed to tourists and I could sort out the problem.

Suez reminded me of Beirut, many of its buildings still showing the scars of rocket attacks. I stopped to ask a policeman for the road to Cairo and he held out his hand and said, 'Money?'. If I had any illusions that Africa might have changed in the two and a half years since I left, they ceased there. I found the road to Cairo and left Suez, accompanied by an entourage of shouting cyclists. The more adventurous accompanied me for a mile or two outside the town, wheeling around me like circling vultures until, still shouting for 'baksheesh', they turned and headed back to the town.

The road to Cairo wound through flat, empty waste-land stretching away to each side. At first the wind was behind me. I could hardly believe it but, true to form, within a few minutes it had turned round and was blowing against me, though fortunately it was not strong. The region was deserted apart from army camps. I was stopped occasionally at army check-points. Most soldiers looked at my visa and were satisfied. At two road-blocks I was asked why the visa had expired and I replied that I had been told at Suez to obtain a new one in Cairo. I cycled seventy of the eighty-three miles to Cairo before stopping for the night, not wishing to enter a city, looking for accommodation in darkness. The following morning the wind had increased and dust was blowing everywhere as I entered the sprawling suburbs of Cairo.

Africa's largest city could not really be termed a haven for cyclists. It contains one quarter of Egypt's forty million population. It also seemed to contain the country's entire population of vehicles. I rode through the heaving mass of Cairo, between, around and, in some cases, almost over, its swarming pedestrians. Blaring horns, screeching brakes, shouting people. Mostly they seemed not to know why they were sounding their horns or why they were shouting. Perhaps they were doing it because it was Cairo and, without the constant din, it would be too much like any ordinary city in the world. If I had patiently waited my turn in the traffic jams, I may well have been sitting there yet. Instead I weaved in and out of the queueing vehicles to the centre of the city. In Tahrir Square I paused and watched in amazement as I observed what must surely rate as the Eighth Wonder of the World – Cairo Bus Station. The sides of each bus seemed to bulge as the prospective passengers jostled and fought to squeeze their way on board. As a bus drew away, people were still boarding, forcing themselves through the packed doorways, scrambling through open windows, and hanging on to the sides and the rear of the vehicle.

Egypt has a comparatively well-organized system of youth hostels and it was at the Cairo Youth Hostel that I slept during my week in the city. My visa problem was solved after countless hours sitting in several offices, waiting or being interviewed by numerous officials. The officials were always very polite and I had the impression that they liked someone different to talk to. Egypt is notorious for its bureaucracy and before long a thick file had been accumulated on my story that the Suez Immigration Officer had told me to renew my visa in Cairo. I moved gradually up the ranks from Immigration to the Department of the Interior and, when I was beginning to think that I would end up knocking on a door marked 'President Sadat', and having to tell him my story, I reached the top of the bureaucratic tree in the form of the State Security Officer, a good-humoured character who immediately authorized my new visa. From the tree-top the message spread downwards along the twigs and branches to the trunk. From there it continued to the roots until a little man in a poky office received the word, and smilingly applied the necessary stamp to my passport. I had received my visa free of charge, I had not been asked to change any of my money into Egyptian currency and the State Security Officer had given me his name and telephone number in case I encountered any further difficulties while in the country.

Once I had retrieved my passport I was able to set about obtaining my visa for the Sudan, from the embassy for that country. The embassy official told me that he could not issue me with a visa to travel by bicycle since it would be too dangerous to attempt to cross Sudan on a cycle so, under the heading 'Type of Transport', where I had written 'bicycle', I crossed it out and wrote 'public transport'. My visa was granted immediately.

While in Cairo I had been asked to speak to the Rotary Club about my travels. The luncheon meeting which I had been invited to attend was in the five-star Nile Hilton Hotel and I was due to speak for ten minutes after the main speaker, the Minister for Land Development. It had been suggested that I display the bicycle in the hall where the luncheon was being held, and it had been my intention to clean it so that it sparkled for the occasion. Unfortunately, the wasted time in the Passport Offices had left me with no time in which to clean it, so I decided that it would look more business-like if I took it in as it had been when I rode into Cairo. I had borrowed a shirt and tie for the occasion, and I arrived early at the Hilton Hotel where I attempted to push the bike through the lobby to the main lift. There had been a shower of rain as I cycled to the hotel, and the wet tyres left a muddy trail across the hotel's plush carpet, making it look as if a snake had crawled across the floor. Within seconds almost every porter on the premises seemed to be blocking my route and urging me back towards the doors, and, after heated discussion, I was eventually able to take the bicycle to the first floor but only by way of the kitchen lift.

It had been suggested that I show some of my equipment to the Rotarians and, among other things, I had chosen the burglar alarm. This had recently developed a tendency to go off at unexpected moments due to dirty connections, and I had still not remembered to clean them. The Rotarians were digesting a very palatable lunch and the Minister for Land Development was mid-way through a very boring speech. I was at the Chairman's table, just to the right of the Minister and the alarm was on the table before me. It could not have chosen a more inopportune moment to sound and, while I struggled to open the casing and silence the gadget, the Minister gave me a look which suggested that I was fortunate that he was merely responsible for Land Development and was not the Minister of Prisons!

At the end of a week, having joined thousands of others in visiting the tourist spots of Cairo and its surrounding area, I prepared to move on again, for I was still well short of the half-way mark of the ten thousand miles that I expected to cycle. I had still not cleaned the bicycle, but it seemed unnecessary to do so since it was working so well. I had a feeling that perhaps the dirt was holding it together and that, if I cleaned it, it might begin to disintegrate, so I left it dirty and vowed that I would definitely clean it when I reached Nairobi.

6

As I left Cairo in mid-December 1978, my spirits were high. I had cycled four thousand miles in the four months since leaving England and felt confident that the pedalling aspect of the journey should not now present an insurmountable problem. I was even becoming accustomed to sitting in the saddle. A leather saddle could never be favourably compared with a fully upholstered foam-cushioned armchair, but at least either the saddle was fitting to my shape or my contours were altering to match it.

Looking ahead, I had six hundred miles of mainly tarmac road to Aswan, then the ferry crossing of Lake Nasser before what I knew would be the most difficult stretch of the journey, the crossing of the Nubian Desert, the section of the Sahara which occupies northern Sudan. The Sahara Desert itself covers three million three hundred and twenty square miles, and I had to cross just two hundred and twenty miles of it. Two hundred and twenty miles is not far to ride a bicycle, but it is a long way to push one, and I anticipated that the softness of the sand would prevent me from riding far. I also knew that the Sudan, that huge desolate country which, covering an area of almost one hundred thousand square miles, is Africa's largest country and more than ten times the size of the United Kingdom, would have other obstacles in store for me, not least of which would be leaving the country. If I was unable to enter Uganda from Sudan, the only alternative would be the little-used route into north-western Kenya. Still looking to the future I also knew, from past experience of the African people, that I would be unable to count on the same kindness and helpfulness that I had experienced in the Islamic countries. In Africa, with its inhospitable climate, terrain and political systems, life is the survival of the fittest, and those who put themselves in difficult situations are liable to realize that they have to find their own way out or pay the price.

I was aware too that time was not on my side. By the time I reached Sudan it would be the New Year and I would have exactly four months to reach Rhodesia to start work on May 1. It was essential that I keep this appointment to earn enough money to fly back to England at the end of 1979, after cycling on from Rhodesia to the Cape of Good Hope. I had no intention on reaching South Africa of turning round and cycling back to England.

I was looking forward now to the six-hundred mile ride to Aswan, down the narrow green strip of the Nile Valley, five to ten miles in width, following Africa's greatest river. The climate was ideal for cycling at that time of the year and, according to the meteorologists, even the wind was supposed to blow from the north, though I had more sense than to be optimistic about that. The road, I knew, would be very flat for once and I looked forward to meeting the people whom I was sure, from my encounters with Arabs so far, would be almost overwhelmingly friendly. 'From here to Aswan should be one of the most pleasant sections of the journey,' I thought to myself as I set out from Cairo, smiling benevolently at the passing motorists and pedestrians who, as always, shot puzzled glances at the laden bicycle.

As always when setting out at the beginning of a day, my first preparations were for food and water, but I knew that the Nile Valley is packed with people, and where there are people there is always food and water. So for the next few days the bicycle would be spared additional weight.

I pedalled thankfully away from the teeming mass of vehicles and people that is known as Cairo, in the direction of Giza. Here I stopped to ask the way to Aswan and received the type of response to which I had become accustomed. The group of Arabs stared in disbelief, first at me, then at one another, then back at me. 'Aswan? By bicycle? It is not possible! It is too far!' Since leaving Europe, the first few times that I had asked the direction of the next major town on my route, which could have been several hundred miles away, it had worried me when I had been told that it was too far on a bicycle and that I should follow the locals' method of putting the bicycle on to the roof of one of the single-decker buses in order to reach my destination; then, it had amused me to see their doubt for, having cycled so far, I could feel confident that I would reach the next town. But after that first few times, it became an irritation to have to explain that I had already reached that point, having cycled several thousand miles all the way from England and that I did not anticipate collapsing of exhaustion during the next section of my journey. To say that I had already cycled from England, however, was only plunging myself into deeper water. The next inevitable question would be a puzzled, 'But how did you cross the sea?' Having then spent several more minutes answering questions and informing the rapidly increasing crowd that I was cycling all the way to Zambia (I had learned on my previous visit to Africa never to say in any country north of the Zambezi River that I was travelling to South Africa), I would again return to my original purpose in stopping and enquire the distance to the next major town, in this case Aswan. And, despite having described my journey from England to that point, the answer still came back the same, 'But it is six hundred miles to Aswan. You must take the bus.' I explained, as always, that I knew the distance, I just wanted to know the direction. Eventually, someone from the throng would point a finger, usually, but not always, in the right direction, and I would be able to set off after shaking anything up to a hundred sweaty hands. The effort of extracting directions from over-friendly Arabs or Africans sometimes seemed not worthwhile, particularly since each time a direction was obtained it was advisable to check at least once before cycling too far. But a few times of pedalling ten or twenty miles along the wrong road and having to go back and start again, had long since convinced me that despite all the efforts it was worth asking, checking and double-checking when unsure of which route to take.

From Giza, I pedalled south along the banks of the Nile. Egyptian tourist information has an annoying habit of beginning brochures with the sentence, 'You can see why Herodotus called Egypt "the gift of the Nile".' But it is easy to see why. The valley is green and lush and though it covers only thirteen and a half thousand square miles, it contains more than seventy percent of the population of Egypt, most of whom appear to spend their time standing beside the Cairo-Aswan road looking for passing cyclists.

As I was leaving Giza I was also leaving the area frequented by tourists. The majority of visitors to Egypt begin at Cairo, visit the Pyramids, the Sphinx and the museums, and then head for the Temples of Luxor, four hundred and fifty miles to the south, by either bus, train, hired car, or aeroplane. Consequently, while those taking the more mundane forms of transport see something of the crowded villages which line the road and through which they pass as they travel south, the villagers see little of the tourists apart from a face leering at them through a window. To the largely uneducated Egyptian villagers, seventy percent of whom are illiterate, living their lives in great poverty, cramped together at more than a thousand per square mile, living in mud huts with thatched roofs, the average tourist must appear to them as a creature from another world. I quickly found that to see one of these creatures in the flesh *and* on a bicycle travelling amongst them was enough to arouse strange reactions in the villagers. The men and children would rush to the roadside, shouting excitedly. The women, devout Moslems, would hide their faces in their shawls and rush into their huts so that this strange male should not see any of their bare flesh. The shouts of the men and children would alert others further along the road who would respond likewise, causing a chain reaction so that as this bizarre creature on his bicycle laden with all manner of mysteries approached, scores of excited villagers would be lining the road, screaming and shouting, jumping up and down and waving their arms, their robes, or anything they were carrying.

Throughout the Middle East I had become accustomed to extrovert displays, particularly from children in some of the villages through which I passed, but nothing compared to the Nile Valley. After the first twelve miles I paused for a respite from this holocaust in a deserted area between two villages. I had just time for a drink from one of my water bottles and to calculate that I had covered one-fiftieth of the distance to Aswan, when shouts behind me alerted me to the fact that my presence had been noticed and a score of villagers were racing along the road towards me waving sticks of sugar cane. I decided that I would not wait to see if they were inviting me to taste the sugar cane, gave a cheery wave, selected a low gear, and accelerated away to the obvious chagrin of the band of villagers who after giving chase for some way, quickly became tiny dots dancing up and down in agitation in the road.

Nowhere on the banks of the Nile is there great distance between dwellings and within minutes I was back amongst the screaming and shouting of excited villagers. The further south I moved the worse it became for the wilder the people seemed to be. Braver individuals would merge from the crowd lining the roadside to try and reach out and touch me or actually make a grab at me as I rode past, and I found that I had to be on constant alert to watch for any movement in the crowds which suggested that an individual might emerge. I found that if an individual did try to pull at me, I had only to raise an arm towards him and he would withdraw with alacrity. Not possessing more than one pair of eyes, however, I could not be watching everywhere and I was frequently being prodded and poked. The strange point about the reaction of the villagers was that, contrary to all the signs, they were not unfriendly. They are simple-minded people who each wanted attention from this strange visitor. The best way to attract attention in a crowd is to make a noise. Unfortunately they were all aware of this so all tried to shout the loudest. Failing there, they would try other methods to persuade the visitor to look at them, such as tugging at his clothing, for there could be no greater privilege for one of these villagers than for a stranger to single him out and to go to him as a friend.

On a number of occasions on the first day of the ride to Aswan, I did stop amongst the villagers, though usually only because I had no choice. A group of them would occasionally stand in the road in front of me and with my path blocked I had no alternative but to stop, controlling the feeling of seething annoyance and placing across my face the largest, most friendly smile I could muster. On these occasions a crowd of dozens of villagers would swarm around each wishing to have his hand shaken, his questions answered, to touch me, and to stroke the bicycle as if it was a St Bernard's puppy. Once stopped, getting going again was an almost impossible task. The steadily increasing crowd would want me to stay longer and would hear nothing of my excuses that I had a long way still to travel that day. The only way to escape was to ride the bicycle slowly into the crowd, causing it to part, until a large enough gap appeared, and then accelerate through the opening. Then the shouts would break out again, usually in Arabic, but with the occasional snatches of English for my benefit: 'Meester, come to my house', 'Drink tea with me', and usually from the children, 'Give me baksheesh'. And the hubbub of noise would raise the alarm in the next village just along the road that something of interest was occurring and they should hurry to the roadside to see what it was.

As I approached the first town of El Aiyat, thirty miles south of Cairo, it occurred to me that if cycling through the villages of Egypt was such a traumatic experience, then the towns, with an even greater concentration of people, were likely to be still worse. I saw visions of being torn limb from limb for having done nothing more provocative than ride on a bicycle. It was with great surprise, therefore, that as I entered El Aiyat, the clamouring hoards vanished to be replaced by the type of Arab to whom I had become accustomed east of the Red Sea. While I cycled I was left alone. If I stopped, polite enquiries would be made as to my health, my needs and, as always, my origins and destination. It was like sailing in a ship at sea during a hurricane, enduring a physical and mental buffeting, and suddenly entering the calm of the eye of the hurricane. As I left El Aiyat I was re-entering the storm, and on the outskirts of the town the hurricane recommenced as I cycled into a wild, shouting, whistling, waving, swarming mass of villagers.

Each main town, situated an average of sixty miles apart, was to represent a brief haven where I could hold a civilized conversation with educated Egyptians before returning to several hours of cycling through the ranks of the 'fellaheen', the peasant farmers. 'It would be the same for us if we tried to cycle through the villages,' observed an Egyptian teacher in the town of Sohag as I prepared to ride on to Luxor. 'An Egyptian with education would never do as you are doing in this country.'

As the evening approached on my first day south of

Cairo it became clear that to follow my normal custom of camping in a secluded spot a little away from the road would be somewhat difficult. Not only were there no spots that could be classed as secluded, but there was scarcely room between huts, people and foliage, to squeeze even a small hike tent. It would have been impossible to camp unnoticed and, despite my burglar alarm, judging from the people that I had seen for much of the day, there seemed a distinct possibility that I might awaken the following morning to find my bicycle missing. In fact it occurred to me that if I was to camp the night near the villages it might be a good idea to attach the burglar alarm to myself rather than to the bicycle.

I always found that after being completely exposed to people and a source of interest to them each day, it was pleasant at night to camp away from habitation and be completely alone. This would be impossible in the Nile Valley and so, as the sun neared the western horizon, I decided that since the 'fellaheen' had been keen to speak to me and touch me all day, I would present them with the opportunity. This would be the best way of assuring the safety of my possessions, for while they were always in danger of being stolen while I was my own host, no true Moslem would give hospitality and then allow his guest to be robbed. So, amid a shouting crowd of villagers, I stopped the bicycle and got off. The shouting gradually died away to a silence as I approached the nearest group and they looked as if they did not know whether to come towards me or to follow the women's example of hiding their faces and streaking for home. Suddenly they made up their minds and crowded around me in a thronging, jostling mass, shouting, laughing, touching. After much excited Arabic discussion between the villagers I was herded to the village police station where the young station sergeant shooed away the crowd as if dismissing a class of naughty school children. With the bike safely locked in a cell the policeman, who spoke good English, took me by the hand and led me around the village. In Europe a male would be a little suspicious if another male expects to hold his hand, but in the Middle East it is merely a sign of friendship and, usually at any rate, quite harmless if somewhat uncomfortable.

The village was typical of those of the Nile Valley; judged by our standards, poor and dirty, and full of the house-flies which crawl unnoticed across the faces of the villagers and which are attracted by the animals. Goats, cows, and donkeys ramble aimlessly around the mud-brick houses, relieving themselves wherever they happen to be when nature calls, as do the humans. Chickens flutter under the feet and build nests on roof-tops. At the small food market, men squat in the dust, their wares arranged on sacks before them – large quantities of healthy-looking oranges, dates, figs, olives and, of the rarer species, small piles of rotting tomatoes. Meat hangs from horizontal wooden bars – at least one assumes that it is meat, obscured as it is beneath a crawling mass of green-bottle flies. Children seem to be everywhere, living with the dust and flies as naturally as British children live in a world of televisions and motor cars, running to us to look more closely at me, until the policeman whips his thin stick through the air towards them, sending them scurrying away, laughing; the little girls running happily in their ragged dresses, teeth flashing beneath large tender brown eyes, for they are not yet subject to the restrictions of the Moslem code which, when they are old enough to attract men, will demand that they be shrouded in black and that they hide their faces. Is it fair, I asked myself, to compare the life of these people with our own in Britain? I remembered the words of a Cairo businessman that it is the ambition of every educated Egyptian living in the smaller towns or the villages, to live in Cairo, and the ambition of every Egyptian living in Cairo to live in Europe.

We stopped at a much larger, white-washed mud-brick

built house which was the home of the chief of the village. The elderly chief, who also spoke some English, took my other hand and gave me a guided tour of the rooms of his house; the room where his ducks, geese and hens lived, that where his cows and goats were spending the night, the next where his donkeys were sleeping, and another where his family lived.

The sergeant, having seen the sights before, returned to the police station, and the chief showed me into his private sitting room where, obviously informed of my arrival in the village, a number of elderly advisers appeared as if summoned by a rub on a lamp. They sat cross-legged on the floor drinking tea, while the chief and I sat in two battered old armchairs which looked as if they had been left behind by the Pharaohs, After I had admired the comfort of the armchair, secretly feeling grateful that I did not have to sit on that all the way to Capetown, the chief dramatically produced one of his most treasured possessions, a portable record player, on which one of his advisers carefully placed a record. From the way that the rhythmical native music vibrated round the room it was clear that whoever the chief had obtained the machine from had not troubled to point out the purpose of the volume control. The record eventually scratched its way to the end and the chief, obviously anxious to please his guest, set out before me a game of Ludo. For the next twenty minutes there was silence in the room, broken only by surreptitious whispers from the advisers and the rattle of the dice in the earthenware pot, as I chased the chief's counters around the board, taking great care not to knock off any of his counters but occasionally to have one of mine removed by him. To the delight of the advisers and much to my relief, the beaming chief won the game; he did not seem the type who liked to lose, and his guffaws of laughter were still echoing around the house when the police officer returned and the advisers took their leave.

After the three of us had eaten bread, cheese, olives and

oranges in the chief's home, the familiar Arab argument developed concerning where I should sleep. Both were determined that I should spend the night in their own home, the policeman arguing that, as the force of law and order, I should stay with him; the chief replying that, as head of the village, I should be his guest. I stood and waited for the discussion to reach a stalemate, aware from past experience that I would shortly be called upon to make the embarrassing decision. Both turned to me to commence the equally familiar attempts at swaying my judgement, the policeman telling me that in his house I could listen to the BBC World Service on his radio, the chief trying to lure me with the promise of fresh eggs for breakfast. I don't care for eggs and I was keen to hear the BBC News. The chief concealed his disappointment well and, back at the police officer's modest little home, I listened to the World News while my new friend conscientiously disappeared on horseback to make his rounds of the village.

The following morning I toured the village again. Meeting the people at close quarters further convinced me that they really were quite harmless if somewhat extrovert. I decided that if I were to stop in each village on my way to Aswan and speak with every individual that approached me, I would undoubtedly reach Aswan without being subjected to the baying wolf pack attitude that I had encountered from the 'fellaheen' on the previous day. Unfortunately to do an American Presidential type of walk-about in the continual line of villages would, from my experience in this one village, take somewhere in the region of ten years, and so the only alternative would be to follow the previous day's policy of riding through the opposition at top speed.

By the time I had again held hands with the police sergeant, further admired the chief's donkeys, and politely eaten enough olives to almost destroy my liver, it was midday, and my hosts were quite upset when I insisted that it was necessary for me to leave.

Returning to the main Cairo to Aswan road was like entering a zoo at feeding time. As I cycled on between the lines of mud huts, the women again hid their faces and ran for cover, while the men and children rushed into the road in front of me or shouted from the roadside the odd English expression, that they had accumulated: 'Yes, please; I speak English good'; 'What is my name?'; 'What time it now is?' As I became more and more irritated the Egyptians learned some new English phrases!

Having made a late start to the day's cycling, the sun was going down when I reached the town of Beni Suef and though I had only cycled thirty miles, I had had enough for the day. I found one of the cheap but very satisfactory hotels which are abundant in Egypt, where I was quickly befriended by a group of Egyptian teachers who sympathized greatly with my 'fellaheen' problem and seemed determined to try to make up for it by making me gifts of food and introducing me to the Egyptian drink of sugar-cane juice. This is made by grinding sticks of sugar-cane in what is basically an old-fashioned mangle, and the resulting sickly brown juice, once a taste has been acquired for it, is an absolute delight. Unfortunately my friends omitted to warn me that, drunk in excess, the liquid is liable to make one feel extremely ill, and it was left to me to discover that for myself in Aswan.

My third day out from Cairo proved no less mentally exhausting than the previous two and I spent the night in the town of El Minya as the guest of a group of young, educated Egyptians who kept up a stream of muttered apologies in response to my tirade against the 'fellaheen'. 'Your journey will become more difficult as you proceed south,' my friends hesitantly informed me, but I confidently assured them that the people could become no worse. I should have reserved my judgement. The next day I left for Asyut, eighty-five miles south and still less than half-way to Aswan, and discovered what is apparently the national sport of Upper Egypt – stoning cyclists. I quickly learned the rules. Though the game can be played by any number of players from two upwards, it is apparently more fun for the majority of the participants if played by several thousand. One person should be riding a bicycle, the remainder of the players line up on each side of the Cairo to Aswan road each equipped with either a stone or a stick of sugar-cane. As the cyclist passes, the stones are thrown in his direction and, if the range is suitable, he is hit with the sticks of sugar-cane. While a general rule was that only males and non-adolescent females may play, minor regulations varied from village to village. For example, in some villages the players preferred to throw olives rather than stones while in others, rather than hit the cyclist with the sticks of sugar-cane, it was more fun to try to poke the cane between the spokes of the wheels. This seemed a silly game to me, but I was the cyclist. Perhaps if I had altered my role to that of an attacker instead of the lone defender, I may have seen the fun in the pastime, but there were not many other cyclists around for me to experiment on. In fact, despite the favourable flat land, Egyptians seemed to have a noticeable aversion to riding bicycles outside the main towns. That was not really surprising since not only did the peasant farmers have their own national game but the lorry drivers and the villagers' dogs had their own versions which I had previously encountered before crossing the Red Sea; the lorry-drivers' game of 'Put the Cyclist in the Ditch' and the canine variant of 'Chase the Cyclist'.

There was only one point in my favour regarding the assault by the villagers and it was that as I proceeded further south their reactions were slower and whereas an Egyptian further north would have seen me coming and shouted and danced at the roadside in anticipation of my cycling past him, it was noticeable that the more southern 'fellaheen' would observe my imminent arrival but stare blankly in bewilderment for several seconds as I approached. By the time they had realized that I was a prime target, I was often leaving them behind, and their only recourse would be to send a few missiles harmlessly after me.

A couple of hours after leaving El Minya my resolve not to respond to the provocations of the 'fellaheen' cracked. A boy of perhaps fourteen tried to catch hold of the bicycle as I rode past and, stopping quickly, I dropped the bike in the road and leaped off. The mass of villagers could not have been more surprised if they had been a pack of hounds in the hunt and the hare had just turned on them. They fled in all directions and, ignoring them all and forgetting about the bike in the heat of the moment, I chased the offending boy. He emitted a high-pitched squeal and ran towards the village while I followed him around the huts and past groups of astonished women. The chase ended when he rushed, screaming and wide-eyed into a group of women clad in their black draperies. They did not know what to do first, protect the boy or hide their faces. Seeing that the cause of the trouble had been temporarily reduced to a trembling, gibbering wreck, I remembered that the bicycle was still lying in the road and sprinted back to find it surrounded by a crowd of curious onlookers all inevitably anxious to touch it and to shake my hand. When I finally left with an aching right arm and sweaty palm, I decided to introduce a new rule to the game. Finding a lump of rock the size of a cricket ball I concealed it on top of one of my panniers ready to seize at a moment's notice. As I approached the next village a loud cry of excitement went up and I could see the sugar-cane being waved in anticipation of some great sport. I cycled slowly until I neared where perhaps two hundred people were jostling for a roadside position in order to be able to poke at me with greater accuracy, and, bearing in mind the famous battle adage about seeing the whites of their eyes, suddenly let out a series of loud shouts of best British colloquial expressions and, waving the rock and making as if to throw it into the midst of them, speeded away as the majority of the participants of the national sport rapidly left the roadside in search of a more peaceful hobby.

As I cycled further south, not only did civilized behaviour on the part of the villagers (and of me!) deteriorate, but so did the quality of the road. The tar surface, liable to cracking under the heat of the sun, was full of splits and holes and for the seventy-five miles between El Minya and Asyut the bicycle had to withstand a great deal of vibration at a time when the last thing that I wanted was for the wheels to be subjected to excess stress. In Asyut I stayed at the youth hostel which was otherwise completely empty and mentally prepared myself for the next day's seventy-mile exposure to the 'fellaheen' as I made for Sohag. Strangely, the following day the people seemed to have improved a little and I was chased by fewer dogs and had less stones thrown at me. Perhaps word had spread that an uncivilized European cyclist was riding through the villages shouting obscenities and threatening to throw a large stone at any person who innocently approached him. Even the road surface was better and a northerly wind had sprung up to help me along.

In Sohag I again found the youth hostel, but was told that it was full. It occurred to me that it was very strange that the youth hostel in the last town had been empty yet this one should have no more room, and I felt it more likely that this youth hostel was also empty and the Warden could not be bothered opening up for one person. However, the inevitable crowd had gathered round me and the bicycle and, realizing that I was English, a young Egyptian informed me that there were English teachers living in Sohag and that he would take me to their home. It was another noticeable difference between British and Egyptian customs. I felt reluctant to appear, scruffy and uninvited, on someone's doorstep, simply because they were also British. The Egyptian, however, could see nothing wrong with this. It was quite natural, under the Moslem code, for me as a stranger to arrive at the house of my fellow countrymen and expect hospitality. In actual fact I need not have worried. The three Englishmen, working for the Voluntary Service Overseas, were amazed when an English cyclist knocked on the door and, as so often in regions like Sohag where tourists do not often stay, were as pleased to have a new face amongst them for the night as I was to be able to speak to English people again.

Word of the wild, rock-throwing British cyclist had obviously not reached the villagers living along the roadside between Sohag and Qena, for the 'fellaheen' were at their riotous best south of Sohag and the ninety miles to Qena was like an obstacle course. By now I had lost all patience with the people in the villages, who seemed to have the mentality of sheep: if one shouted they all shouted, if one jumped into the road in front of me they all followed him, if one threw a stone the result would be like a hailstorm, and I had found that the only practical method of negotiating the route was to play the villagers at their own game, deciding that the best method of defence was attack. As soon as I saw a village ahead, I would slow down, engage a low gear ready for quick acceleration, and conceal my hunk of rock in my fist. The shock tactic of my sudden shouting coupled with the sheep instinct of the masses, gave the desired result. As I rode at them, threatening to throw the stone, they scattered, and though a few stones came rattling harmlessly along the tarmac after me I was through the village, my legs revolving like the rotor arms on a helicopter. It was a good method of making enemies and if I had had a blow-out before having completely cleared a village, I would probably have been a hospital case, but the tactics saw me along the route with a great deal more peace than I would otherwise have had, though I have often wondered how the next cyclist down that road fared.

In Qena, I again found the urban Egyptians to be considerate, hospitable, and unable to find enough adjectives to put before the word 'sorry' when emphasizing their apologies for the antics of the 'fellaheen'.

The next day saw me in Luxor, a sure stop-over place for any tourist in Egypt. I spent two days in making a rapid tour of the magnificent historical sights: Karnak, the Valley of the Kings, the Tombs of the Queens, the Ramesseum, Queen Hatshepsut's Temple and, for me the most impressive, the Collossi of Memnon. Since many tourists hire bicycles in Luxor in order to cycle from one monument to another, the locals were quite accustomed to seeing strangers using this method of transport, and it made a pleasant change to be able to ride unmolested. While two days is only a fraction of the time that should be spent in a town with as much history as Luxor and its surrounding area, it was all the time that I had available and as long as I could happily spend in such a tourists' paradise, where every visitor is seen by the locals as a gold-plated dollar sign.

Eight days after leaving Cairo I cycled into Aswan. It was Christmas Day 1978, and there could have been no better Christmas present for me than the knowledge that I had no further to cycle in Egypt.

7

Aswan, Egypt's most southern town, has, like Luxor, been made into a tourist centre. Its setting beside sand-dunes sloping down to the river, with tourist-shops on the waterfront makes it seem like Bognor Regis on a sunny day. It is difficult to imagine in this idyllic haven, that those sand-dunes belong to a savage desert and that beyond them lies tropical Africa.

In the youth hostel I found about fifteen other Europeans waiting for the ferry that would take us across the Lake Nasser to the Sudanese town of Wadi Halfa. No-one was sure when the next boat would leave for, as usual in the countries of the Third World, a different story had been given in answer to each enquiry. The consensus of opinion among the travellers was that the boat that was due to leave the next day would actually leave the day after. The next day, a Tuesday, I drank a few glasses of the very cheap and tasty sugar-cane juice for breakfast and then visited the Aswan office of the Nile Navigation Company in the hope of finding out definitely when the ferry would sail. I found the office, situated in a recently constructed building, looking smart and modern. The immaculately dressed official behind the desk was the picture of efficiency as he greeted me – until I asked for information on sailing times. Yes, the boat to Wadi Halfa departs every Tuesday and every Thursday, I was told. Would a boat be leaving today? No, today's sailing was delayed until tomorrow. Would the boat definitely be leaving tomorrow? Yes, I was assured. Definitely. Unless it was delayed until Thursday, in which case Thursday's ferry would be delayed until Friday though the crew would not load the boat on the Moslem Sabbath, so that would mean Saturday.

I began to understand why such a confusion of stories had abounded among the travellers in the youth hostel. I stopped at the nearest roadside café and had another couple of glasses of sugar-cane juice and lunch of the traditional Egyptian meal of 'fool', unleavened bread and a kind of haricot bean and washed it down with more sugar-cane juice. Returning to the youth hostel to compare the nonsensical information that I had accumulated concerning the ferry, with any stop-press bulletins, I found that tomorrow's ferry, which had been delayed until the day after, had actually left today and that those who had heard the news in time had hurriedly packed their rucksacks and taken the train to the ferry terminal.

At the shop across the road from the youth hostel I drank a few more glasses of sugar-cane juice and decided that the only way to be certain of catching the next boat was to go down to the ferry terminal beside the Aswan High Dam and sit there as if I was back in Britain waiting for a bus. After a last glass of sugar-cane juice and then another for the road, I set off back to the youth hostel, speeding up considerably as I felt the sugar-cane juice catching up with me. My pace increased as the effects of the drink increased and, by the time I reached the hostel, I was rapidly covering ground in the direction of the toilet, the last few yards being taken at a fast sprint. The remainder of the day was spent either in state or rolling on my bed clutching my stomach, and over and over I cursed the quantities of liquid sugar that I had consumed over the last few days, and particularly during the last few hours.

The next day I left Aswan and cycled rather slowly and painfully southwards in the direction of the ferry terminal at the foot of the High Dam, stopping frequently to disappear at high speed among the rocks and boulders which were strewn across the desert landscape. At least there was peace, the vitually unpopulated district around the Aswan Dams being classed as a Military Area so I had no problems from the 'fellaheen'. Instead, a problem arose as I approached the Aswan Dam, the original Dam wall which was opened in 1902 but had since been made obsolete by the building of its big brother, the High Dam, four miles to the south. The wall of the Aswan Dam is just wide enough to allow two directions of traffic to pass over it, but it was deserted, apart from an armed soldier who leaned against a sentry-box by the roadside. He spoke no English but indicated to me that pedestrians and cyclists are not allowed to cross the wall, only motorized vehicles. I say that he spoke no English but he did know one word. The hand not holding the rifle stretched out towards me: 'Dollars!' My Arabic was scarcely more fluent than his English, but I knew enough to reply, 'La', which, with a determined shake of the head, put the message across. He shrugged his shoulders and resumed his stance supporting the sentry-box and I set off, pushing the bicycle towards the top of the dam wall. He shouted to me and waved his rifle and I decided that negotiation might prove more advisable than provocation and returned to reason with him using smiles and gestures, but to no avail. After perhaps ten minutes two more soldiers arrived. One of them spoke English, and he explained to me that though cyclists were not allowed to pass along the dam wall, his friend was willing to let me cross in exchange for a small sum of money. I relied on the system which is usually successful in situations where a bribe is being asked for, by saying that I had no Egyptian pounds left and that all my other money was in travellers' cheques; no dollars, no sterling, no deutschmarks. For a further ten minutes the guard refused to let me cross but, knowing that travellers' cheques bearing my signature would be of no value to him, and not knowing that I was lying, he realized that he was not going to become rich quickly after all and eventually told me, through his fellow-soldier, that I should hurry across the wall. After a hand-shake all round, I quickly cycled the one and a quarter miles along the wall, by which time I was ready to make another dash into the rocks.

The Egyptian tourist brochures imply that Egyptians have always been great builders and engineers. First the Pyramids, then the Suez Canal and the Aswan High Dam, have all been building projects of great magnitude, milestones in Egyptian history. The brochures will be less ostentatious in proclaiming that neither the Canal nor the Dam were due to Egyptian technology, the Suez Canal having been engineered by the Frenchman, Ferdinand de Lesseps, in 1858, while the Aswan High Dam was built during the 1960s thanks to Russian money, equipment and engineers, though the Egyptians do proudly point out that thirty-five thousand Egyptian labourers worked on its construction.

There was no difficulty in cycling the two miles along the wall of the High Dam which, planted with grass and young trees beside the road leading across the top, and with the waters of Lake Nasser three hundred and sixty-four feet below, makes an attractive ride. It was easy to trace the whereabouts of the ferry by the mass of Arabs waiting on the shores of the lake. Tied up to a jetty and looking completely deserted was the boat, or rather the boats, for the ferry was actually three ancient, flat-bottomed river-boats tied together. The idea of linking three boats together, I was later told, was far more practical, since not only could more people be carried, but if one boat began to sink, everyone could crowd on to the other two and the sinking boat would then be cut loose. By the looks of the three boats I was not sure that we would complete the two hundred miles to Wadi Halfa without all three of them sinking, but one does not let one's imagination dwell on such matters when intending to travel on African ferries. The prospective passengers squatted patiently on the lake shore, or wandered between groups. Most were men and, dressed in their long white cloaks, the scene resembled a picture of Biblical times beside Lake Galilee. From a distance it seemed like a nest of ants as the figures moved to and fro, and I wondered briefly how so many people were going to fit on to the ferry, but having witnessed the way that Cairo buses would almost bulge at the seams as more and more passengers squeezed on to them, I quickly dismissed the thought that any of these people would be left behind.

I threaded my way between the bodies which stood, sat, or lay around, until I found someone who, wearing a peaked cap and a uniform, looked reasonably official. I managed to decipher from his odd words of English that the ferry would leave the next day, Thursday, 'Insch Allah', if Allah wishes it. There being nothing more I could do I cycled back in the direction of Aswan, before finding a track which led away from the road into the isolated, barren region designated as a Military Area where, when I was not squatting amongst the rocks, I set up my tent. One of the best aids to curing a bad stomach is to eat nothing for twenty-four hours and, since nothing had gone into my body that day, but plenty had come out, I was feeling quite shaky. I decided it was time that the diahorrea was stopped, and got out from my First Aid kit my small jar of Lomotil pills. Lomotils, I am told, are the tablets that Neil Armstrong and his crew took with them to the moon in case of stomach troubles and, after calling on the service of these tablets numerous times during my three years in Africa in the Land Rover, I had no doubts that a dose of these would solve my problems. I had not taken any up to that point, believing that it is better to clear some of the complaint from the body first, but I was not expecting to find five-star toilets on board the Lake Nasser ferry and was not anxious to have a bad stomach while on the boat. The recommended dosage of Lomotils is four tablets followed by two at four hourly intervals. From my experience, two tablets will generally stop a person from needing to go to the toilet for the next few days, and four tablets at once would be enough to cure a diarrhoetic elephant. I took two and, with two more after the boat had sailed, ended my problems. I also vowed to severely restrict my consumption of sugar-cane juice in the future. As I pushed the bicycle away from my camping site the following morning, a wizened old Arab was making his way toward where my tent had been, a hopeful expression on his gnarled face. He would be looking for anything that I had left behind and I mentally wished him the best of luck for, if he looked between the rocks, he would find I had left plenty; though I doubted if what I had left was exactly what he had been hoping for.

Back at the ferry terminal the same sight met my eyes. The decks of the boat were again deserted and the ants nest of Arabs still swarmed at the lakeside, except in even greater numbers than on the previous day. The train from Aswan pulled in at the nearby station, disgorging still more prospective passengers, including six Europeans from the youth hostel. When we learned that the ferry would not be leaving that day, nor the next since it was the Sabbath, the Europeans returned to the youth hostel while I cycled back into the Military Area to pitch camp again. 'Saturday. Maybe leave nine, maybe ten, maybe eleven,' we had been told, and so I spent the intervening period in preparing the bicycle for its desert crossing, and in reading one of the paperback novels that I always carried.

When I returned to the ferry at eight o'clock on the Saturday morning, it was with relief that I observed signs of life on board the boat. I made my way through the Arabs and their vast quantities of goods which they were taking to Sudan either as gifts or to trade, towards the gates of the metal fence which separated the ferry from the crowd. I was anxious to board the boat as quickly as possible, partly to select a decent place to put my sleeping bag, but particularly to find somewhere to put the bicycle where it would be safe – and that meant immediately next to where I would be sleeping. To my surprise, I was allowed through the gate by the Customs Officers almost immediately, as it appeared to be their policy to allow tourists to board the boat first. As a result I was the first passenger aboard and was able to choose at my leisure the spot where I would spend the next two days and two nights. The three boats fastened together gave a good choice of places to occupy, at least while no-one else was on board. The traditions of the ferry dated back to when it was first used as a river boat on the Nile in the 1930s and, standing there on the deserted boat, it was not difficult to imagine the British colonialists cruising up or down the river, making use of this valuable system of transport or simply for a holiday 'booze cruise'. The boat would have been immaculately clean, the only Africans to be on board would normally have been the crew and an army of uniformed waiters ready to obey the slightest command, the fans in the cabins would have provided air-conditioning, and the luggage would have been neatly stacked below decks. Now, only remnants of this life-style exist. Wealthier Europeans travel by air not on a ferry. The cabins are still there, but those purchasing first or second class tickets have the dubious privilege of squeezing into what is now shared accommodation where, though they have the advantage of a bunk on which to sleep, it is doubtful that they will sleep well during the voyage for the fans rarely work any more and the heat in the cabins is unbearable. The days of the boat being scrupulously cleaned are also past and, though the decks are washed after each voyage, in today's crowded conditions of travel it does not take long after setting sail before hygienic conditions on the ferry are such that even the strongest European stomach would turn over.

Each of the three boats had three tiers, the water-level

deck and an upper and a lower. I selected the middle deck on the middle boat and found a section that was perhaps once used as the purser's office, an area of approximately twelve feet square, walled on three sides and with a three-foot high wall and a gate on the fourth side. I moved the bicycle into a corner of this section, spread my sleeping bag on the floor and set up a position obstructing the gate to discourage anyone from joining in my area, like a blackbird defending its territory. It was two hours, however, before the next passengers arrived on board, fifteen other Europeans, most of whom had been staying at the Aswan Youth Hostel and who had arrived on the train. They were a mixture of nationalities and included archaeologists, expatriates working in Egypt and travelling into Sudan as a holiday, and trans-African hitchhikers. Some had cabin-tickets but the remainder were, like me, travelling third class, and opted to stake a claim to a part of the upper deck of the boat in the sunshine. It seemed an attractive spot but, after a few hours, with no shade from the Egyptian sun, they regretted their choice. They regretted it even more when night came and there was no protection from the cool breeze which swept across the lake.

Around noon the gates in the metal fence behind which the Egyptians and Sudanese had been waiting were opened and the crowd surged forward like a huge tidal wave. They did not get far at first as men, women, children, luggage, pots and pans, goats and donkeys, all became jammed in the narrow gateway in the rush to board the boat. Amid much shouting, clattering, squealing and braying, the first figures emerged from the confusion. I stood in my territory, glaring at anyone who looked as if they had thoughts of joining me, until five o'clock that afternoon when the ferry finally set sail and I decided that everyone seemed settled enough in the positions which they had claimed, to be able to leave my section and take a quick walk around the boat.

Touring the decks once the remainder of the passengers had boarded was not the easiest of matters. Prostrate, cloaked figures were everywhere and one had to step between them with extreme care to avoid trampling on someone's face or fingers. On the decks, in the passages, in one of the toilet closets, people were sleeping, lying beside their packages of pans or bundles of cloth, covered by their 'galabiahs', the long white robes, as if they had gone into hibernation for the duration of the voyage. The most amazing sight was in the lower decks, obviously the most popular quarters, where the people sat or lay so closely packed together that it seemed they must have been slotted in according to their shape to make them pack tighter. These lower decks were enclosed and the chatter and shouts of scores of people filled the air, children's screams and the donkeys and goats which had been herded into a corner, adding to the clamour. Above the crowd and the noise arose the smell of the people, their wares, their food, their animals, their offal; and this was less than one hour after leaving Aswan. Two days later the stench coming from the lower decks was indescribable, and I muttered a word of gratitude to Allah that, when I had first boarded the ferry, I had not opted to make my living quarters on those lower decks. Had I done so, I would surely have needed an oxygen mask by the last day.

Two hours after leaving the Aswan ferry terminal for the two hundred mile voyage to the Sudanese town of Wadi Halfa, the boat, because it had left so close to sundown, was stopping for the night, as sailing in darkness in that area of the lake was considered unsafe. Already running four days late, it was to be delayed by a further twelve hours because it had been late leaving on that fourth day. We Europeans on board had to feel thankful that at least it had commenced its voyage and not waited in Aswan until the next morning for by then there may well have been some other reason for delaying departure.

The following morning I was awakened at first light by the Sudanese Immigration Officers who were following the sensible practice of performing their duties on the boat rather than causing chaos at Wadi Halfa. It appeared that the area that I had claimed for my living quarters was actually the Immigration Office, which perhaps explained why no Arab passengers had joined me there when they first boarded. The Moslem Immigration Officers would not have been so discourteous as to ask me to move elsewhere, however. They merely asked me to move my sleeping bag a little towards one wall, to make room for the table that they were bringing in. During the remainder of the day the five Sudanese Immigration Officers ate three meals in my 'cabin' and they invited me to join them in each. Our Western customs tend to make us refuse to join others in a meal out of politeness, but to the Arabs it is polite to accept their invitation and bad manners to refuse, so I joined them on each occasion, squatting on my haunches with them around a large, round enamel bowl on the bottom of which had been laid a thin piece of lightly baked pastry heaped with a mixture of chopped beans and vegetables. At first I would watch the others to see how they ate, but soon realized that table manners are few and simple. Since they picked up the food in their fingers it was really a matter of practice at holding the pastry between the fingers and scooping vegetables into it. The only rule to remember is to dip the right hand into the food bowl, since the left hand, used to perform ablutions, is unclean. I found this something of a problem as, being left-handed, I experienced considerable discomfort in breaking the pastry and collecting up the vegetables inside it using the fingers of my right hand. It put me at quite a disadvantage since no matter how quickly I ate I could never keep pace with the Arabs who always seemed able to operate with the efficiency of a mechanical excavator, scooping huge quantities of beans into a large handful of pastry and transferring it to the mouth before the hand dived back into the bowl for another fistful. The bowl was usually half-empty while I was still trying to break off my first piece of pastry. After the first two meals with them I explained my difficulty, and they appeared quite happy to see me eat using my left hand. Crouching around a bowl, eating with Sudanese, was to become a way of life for the next few weeks as I journeyed through the country, for I never met a Moslem in the Sudan who would be eating and who would not insist that I joined him.

The two days spent on the boat were not really my idea of pleasure, although some may have enjoyed them. There was nothing to do except talk with the other Europeans and with the Arab passengers of whom those who spoke any English would have been happy to spend the full two days in non-stop conversation. Though the sun was hot, there was a slight breeze across the lake which made lounging on the upper deck quite pleasant for limited periods. A lot of time was spent by we Europeans in watching the barren shore-line, as such empty desolation always seems to hold a fascination for those who are not accustomed to it. To each side of us barren rocks and low mountains reached down into the lake. Sometimes, particularly to the west, the rocks would be covered with golden sand and occasionally we would see large drums. We saw no settlements apart from a tiny village beside the El Sibu Temple on the eastern shore, one of the temples which were moved back from the flood waters when the lake was formed. The most famous of these is Abu Simbel on the western bank of the lake and we were disappointed that we sailed by this during the night and were unable to see anything except a few lights on the shore. Apart from these signs of habitation we saw no other evidence of life.

At ten o'clock on the morning of New Year's Day 1979, the ferry reached Wadi Halfa and complete chaos ensued as several hundred people with their baggage and animals all tried to leave the boat at once. They leapt from the middle deck, or dropped their luggage and then themselves from the upper tier of the boat, swarmed, pushed, jostled, falling off the boat on to the shore or into the water, laughing and shouting in the apparent hope that the more noise they made the quicker they would be able to leave the boat. I was in no hurry since I had been told that it was a public holiday in the Sudan and the Bank in Wadi Halfa would be closed. From discussion with my fellow travellers on the boat I had learned that we would be unlikely to find a black market on which to exchange money so I would have to wait in Wadi Halfa until the next day. It was from there that I knew the most arduous section of the journey would commence: crossing the Nubian Desert.

The two days on the boat had given me the time to calculate a time-table for the remainder of my journey to Rhodesia. In exactly four months I had to be in Salisbury to commence work, and I had more than five thousand miles to cover before then, of which nearly two thousand would be across the Sudan. Though I had not wanted to resort to public transport to speed up my journey, there was now no doubt that I would have to do so. Furthermore, this would have to be through the Sudan for otherwise I could spend the full four months in simply traversing this country. However, the Nubian Desert was the one section of the Sudan that I could not permit myself to cross on public transport. Too much had been made of this stretch of desert before I had left England. Jokes, cracked by friends who were amused by my plans, had invariably involved the Nubian Desert. Pictures had been doodled on the back of beer mats in local pubs, of a matchstick character which was supposed to look like me, waist deep in a sand-dune, or cycling towards a mirage the centre of which was dominated by a brewery. More important, however, was my personal satisfaction. Since first considering the journey I had looked at the Nubian Desert as being the greatest obstacle. I was not for one moment so foolish as to believe that if I ever succeeded in crossing the desert with the bicycle, the rest of the journey would be easy, but the thought of crossing the Nubian Desert had always been the major headache of the journey. Not for the sake of time, or for any other reason, could I simply jump on a train now that I had finally come face to face with my ultimate adversary. So I waited six hours until the boat had cleared of the other passengers and then wheeled the bike down the gang-plank on to the desert sand and set off to ride the half mile into Wadi Halfa.

As I rode away from the boat I soon began to learn the difficulties of cycling in sand. The first two hundred yards had been flattened to a firm surface by thousands of people walking to and from the ferries but as the distance from the ferry increased the passengers' route had become more spaced out and the sand was less firm. The narrow wheels, coupled with the weight of the bicycle and its luggage, caused the rims to sink into any surface which was even slightly soft. The only way through soft sand was to dismount from the bike and push it on until I reached a harder surface where I could remount and ride again. It did not take many times of performing this on-off-on-off ritual, before I realized that more progress could be made by continuous, rhythmic pushing than by mounting and dismounting every few yards.

The town of Wadi Halfa presents an even more typical view of a typical desert town than does a typical desert town, probably because it has so recently been built. The ferry had sailed over the old Wadi Halfa, for that town now lies beneath the waters of Lake Nasser, Sudan having agreed prior to the construction of the Aswan High Dam to the relocation of the town's residents in exchange for a twelve and a half million pound resettlement grant from the Egyptian Government, an inadequate amount as things turned out since Sudan later claimed that it had cost twice that amount. Built of sandstone and mud, the buildings are the same orange-brown colour as the ground on which they stand and if it was not for the roofs of corrugated tin Wadi Halfa would probably be invisible from the air. The streets are wide and there are very few vehicles. The residents rely on their feet for transport, bare or wearing sandals so that the soft sand on which they are walking does not stick inside their footwear. There are few trees and little sign of activity. Indeed, from a distance the town appears deserted. Only at close quarters can voices be heard. Most of the male inhabitants can be seen lying lethargically on the sand near the town centre, the shade of the buildings protecting them from the relentless sun which beats down from the cloudless blue sky. Women are few and far between, an occasional form, shrouded from head to toe in black, drifting by like Scrooge's Ghost of Christmas Yet to Come. Women's Lib seems a million miles from here. One cannot imagine the women of Wadi Halfa dancing around a bonfire of burning bras.

I pushed the bicycle through the western outskirts of Wadi Halfa until, to the south of the village, I saw what I was looking for – the single-track railway, stretching away to the distant horizon. The railway is the only recognized form of transport linking this outpost of the Sudan with the rest of the country and it does so via the slightly larger town of Abu Hamed, two hundred and twenty miles to the south. Between the two is the barren area of rock and sand known as the Nubian Desert, one of the most desolate places on earth, covering one hundred and twenty thousand square miles and stretching from the eastern bank of the Nile to the mountains of the Red Sea coast. There are no villages between Wadi Halfa and Abu Hamed, but I had been assured by people whom I had met in Egypt who had crossed the desert on the train, that there are ten railway maintenance stations equally spaced along the two hundred and twenty mile stretch. It was on the maintenance stations that I would be relying for water. It is possible to drive a vehicle from Wadi Halfa to Abu Hamed but there is no recognized track and the occasional four-wheel drive vehicle that makes the journey usually follows close beside the railway, at times driving on the track with its wheels each side of the lines. Few travellers with their own vehicles come to this corner of Africa because of the difficulty of transporting the vehicle across Lake Nasser. Those that do bring their vehicle to the Nubian Desert, tend to arrange for it to be carried between Wadi Halfa and Abu Hamed on the train.

It was my plan to ride the bicycle across the Nubian Desert by following the railway track. Where the sand was too soft to allow riding I would push the bike. When I had mentioned my plans to other travellers, the reactions varied from gentle advice not to take the risk to outright statements that my head must be full of Nubian Desert sand. The railway was built by General Kitchener as part of Cecil Rhodes' dream of an unbroken line of British influence from the Mediterranean Sea to the Cape of Good Hope. When Kitchener had voiced his plans to take a railroad across the Nubian Desert, he met with similar response to that which I encountered when I talked of taking a bicycle across. Eminent railway engineers had unanimously advised Kitchener that such a railway was impossible to construct, distinguished soldiers had replied that the scheme was not only impossible but absurd, and many other persons who were not asked gave their opinion anyway, that the whole idea was that of a lunatic. They predicted ruin and disaster to his expedition. Kitchener listened to the advice, reflected on it, and ordered the railway to be constructed without further delay. I received no further encouragement for my plan of cycling over the desert, which did not worry me unduly because, unlike Kitchener, I was only risking my own neck and not the lives of hundreds of others.

Having found the railway line on this warm, desert evening, I continued to push the bicycle towards it, a little way to the south of Wadi Halfa. I had no wish to be observed by any Sudanese since I had heard that any vehicles intending to drive across the desert are only allowed to leave Wadi Halfa in a convoy of two or more. If this was so, I did not expect to be allowed to set off cycling alone, and I did not intend to sit around and wait for the next trans-desert cyclist to arrive. In parts the sand was very soft and I had to almost drag the bicycle through these patches. As I reached the railway I saw that the track was raised on a bank of rock and sand about three feet above the desert floor. The sides of the bank were soft and it was quite a difficult task to pull the bike up the slope on to the level of the railway line, where I found that the lines were lain on a firm surface of sand. At each side of the rails the top of the bank had a width of about two feet before dropping down at forty-five degrees to the desert surface. What filled me with optimism, however, was that there were no sleepers visible between the lines, these having been buried by sand. The surface between the lines was flat and firm. Instead of having to try to ride or push the bicycle along a sleepered track, the way was completely smooth. At worst, pushing the bike between the rails would be relatively straightforward, at best the surface would be firm enough for me to ride along. I mounted the bike, engaged one of its lowest gears, and tried to cycle. It was a success! Pedalling was not easy, the rims sunk into the sand a little way causing an unsightly furrow on the smooth surface between the lines, but I could ride at about eight miles an hour. I was ecstatic! My problems were over! If I set out for Abu Hamed now, and the surface remained as firm as this all the way, with two hours to cycle before darkness tonight and then thirteen hours on each of the next two days, I could be across the desert by the day after tomorrow. I resisted the temptation to set off there and then, lowered the bicycle down the railway embankment to the desert surface and walked a little way from the track before setting up my tent for the night. All being well, two days would see me on the other side of the Nubian Desert.

8

On the morning after my arrival in Wadi Halfa I pushed the bicycle, with difficulty, along the sandy streets into the main part of the town. I was still feeling far from one hundred percent fit, my stomach complaint in Aswan having left me with a general tiredness and with my legs feeling rather shaky. The last few months had taught me, however, that when feeling below par the best cure was always to 'cycle it off', and I was hopeful that the next few days would see me in Khartoum and back to full fitness. It was perhaps fortunate that I was not prescient.

Wadi Halfa presented the same picture as on the previous afternoon. Arabs wandered aimlessly about the streets or sat in the doorways of cafés drinking tea, flies droned incessantly irritating you with their persistent determination to crawl over any exposed part of the body, and traders stood in the shady doorways of their sparsely stocked shops waiting for custom that would rarely arrive. Having already established from other travellers that there would be no black market on which to change money in Wadi Halfa, I visited the bank to change some of my travellers' cheques into Sudanese pounds. The bank was pointed out to me by a policeman who, after I had thanked him for his help, gave the traditional reply of the Sudanese after they had helped someone, 'Thank you for the duty'. Bread was next on my list and I managed to buy five loaves of the unleavened variety which is often the only type available in desert climates where yeast cannot be preserved. I stored this in my panniers with my other food supplies: two tins of jam, nuts, raisins and, most valuable of all, several pounds of dates – the 'staff of life' of the Nomadic Arab, a great source of energy, a complete food in themselves, containing seventy-eight percent sugar and being rich in iron, calcium, phosphorus, potassium and vitamins A and B_3, the latter providing stamina and drive.

Pushing the bike through the soft sand of one of the town's streets I encountered some of the European travellers who had been on the Lake Nasser ferry. They had hoped to be in Khartoum by this time, having hurried the previous afternoon from the quay to the station to board the train to Abu Hamed which was intended to connect with the ferry. Unfortunately for them it appeared that the train was delayed for two days and in the meantime they were stranded in Wadi Halfa. We ate some 'savnak', Nile perch fried in animal fat, while the other travellers gave a final dissertation on the folly of solo bicycle rides into deserts, advising me to accompany them on the train. While their voices blended with the background drone of the flies to produce a distant buzzing sound, I enjoyed my fish and mentally checked my provisions. Having twice driven through the Sahara and crossed both the Kalahari and Namib Deserts by Land Rover, I was reasonably confident that my experience of living in the desert would help me to survive most mishaps that might befall me. The golden rules are mere common sense: not to wander away from your possessions since it is surprising both how difficult it can be to backtrack and how quickly a dust-storm can blow up, to stop and take shelter if there is a sandstorm and, above all, to drink plenty and to always keep a little water in reserve. Dehydration is the greatest danger to desert survival and so minimizing water loss is essential when supplies are limited, as mine were. It is recommended that a person sitting beneath the desert sun and pursuing no form of activity whatever, drinks at least one gallon of water per day to compensate for what he loses through sweat. I had purchased some one-pint and two-pint plastic water bottles in Cairo and these, added to the aluminium bottles which I had carried on the bike since England, gave me a potential capacity of two gallons of water. Cycling in sand is not an activity calculated to aid the retention of body fluids and I anticipated that two gallons would be a minimum requirement. Even if I was not able to reach Abu Hamed in the two days that I hoped, I should reach the ten railway maintenance stations at sufficiently frequent intervals. If a water shortage ever appeared imminent I was familiar with the methods of minimizing loss of body fluid: travelling only at night and resting during the day; wearing extra clothing during the daytime rest hours to reduce evaporation by creating a zone of more humid air around the body; resting out of the wind in a spot where the air is still and which is shaded – though where one finds a shaded spot in the middle of the Nubian Desert never became clear to me. One thing that I did not need to worry about was getting wet. Rainfall in the Nubian Desert averages five inches per annum and no-one was expecting it to arrive in the foreseeable future.

When the fish and the advice were both finished I left the other travellerrs, found a tap from which to fill my water containers and pushed the bike back towards the railway track. It was late morning, not the best of times to be setting off, as I again hauled the bicycle up the bank and on to the railway track. To each side of me were the low, rugged mountains of the Nubian Desert. Ahead the land was completely flat, the railway stretching as far as the eye could see to the horizon where the blue sky sloped down to the sand, and towards Abu Hamed, two hundred and twenty miles to the south. Engaging a low gear, I began to cycle between the railway lines, away from Wadi Halfa. Steering was not easy since, to avoid putting too much weight on to the back wheel, I was carrying a considerable amount in the front panniers and in the handlebar bag. With twenty pounds of water, several pounds of dates and a considerable amount of other food, besides the tent, sleeping bag, clothes, tool-kit, spare parts etc., the bike was weighing over one hundred and twenty pounds and it was difficult to ride in an exact straight line between the railway lines. However, the first five minutes was exactly as I had anticipated and I was able to make steady progress. Then, with less than a mile covered, I was suddenly jerked forward as the rims sunk into the sand and the bicycle came to a dead stop. Although the tyres had only sunk into the surface by a fraction of an inch it was impossible to cycle. My hopes of a straight ride across the desert had collapsed as suddenly as the bicycle had stopped, and the only way now would be to push and hope that I would come to a firm surface again, maybe in a mile, maybe in fifty miles.

Relieved of my weight, the wheels rested on the surface of the sand again and pushing was not difficult. Indeed I consoled myself that pushing a bicycle was probably easier than ordinary walking since it provided me with something on which to lean and, exposed to the full force of the midday tropical sun, a support was helpful.

The main problem at this time was the house-flies. They were everywhere – on the bike, on the panniers, on me, or just buzzing in front of my face. Occasionally the ground would seem firmer and I would remount the bicycle and try cycling again. Usually it was impossible to move and I would have to dismount and continue pushing. Sometimes I would be able to ride for stretches of a few hundred yards before the bike stopped so sharply that, because of its weight, I would be in danger of overbalancing and having it fall on top of me. To remove this problem I reduced the height of the saddle to its lowest position. It made cycling a little uncomfortable but at least the sudden stops when I encountered a softer surface were less of a problem as I could instantly put my feet on to the ground.

Experimenting, I lifted the bicycle from the railway and down the embankment to try cycling on the ordinary desert. This was a wasted effort. The desert surface was softer than that on the embankment and I expended considerable valuable energy in hauling the bike back up the soft, three-foot high banking on to the railway track. Still trying different ideas in an attempt to find a method of riding the bicycle instead of pushing it, I tried to cycle on the narrow strip between one of the lines and the top of the bank. This too proved unsuccessful. I swayed off course in a patch of looser sand, lost my balance, and the bike toppled over the edge of the bank. I managed to jump off quickly and skidded down the bank, the bike turning a somersault and rolling after me. I could have cried with anger and frustration but had to satisfy myself with kicking the bike and a spell of berserk fly swatting.

Eventually I had to concede that there was no alternative to pushing the bicycle. Mounting, riding for a few yards, dismounting, pushing for a few yards, remounting, and so on, was not worth the effort. It was more practical to maintain a steady rhythmic push and, even though it was going to take a long time, I should eventually be able to cover the distance. Even allowing for the hot sun and the flies, walking with the bicycle was not too difficult while the sand was firm enough to allow the wheels to turn freely. Occasional patches of softer sand were liable to cause the wheels to suddenly skid away from me, and such events were hard on the wrists as the full weight of the bike and its load was instantly transferred to them; but there were also firmer sections where, by resting the wheels against the inside edge of the rail, it was the rail that took most of the weight. The latter method tended to leave a black rubber mark on the side of the line where the edge of the tyres was being worn away, but that was the least of my worries – I wasn't paying for the tyres!

As I wheeled the bicycle deeper into the emptiness, along the track which Kitchener had named The Desert

Railway when it was constructed in 1897, I counted off the small concrete kilometer posts which had been fixed into the sand to the eastern side of the railway. The distance between each of these posts was divided into eighteen sections marked by telegraph poles and these too had originated from Kitchener, for every consignment of railway sleepers delivered from Wadi Halfa to the railway construction team had been accompanied by a proportionate number of telegraph poles, insulators and wire. Had it not been for the kilometer marker posts I would have had no idea of the distance that I had travelled and little clue as to the speed that I was making. Such information was essential to allow me to use my water supplies according to the distance to each maintenance station.

I had been told that there were ten maintenance stations equally spaced along the two hundred and twenty mile stretch and when, after I had covered only a few miles, I spotted a tiny speck on the horizon I was unsure what it would be. Although the travellers in Wadi Halfa had been informed that the train would not depart until the following night and although I would certainly have heard it coming even if it had set off early and was approaching me from behind, it is rather unnatural to walk for miles along a railway track and so I had, at first, a habit of glancing nervously over my shoulder at frequent intervals as if anticipating the sight of an immense locomotive mercilessly bearing down on me from the rear, as I trudged unsuspectingly on my way. My first thought when I saw the dot was that it was a train coming from Abu Hamed.But when, a few minutes later, the speck had scarcely increased in size I concluded that if it was a train it was not approaching very quickly and, as only my advance caused the shape to grow, I realized that it must be the first maintenance station. I approached the collection of ramshackle huts. The six Sudanese at the camp looked at me uncertainly as if trying to decide whether or not I was a mirage. As I pushed the bicycle to where they were stood they all broke into excited conversation of which I understood not one word. Arabic seemed to be the only language that they spoke but this was, by now, a familiar situation for me and I had already learned how relatively easy it is to make oneself understood by sign-language. I had timed my arrival well for they were about to eat, and so I sat on my haunches among them, around the large enamel bowl, dipping in my hand and helping myself to the mixture of pastry and vegetables soaked in sauce. Sign-language is not perfect, however. Before I left them they seemed to be telling me that the next station was only ten kilometers further on down the line and I set off, unable to reason that it could be so close, but at the same time hopeful that it would be.

After I had walked for several more miles, the sun began to go down and it was clear that either the crew at Maintenance Station Number One had their figures wrong or that I had misunderstood their message. The horizon remained empty, the railway and its accompanying line of telegraph poles extended endlessly into the distance, and the only good news for me was that the flies were gradually disappearing with the heat of the day. I had left the rocky hills of Wadi Halfa behind and now the land was completely flat all around, beneath a covering of fine, gritty sand. At 6 pm a quarter moon was up, it was almost dark, and I had had enough. The banking had now disappeared and the railway line ran on the surface of the desert, so I pushed the bike away from the railway, leaned it against a telegraph pole and, before erecting my tent, traced a large arrow into the sand with my foot, pointing towards Abu Hamed. Knowing my reactions first thing in the mornings, it would not have been inconceivable that the next day might find me pushing the bike back into Station Number One. As I pitched the tent I was surprised at the feeling of utter isolation which, though travelling alone, I had never felt so intensely when camping outside the desert. From the kilometer posts I calculated that I had covered seventeen miles. I had averaged little over two miles per hour. So much for reaching Abu Hamed within forty-eight hours! I ate some of my supplies: jam and bread and nuts, following them with salt tablets and my daily multivitamin pill, and found that I had lost the knife, fork and spoon set which I had brought with me from England. They must have parted company from the handlebar bag when the bike performed its gymnastic display down the embankment. As on most nights during my journey I climbed into my sleeping bag and went straight to sleep. Pushing a bicycle across a desert is a marvellous cure for anyone's insomnia!

The following morning I awoke at seven o'clock feeling the effects of the dust in my throat and glad of the sweets that I had bought in Egypt. I felt enthusiastic about the thought of doing battle with the desert, however, and though I realized that I might well have to walk the whole way to Abu Hamed, if I could cover twenty miles and pass one maintenance station each day, I would be making satisfactory progress.

By the time I had packed the tent, checked with my arrow-head that Abu Hamed was in the direction that I thought it was, and pulled the bicycle back through the soft desert sand on to the slightly firmer surface between the railway lines, the cool of the desert night and early morning was rapidly fading and the air was beginning to feel uncomfortably warm. I had decided to travel for an hour before a breakfast of dates, to give me something to look forward to, and I had only been pushing for half an hour when I saw movement ahead. The black dot rapidly approached and proved to be a hand-powered, open sided, waggon bearing six Sudanese from the next station. Since they were supplied with shovels I assumed that they had been working on the railway and, though it was only 8.30 am, they seemed to have finished for the day. They indicated that I should lift the bicycle on to the trolley and travel on to the next station with them, but I resisted the temptation and, by waving my arms around, enquired how far the next station was. One of them held up three fingers and I felt a surge of encouragement. Three kilometers! I would be there in half an hour. I waved to the departing waggon and its contents, who were watching me in perplexity as they diminished and finally disappeared from sight in the distance. I continued on my way, straining my eyes for a mark on the horizon which would be the first sign of the station, but I could see nothing except the railway, the line of telegraph poles and the flat desert on each side. As the sun warmed the air still further the flies recommenced their maddening attacks of the previous day and I would often have to stop and swat at them with my hat. They appeared to have suicidal tendencies but it seemed that as one was liquidated, two replaced it.

On one occasion I noticed that the tyres were not breaking the surface of the sand and, mounting the bike, I was able to ride for about ten minutes before the wheels suddenly dug into the track and I was brought to a sharp stop. The most successful method of pushing, I again found to be resting the wheels against the inside edge of one of the lines. If the wind had blown sand into a small drift against this edge, I then had to push in the middle of the track, which was considerably more difficult since the wheels were prone to skid sideways unexpectedly.

Perhaps the member of the maintenance crew who had held three fingers up was blessed with powers of extrasensory perception and had meant not three *kilometers* before I reached the station but three *hours*, for it was almost noon when I pushed the bicycle to the little group of huts beside the railway. By that time I was feeling very tired, due to having been under the impression for three hours that I would be reaching the station at any time. I had eaten nothing apart from a few dates, hoping that the maintenance crew, knowing that I was on my way, would have prepared food for me. I had overestimated their intelligence, however. They looked at me blankly as I wearily walked towards the group, and then flickers of understanding dawned across their faces; it seemed that they appreciated my need after all. But again I had given them too much credit. They stretched out their hands towards me; 'Whisky,' pleaded one, 'Cigarettes,' whined another. Though they could not have understood my words, they must have read the look of disgust on my face as I asked them which brand of cigarettes they preferred and whether they would rather I gave them Irish or Scotch Whisky. 'How did you know that I am pushing a bicycle load of cigarettes and liquor across the desert?' I asked their uncomprehending ears.

Since I was clearly not going to be offered food at this station, I filled my plastic containers with the stagnant, evil-smelling water that was kept in large tanks at all the camps for drinking and for powering the steam-driven railway engine, and then took the bike into the shade of one of the wooden huts where, on my small primus stove, I cooked one of my dehydrated meals, a tasty beef curry. Having no knife, fork or spoon, I stirred it with a tent-peg and ate it with my fingers. By the time I had finished it was one o'clock and, having covered about half of the twenty miles that I was aiming for, I decided to rest in the shade for half an hour. The attempt was unsuccessful. Two of the maintenance crew arrived, bringing hundreds of flies with them, and determined to converse with me in Arabic. They were greatly distressed when I prepared to set off pushing the bike out into the desert, having presumably concluded that I was going to sit at the station until the train arrived. They contorted themselves into a variety of strange positions to impersonate a train, insisting that I should wait until it arrived, indicating by drawing Arabic numbers in the sand that it was due at 6.30 that evening.

As I pushed the bicycle out of the shade and back onto

the railway track, the heat hit me as if someone had just opened the door of a giant furnace. I continued on my way hoping that future maintenance stations would prove more hospitable than the last. The going for the remainder of the afternoon was more difficult than it had been that morning, the ground between the lines proving quite soft, so that I had to keep the wheels up against the inside of a rail despite the fact that there was also a slight furrow of sand resting there through which I had to be continually forcing the bike to persuade the wheels to turn. I removed the rear pannier from the left-hand side, the side on which I was walking, since it was continually bumping against my leg, and hung it on the cross-bar on the right hand side. At each kilometer post I would stop to rest for a minute or two and every three kilometers (forty to forty-five minutes), I laid the bicycle on the track and sat on the small concrete post for five minutes. There was no scenery and no sound; a flat expanse still stretched all around and I could turn through three hundred and sixty degrees and see not the slightest protrusion to break the monotony of the horizon. Apart from the flies, the crew of the station, a couple of lizards, and two Egyptian vultures, I saw no other signs of life. The latter creatures, easily distinguishable by their white heads and yellow beaks, I noticed sitting on the telephone wires late in the afternoon when my pace was flagging. They were watching me with apparent curiosity and I could almost see them licking their beaks in anticipation of a good meal, but after circling overhead for some minutes, they must have decided that I was in more healthy condition than I looked, and they soared away.

In the evening, around five o'clock, I came to a section of track where a vehicle had driven along with its wheels on each side of the rails, pressing the sand into a firmer surface. By positioning the wheels of the bicycle into one set of the vehicle's tracks, I found that I was able to push the bike almost as easily as if I was doing so on a tarmac road. My speed increased and far less effort was required. I was able to complete two kilometers at a time without a pause provided I was careful to keep the bicycle wheels running directly in the car's tracks. After a while the compacted surface became firm enough for me to ride along and I was able to pedal until darkness, with only occasional skids when I lost my concentration and allowed the steering to wander from the vehicle's tyre marks into the softer sand. When, with twenty-one miles completed that day, night moved quickly in and the heat of the day was rapidly lost into the clear atmosphere, I pitched the tent to rest for the night I was feeling encouraged by my progress in the last hour and hopeful that the vehicle had continued to compress the surface for some distance yet to come.

During the night I was awakened by a great roaring which shattered the silence of the desert. It was the train from Wadi Halfa to Abu Hamed and it was little consolation to know that by the time I set off the next morning – my third day in the desert – my fellow travellers from the Aswan ferry would be virtually in Khartoum. When the sky began to grow grey in the east I packed my tent and returned to the railway line, shivering in the desert dawn but optimistic that I would be able to continue cycling for some distance in the tracks of the unknown vehicle. Two miles later my optimism ceased abruptly as the tracks of the vehicle swung away from the railway and back on to the desert. I would have liked to have had a word with the driver at that point but, after testing the car tracks on the desert floor and finding them too soft to ride in, I put my head down and continued to push along the railway track. The sun rose and the heat swept across the flat emptiness with startling suddenness. Nothing moved. The only sound was of the wheels scraping the sand. Then, as the temperature rose, the first fly came, landing gently on the back of my hand and tickling irritatingly. As I brushed it away I noticed a second on the handlebars and a third apparently unhurriedly washing itself as it perched on a pannier. Another arrived, and another, until the air seemed to be filled with their incessant drone as they circled my head, looking for an exposed part of my body on which to land. 'Musca Domestica', the common house-fly, the occasional inconvenient visitor to the British household, seems to take on a new personality in the Nubian Desert. He hovers, he lands, and he tickles. As you prepare to swat him he withdraws to attack again. He has the speed of a mirage fighter, and anyone who says that a house-fly has no intelligence, should study the house-fly of the Nubian Desert. He seems to know the moment that you are about to swat him and he takes off, to return again, around your eyes, your nose, your lips, your ears, any fraction of exposed flesh, until you feel that your whole body is crawling and buzzing, because he is doing it not by himself, but with a thousand of his friends.

I put on the long-sleeved cotton shirt that I had bought in Cairo with flies in mind to keep them from landing on my bare arms, but coating exposed flesh with fly repellent cream was a waste of time – the flies seemed to love it! I took paraffin from my primus stove and daubed it on my hands and around my face, but they appeared to thrive on it. I tried to ignore them, pushing the bike despite the constant buzzing and their attempts to climb into my mouth and nostrils, reminding myself of books that I had read which categorically stated that the desert is a sterile environment and that there are no flies whatever to be found therein. I swatted at them, spat at them, shouted at them, but if I had to credit them for something it was for their determination. Only death seemed to deter them, and death came to scores of them that day, as it was to do on each subsequent day of my trek across the desert. As my forbearance became periodically exhausted I would momentarily forget the bicycle, letting it fall on to the railway track, as, possessed of a hatred that I had never experienced before, I mounted frenzied assaults with my hands, hat, or any other suitable item, on those countless, soul-destroying insects.

After two hours of pushing, the sun high in the sky, I saw in the distance a huge city surrounded by sparkling reservoirs and with sky-scrapers and minarets pointing into the sky above the city. I knew that it was really the next maintenance camp for the railway, shimmering in the heat, and that as I approached the water would change to sand and the lofty concrete buildings would become wooden huts. I had quickly grown accustomed to seeing lakes gleaming tremulously in the distance, receding or shifting as I drew near, sometimes appearing to leave me stranded on an island surrounded by glistening water; or to observing strange, science-fictional creatures, their distorted, spindly legs seeming to bear them over the sands as I watched.

While the maintenance station was still hovering indistinctly in the distance I noticed a small, black creature bearing down on me. It quickly became recognizable as another hand-powered railway waggon with four station crew on board who had obviously observed inexplicable movement in the desert and had come to investigate. Again, no English was spoken by the men but this time they did not offer me a lift to the station. Had they done so I would again have refused their offer, but they probably thought that if I was stupid enough to walk so far voluntarily, I did not deserve a lift anyway. The station was still too far away for me to assess the exact distance and, as I had done on the previous day, I pointed to myself, then into the distance, and then to the nearest kilometer post to enquire how far away the buildings were. One of the Sudanese replied by putting two fingers up – leaving me uncertain as to whether he meant that the distance was two kilometers or that I would not be welcome!

I followed the departing waggon to the camp, but again

received no food. If the bicycle and I had suddenly hatched out of a giant egg the six station staff could not have looked more confused. They watched my every movement, their mouths open and their wide eyes rolling. I wheeled the bike in, helped myself to water and continued on my way.

Soon after noon I stopped to cook a dehydrated meal. While I was eating, the soft breeze which had been blowing from the north, and therefore to my advantage, increased in strength. At last, in this Godforsaken wilderness, something was happening which did not seem to have been sent by the devil himself. As soon as I had eaten and scoured my pans with sand, I set off again, and though the sand was mainly still soft enough to make pushing more difficult than on a hard surface the strong breeze helped me considerably, pushing me along on the firmer sections so that I was almost trotting with the bike, and decreasing both the heat and the number of flies. Later in the afternoon another speck appeared on the horizon. I assumed that it must be the next station, and was still recovering from surprise that I should be reaching another station so soon when I realized that it was heading towards me. Maintenance stations do not normally move, so I decided that I had better leave the line quickly as it must be the train from Abu Hamed to Wadi Halfa. As I stood with the bicycle by the line and waved at the train as it passed, heads jerked in surprise from windows and doorways, bemused expressions on the faces that peered at the unexpected figure in the desert.

Towards evening the next station did come into sight, and there I had the pleasant surprise of being able to converse with a Sudanese who spoke a little English. He explained that there are not ten maintenance stations on the Desert Railway, but fourteen: ten original stations from when the railway was first constructed and four additional maintenance points which have since been added, this one between Stations Three and Four, another between Stations Four and Five, one between Five and Six and a fourth between Seven and Eight. This was good news for me since it meant more watering points. I would have been quite happy had I been told that there were stations at half-mile intervals. I left the camp with a few pieces of bread that were given to me to add to my own rather stale supply and, as the sun went down and the wind became chilly, camped beside the railway having travelled twenty-one miles during my third day in the desert.

It seemed that the deeper I moved into the desert the hotter the days became and the colder the nights. The third night I spent huddled in my sleeping bag, contemplating how I could possibly have complained that it was too hot during the day. By nine o'clock next morning, as I pushed the bicycle beneath the baking sun, I wondered why I had not derived intense pleasure simply from the sensation of shivering with cold. Mid-way through the morning I reached the fifth maintenance camp, Station Number Four. It had been here and at Number Six Station that, eighty years earlier, Kitchener had received a tremendous boost to morale during the construction of the railway, when a well had been sunk and water discovered. I was taken into one of the huts and offered an enamel bowl containing what appeared to be the left-overs of the crew's breakfast, a mixture of vegetables and bread. A few weeks earlier my stomach would have churned at the sight of the mixture but after dispersing from the bowl the crowd of flies that swarmed over the food I hungrily consumed it by the handful. After the meal I sat for a while in the shade with the maintenance crew, then filled my water containers from the railside tanks and continued on my way.

It was mid-afternoon when the consistency of the sand abruptly changed. I noticed its slightly lighter colour from a distance and wondered if the surface would be firm enough to enable me to ride again. The change in colour, however, now meant exactly the opposite. As I pushed the bike across the desert, staring at the empty horizon, with the flies making their constant maddening attacks, the wheels suddenly sank several inches into the sand. The bicycle stopped and it was impossible to push it. I heaved and strained but the wheels would not revolve through the sand. After half an hour of exertion attempting to drag the bike, I sank down exhausted. There was no possibility that I could wheel the bike across that surface. The sun beat down. Apart from the incessant droning of the flies, which I could no longer even be bothered to brush away, there was total silence. At that moment, as I gazed across the empty landscape, I could happily have dug a hole in the sand and climbed into it. After almost four days and a third of the way, it seemed that the desert had beaten me. I would have to sit there until the next train came past on its way to Abu Hamed, flag it down, and cross the remainder of the desert on that. Then an idea came to me. One last possibility. If a train could run on rails, why couldn't a bicycle? With new hope I hauled the ungainly weight of the bike on to one of the lines and, balancing it there, began to push. The wheel was one and a quarter inches in width, the line was about one and three-quarters. Within a few yards there was a jarring lurch as the bike dropped off the line, back on to the sand. I tried again and managed a little further. I moved all the luggage from the front of the bicycle on to the back so that I had a closer view of the essential spot – the point where the front wheel came into contact with the line. I set off again. It took time to adjust to the balance of the loaded bike. If I took my eyes from the front wheels contact point for a second, the bike would leave the rail, and with the weight of all my equipment now to the rear, it was not an easy task to lift it back and balance it again on the line. After an hour I had covered approximately two hundred yards. It was almost funny: Kitchener, on one particular day, had laid five thousand three hundred yards of track. He had built the railway faster than I was travelling along it! And I didn't have Kitchener's difficulties! I didn't have to feed two thousand platelayers in the middle of the desert, and I wasn't expecting an attack from several thousand dervishes at any moment!

I knew from previous experience the danger of travelling in a desert with limited water but I had to reduce the weight on the bicycle somehow. A gallon of water, half of my precious supply, was poured on to the sand. I disposed of some of the spare nuts and bolts that I had been carrying as well as various spare bicycle parts. And, as I pushed the bike along the rail, I gradually improved and was soon able to wheel it for stretches of up to a hundred yards without it dropping from the line. It demanded absolute concentration on the path of the front wheel, which was almost impossible to give because, with both hands engaged, I could do nothing to prevent the merciless attacks of the flies which often reduced me to throwing down the bicycle and waving my arms wildly round my head in a fruitless attempt to drive them away, screaming insults at the top of my voice. But by the time evening came I knew that I had faced and overcome the ultimate test of the desert and that now, no matter how soft the sand became, nothing was going to prevent me from reaching Abu Hamed.

During the heat of the day it had occurred to me that it would be a good idea to continue my journey during the night, and with bright moonlight to help me I was able to continue after sunset though only with increased difficulty. Yet I had to have some sleep, and with no shade and respite from the flies it was impossible to sleep during the day. After two hours of darkness, with a cold wind sweeping across the desert making my hands almost too numb to grip the handlebars, I erected the tent at the end of the fourth day, having travelled eighteen miles and feeling thankful that when Kitchener's Chief Engineer, Percy Girouard, designed the railway, he did not use rails that were half an inch narrower.

They say that the extremes of temperature between day and night in the desert causes rocks to crack. I could easily believe that. After a day where the sweat poured from me in a continuous stream and a night where it was too cold to sleep for much of the time, I would not have been surprised if the bike frame had split! Next morning, after a difficult first few hundred yards, I soon became reaccustomed to the balance of the bicycle and to concentrating on the point where the front wheel met the line, and, though every few minutes the wheel and the line would fade into a blur, or the flies would become unbearable and I would have to relieve the situation by butchering several with my hat, and in either case the wheels would promptly drop from the rail, I was making quite good progress. Now that the bicycle was running on the rail, there was no resistance to the wheels as there had been from even the shallowest of sand. Before long I was able to walk at a fast pace, my eyes glued to the track and my arms supporting the bicycle firmly, with the bicycle leaving the line only two or three times per kilometer. By mid-morning, the sun was burning down, the flies were buzzing and the flat sand stretched away all around. In the distance I spotted the shape of buildings and correctly guessed that it was the extra maintenance station between Numbers Four and Five. This station was to prove the turning point in the way in which I was received by the maintenance crews. At the previous stations hospitality had been noticeably lacking by Arab standards and it had seemed that the staff had viewed me as some kind of lunatic who would soon learn sense and either meet with an accident of give up and take the train. From this station, however, the maintenance crews appeared to consider it a worthy achievement to have reached so far. They indicated now, by motions, that word of my journey had been relayed to them by telephone from Station Four and, as my hand was shaken and I was patted on the back, I had the impression that had there been a convenient red carpet I would have found myself pushing the bicycle on that. One of the Sudanese took the bicycle from me as gently as if he was handling a bone china tea-service and propped it in the shade of a hut. I was led into one of the wooden huts, which was marvellously cool and, for the first few moments, pitch black after the glare of the sun. The hut, like others into which I had looked at previous stations, was bare apart from a little furniture: two beds, wooden stools and a table, and a few tin cans and bowls. I sat on one of the beds and, had it been a fully sprung, de-luxe mattress, it could not have been more comfortable. It was made in a similar fashion to a hammock, consisting of interwoven string between a wooden frame and mounted on low legs. After my exertions of the last few days, two nights with little sleep, and now sitting on a comfortable bed in a cool, dark room, I had a sudden desire to lie down and sleep. Yet I knew that in this torrid zone with its paradoxical temperatures, I must cover as many miles as possible during daylight, for not only was there the bitter cold of the desert night, but there was the additional difficulty of keeping the wheels on the rail with only the moon to provide illumination. Besides, my six hosts were too intent on trying to make polite conversation to allow me to sleep – though of course they could not speak English. One of them rushed away, to return a few minutes later bringing me a glass of the hot, sweet, milkless tea which is so popular and so refreshing. Another, presumably the head chef, poured flour and a mysterious looking liquid into an earthenware bowl and, dipping a stick into the mixture began to rotate the utensil enthusiastically between his hands. It was obvious that the station cook did not often have the privilege of entertaining guests for dinner and that he was determined to take advantage of the opportunity to demonstrate his culinary expertise. A few minutes later a dish containing the freshly baked pastry was laid before me, together with another dish containing a black, syrupy fluid which looked and tasted remarkably like cough medicine. As usual the food was not the type to which the European palate is accustomed, but in the circumstances I could not have appreciated it more had it been a medium-rare grilled porterhouse steak. The staff sat on the floor and watched my every movement as I ate, the cook's eyes following me so closely that it seemed he must be tasting each mouthful. As soon as I had finished eating and smiled my approval they leapt to their feet and began to rush around, falling over each other to fetch and carry. Two of them took away my dishes, while a third produced a bowl of water in which he indicated that I should wash my hands. Another hurried in through the doorway with a glass of tea which he put before me. When I left the station at midday, a little over an hour after my arrival, I knew the maintenance crew had done for me all that they were able and all that was needed. As I found before, such hospitality provided not only physical sustenance but was of great encouragement psychologically.

In those conditions, however, the mental inspiration soon fades. Progress was warm work and was made increasingly difficult by the flies. It became impossible to concentrate on keeping the wheel on the rail because of their swarming on my hands and buzzing around my face. Within two hours I had reached the stage where I was shouting at the flies, hitting and kicking at them, anything to return just a fraction of the torment that they were inflicting on me. I decided it was time to take some respite from the flies and the sun and, throwing the bicycle down on to the track, I ran to the shade of the nearest telegraph pole where I spent twenty minutes sitting in its shade – though even with careful positioning a telegraph pole is only wide enough to shade the middle part of a human head, not each side of it. The move seemed to confuse the flies for the first few minutes and they continued to plague the bike, but they soon picked up my trail and turned their attentions back to me. I would have to find some way of foiling the flies, so returning to the bicycle after my rest, I put on my long-sleeved shirt. The only cloth I had available was an oily rag that I carried with which to periodically wipe dirt from the chain, but I wrapped it, Arab fashion, around the lower part of my face just below the eyes and back over my ears and forehead, holding it in place by tucking it under my hat. That left only eyes and hands exposed, and those I covered with sun glasses and socks respectively. As I set off again the flies buzzed in mad frustration around my sun glasses. Beneath all the clothing I sweated profusely, which excited the flies even more. The buzz of their wings around my face seemed to be echoing across the desert and they swarmed on the lenses of my sun glasses, but now I was able to laugh at their attempts to reach me, except on the occasions when one would suddenly find its way through the slits between the rag and sun glasses and become trapped inside the sun glasses, buzzing madly between the lens and my eye.

Later in the afternoon a strong north-easterly wind blew up, and as the temperature dropped the flies gradually disappeared, though I was never able to guess where to. At five o'clock I reached Station Number Five, stopping first to disrobe since I must have looked like a creature from outer space. Here I received the usual large enamel bowl, this time containing a type of cous-cous, the traditional North African meal of steamed semolina in a vegetable soup. I refused the invitation to sleep at the station, as I again hoped to cover ground in the cool of the evening, and was on my way again within half an hour of my arrival. To my delight, I found that the sand between the rails was firm enough to allow the wheels to turn, and I pushed on into the darkness with the wheels resting against the inside of the right-hand rail. By seven-thirty, having walked twenty-one miles during my fifth day in the desert, the cold wind drove me into the tent for the night.

The entry in the diary that I kept daily during my

bicycle ride to the Cape of Good Hope, began, after my sixth day in the desert: 'God, this is a hell of a place. Too cold to sleep well at night; too hot to think during the day; and so many flies it's unbelievable.' I had been awakened at dawn on that sixth day by the sound of a howling wind and with grit lashing the tent. I could hear the sand hissing as the wind drove it across the desert, and a corner of my tent flapping wildly where it had obviously wrenched free of the rock which had held it down. For the last three nights the desert had been too soft to allow the use of tent pegs, and as I pitched camp each night it had been necessary to select some of the large stones which littered the desert to act instead of pegs. Looking through the tent door, on my sixth morning, the scenery looked even more bleak and depressing than usual. Sand swept in waves along the desert floor and flew through the air like spray from the sea. The sky was overcast with grey and the sun completely blotted out. I had four pints of water to last me until I reached the next station which, even assuming that my source of information had been correct and there was a new station between Stations Five and Six, was still several miles away. I waited for two hours, during which the wind abated slightly and less sand was whipped up. Then, knowing that by following the railway track I could not possible become lost, I defied the wind by lowering the tent and bundling it into a ball, and then set off. As the flies had attacked exposed flesh, so did the sand, stinging like tiny pins as it was driven against me. The oily rag, which the previous day had protected me from flies, I now used to shelter my face from sand. At noon I reached the station that lies midway between Numbers Five and Six. This was good timing as I was able to join the crew around their bowl for lunch. By the time we had completed the meal the wind had died away, the desert become calm, and the heat and the flies returned. By five o'clock that evening, long after soft sand had forced me to return to wheeling the bicycle balanced on the rail, I had reached half-way across the Nubian Desert, but I had resigned myself to travelling during the cold night rather than the heat of the day. The flies that afternoon had been even worse than any other day – so bad that, with my face swathed in the cloth despite the heat of the afternoon sun, I had scarcely been able to see the railway line for flies swarming in front of my sun glasses. My tormenters accompanied me, even in semi-darkness, to Station Six which I had been told was the largest of the maintenance camps. There were ten men there, one of whom spoke quite good English. They brought a large enamel bowl containing water and, as I wondered how I was supposed to drink from such an ungainly vessel, the English-speaking Sudanese explained that it was for me to wash my feet in. After washing, I was invited to lie on one of the string beds while food was prepared for me. Half an hour later a mixture of bread, vegetables and some pieces of gristly meat that looked as if the animal they came from had suffered from an unpleasant skin disease, were set before me in an enamel bowl which looked very similar to the one in which I had so recently washed my feet. Having finished the meal I declined the offer of accommodation for the night and, by the light of the large moon, set the wheels carefully on to the line again and pushed the bicycle away into what was now a bitterly cold night. During the next four hours, until midnight, I travelled ten miles, and by then it was all that I could do to erect my tent before falling asleep – despite the cold.

By the seventh day of my desert journey it was only the heat of the sun on the tent that persuaded me not to stay in my sleeping bag for the entire morning. By seven o'clock however, the rays of the dawn sun made the atmosphere stifling inside the tent, and I quickly packed the panniers and returned to the railway. Inexplicably, the fly situation had improved considerably. I wondered if they had been offended by my insults of the previous day and had decided not to accompany me today, for there were far fewer, though even a few persistent flies can make life very difficult.

I reached Station Seven at noon; again an appropriate time for I was able to squat with the men around the communal bowl, eating the cous-cous which appeared to have been liberally seasoned with dead flies. After the meal I was led to one of the huts to rest and there discovered the apparent reason for the lack of flies in the desert during the morning – they were all in the hut! While I lay on the bed the Sudanese, untroubled by the flies circling their heads and walking across their faces, sat in a corner of the hut and talked to one another.

When the sun began to sink I was given another meal and then set out again, finding to my surprise that the sand between the lines was hard enough to enable me to cycle. The wheels kept suddenly skidding sideways again sending me sprawling across the track, but I was helped by the bright moon and was able to ride most of the twelve miles to the station midway between Numbers Seven and Eight. It was nearly ten o'clock when I reached this station and everything was in darkness, the maintenance crew obviously all asleep. It seemed a pity to waken them – they had probably only slept about fifteen hours that day – so I took some water from the railside tanks and was about to continue on my way when it occurred to me that it would be a waste not to leave some evidence of a moonlight visitor to the station. So, without making any noise, I altered the positions of any items that I could find outside the buildings. I built a small tower with the enamel bowls that were lying on the sand, filled empty drinking vessels with water, collected tools that were scattered around into a pile near to which I built a low cairn of stones and drew strange looking animals in the sand with a stick. I set off along the railway track, amused at the thought of the expressions on the faces of the maintenance staff when they awoke next morning, for, knowing that no train had passed during the night, they would not imagine that any human would have visited the station by night. Aided by a strong, if cold, wind at my back, and the psychological benefit of being able to ride the bike in stretches, I continued travelling until midnight, by which time I had covered thirty-two miles on my seventh day.

The following day I arrived at Station Eight in time for lunch, and travelled twenty-eight miles before, at 7 pm, the cold was so intense that I was driven to the shelter of my tent. I was able to cycle about half of the distance on that day but the maintenance crews of Station Eight appeared to have been in industrious mood, as the track had been liberally spread with small stones across which the bicycle bounced and skidded, and I was constantly expecting spokes in my rear wheel to break.

On my ninth morning I was again treated to the dubious privilege of a desert dust-storm, but I had calculated Station Nine to be only two miles on from where I had camped and felt that all the flying sand in the desert could not have prevented me from continuing as far as the station. Nevertheless, it seemed as if the desert had a mind of its own and, having failed to stop me with extremes of heat, cold, and its plagues of flies, it had again exploded into a fury of sweeping sand in a desperate attempt to defeat me. As I pushed the bike towards the last-but-one station, I wondered what other tricks the desert still held in store up its proverbial sleeve. At the station I was again well received. The crew produced a mirror and delightedly showed me my reflection; I nearly had a heart attack! Unwashed, unshaven, the sand caked to me where it had stuck to the sweat on my body, eyes red from the sand, and lips black and cracked.

As before the dust-storm died down towards midday and I was able to leave the station and set out pushing the bike along what I estimated to be the last forty miles of the Desert Railway. The sand between the lines was again soft and I felt no enthusiasm whatever as I walked along the railway, carefully balancing the wheels on the line. To the east a low range of mountains appeared and as the railway drew closer to the foot of these, the desert on each side of the railway, particularly to the east over an area of perhaps eighty square miles, underwent a strange alteration. Instead of the monotony of sand and rocks, everywhere was suddenly green beneath intermittent patches of short, wiry grass. Occasionally there were bushes and small trees, and a thick twining vegetation whose tendrils weaved their way like countless serpents around the trees and bushes, trying to extend their own lives at the expense of others. And, as I pushed the bicycle through this area of luxuriant growth, the sun beating down and my throat dry from the morning's dust-storm and due to my limited supply of water, I saw fruit. It lay beside the railway, green with yellowish markings, melon-sized and looking as sweet and appetizing as any water melon could. It was like seeing an apparent mirage and, on reaching it, realizing that it had never been an illusion but was a hope fulfilled – any desert traveller will testify that there is nothing that the imagination dwells on more than the thought of fresh, juicy fruit. I had an almost overwhelming urge to pluck one of these melon-like fruits, tear pieces from it and hold them between my lips, sucking in the thirst-quenching juice that must be contained beneath the rind. But, somehow, I had already been struck by the alien atmosphere of this lush region apparently so green and fertile, yet uninhabited. On previous days in the desert I had seen occasional dead birds, usually types of vulture, but here corpses of a variety of birds were scattered liberally amongst the greenery. I picked one of the fruits and dropped it on to the railway line, where it burst open revealing its sickly, mushroom-like white contents. So this was one more trick of this Godforsaken wilderness, a last, desperate attempt to trap the traveller. After the blatent malevolence of its heat, flies, sandstorms, mirages, solitude, it was now subtly offering this enticing fruit from a huge lush garden. An inedible gourd which, if tasted, would provide its reward not with sweet satisfaction but with illness, even death. For three hours I pushed the bicycle through the evil atmosphere of this rich, damp region, re-emerging into the familiar, almost welcome, barrenness of the true desert at dusk, and after another three hours I reached the final maintenance station of the Desert Railway.

I found Station Ten to be large enough to accommodate sufficient staff to work on the branch line which ran to Karima, one hundred and fifty miles south-west. The staff immediately presumed that I would be staying the night, an assumption with which I had no inclination to disagree. I was taken by three of the Sudanese into a hut illuminated by paraffin lamps and warmed by a small wood fire which had been built on the sandy ground in the middle of the room. A fourth string-bed was carried into the room for my use, and we ate a tasty meal of a kind of stew, the ingredients of which I could not identify and felt it better not to enquire about.

With just seventeen miles to Abu Hamed, I set off at first light the next day. For short stretches I was able to ride, though in parts the sand, which had covered the sleepers of the railway up to this point, had been eroded giving an effect of cycling on a sea of petrified waves. The wheels of the bicycle, particularly the rear, were again subjected to a tremendous jolting and in the sections where I was able to ride I did so with clenched teeth, knowing that such ill-treatment of the wheels could proved disastrous later. Had I known then how true this would be, I would undoubtedly have refrained from riding over such broken up sections and been satisfied that the ground was firm enough to allow me to push the bike. Even the wind, which when it had blown during the last few days had been at my back and a great help, had now turned against me and blew strongly from the south. At least the strong wind gave the consolation that there were fewer flies to trouble me – or perhaps, in view of the number that I had killed recently, there were not many left!

At noon on my tenth day in the desert I spotted a tiny speck in the distance. Abu Hamed was near. At two o'clock that afternoon, I reached the outskirts of the village where I was surrounded by curious onlookers some of whom asked in broken English how I could say I had come from Wadi Halfa when no train had arrived for several days. Before long, however, word spread around the small desert town that a traveller had crossed the desert by bicycle and, as I pushed the bike along the dusty streets in the centre of the town, the usual stares with which I was received in all small towns of the Middle East and Africa were accompanied by mutters, of 'Wadi Halfa', 'Abu Hamed', 'SaHara'.

I doubt if anyone has crossed the Nubian Desert on a bicycle before. Nothing would persuade me to do it again. I had achieved what I had set out to do and I was adequately satisfied that I had been able to cross the one section of my journey that I had been categorically assured was impossible, but I was aware that I had now lost valuable time. Already it was almost the middle of January, leaving only fifteen weeks to travel the vast distance that still remained to Rhodesia where I had arranged to start work in May. While Abu Hamed is connected to the capital city of Khartoum by a considerably more conventional road than the one I'd just travelled, the surface is not exactly of M1 standard. In fact I had previously learned that the road is a mere desert track through the sand and knew that I would still be unable to cycle. Leaving the bicycle locked in a cell at the Abu Hamed Police Station, not difficult to locate since it was situated on the platform of the railway station, I walked for several hundred yards along the railway track in the direction of Khartoum. I was hoping that by some miracle the sand between the lines might be firm enough to allow me to ride along the railway track as I had done when leaving Wadi Halfa, but the sand was again so soft that it would have necessitated balancing the bicycle on the rail again, and I had neither the time nor the inclination to walk the three hundred and fifty miles to Khartoum under those circumstances. I reluctantly made my decision that it would be necessary to take the train on to Khartoum.

I was told the train to Khartoum would arrive from Wadi Halfa that night and leave Abu Hamed 'before to-morrow', which I assumed would be in the early hours of the morning. Abu Hamed was not exactly the focal point of African social life, but at least there was a tap at the railway station where I was able to wash, and fruit – mainly oranges and grapefruit – in the shops. In the evening I joined the bicycle in a police station cell. As I entered the small, dark room, the friendly Sudanese policeman informed me that he would lock the metal-barred door behind me as he was responsible for my safety and did not want me to be attacked during the night. I was too tired to argue and slept on the low wire-mesh camp-bed until midnight when I looked through the bars of the cell door to see, by the light of an oil lamp, the policeman slumped over his desk fast asleep. After several minutes of calling, he awoke and I realized that it was a different officer. He had not even known that I was in the cell and was startled to see me there and most unhappy at having his sleep disturbed. I explained that my train was due to leave in less than two hours and asked if he would let me out. 'Why is the cell door locked?' he asked me. 'To keep me safe.' He gave me a look as if to say he had heard that excuse before and asked where I had come from. I told him that I had just arrived that day, from Wadi Halfa. 'How can this thing be? There has been no train since one week.' I uncomfortably explained that I had just emerged from the desert on a bicycle, upon which he gave me a strange look and put his head down to go back to sleep. It took a considerable amount of noise to make him raise his head for a second time and he pointed out that he could not release me from jail without permission. Eventually he disappeared to seek permission and it was almost 2 am before the door was unlocked and I was able to wheel the bicycle on to the railway station platform where the train to Khartoum was now ready to leave. I hurriedly pushed the bicycle from the platform to the back of the train where the guard's van stood, climbed aboard and struggled to pull the bike up after me, three feet from the ground and through the narrow doorway of the waggon. The bicycle, with its pannier at each side, was considerably wider than the doorway, and though I manoeuvred the handlebars into the waggon the rear end of the bicycle refused to enter the van. The train set off with the bicycle still half in and half out of the guard's van, and an agitated guard running along the platform, desperately pushing the bike from the rear and, with the door blocked, unable to climb into his own van. It was some minutes before I was able, by leaning over the bicycle and removing one of the rear panniers, to bring it fully into the waggon. By then the guard was a mere speck in the distance.

I slept the remainder of the night in the guard's van and during the day was able to look out on to the arid semi-desert. The soft sand which lay everywhere told me that I had made the correct decision in travelling by train. It would have taken a long time to push the bike on to Khartoum. The train stopped occasionally at stations, occasionally to pick up railside passengers, and frequently for no apparent reason at all. At the stations I was able to walk the length of the train to examine it more closely. There were four classes of passengers: First Class had the comparative luxury of cramped sleeping compartments; Second Class would have made Second Class passengers on British Rail feel like VIP's; Third Class where the wooden benches in conjunction with the swaying of the train could be guaranteed to cure any slipped disc; and Fourth Class which resembled pictures of those trucks in which Stalin's fallen friends were taken to spend their Siberian holidays. As I toured the train I would see fingers pointed at me and hear similar whispers to those that I had heard in Abu Hamed: 'Wadi Halfa', 'Abu Hamed', 'SaHara'. Sudanese would approach, courteously greet me with 'As-salaam alaikoom', and ask me if it was true that I had crossed the desert by bicycle. At first it was flattering, then the same questions demanding the same replies became irritating, and I remained in the guard's van where a substitute guard, perhaps grateful to me for helping to find him employment, invited me to eat with him and his friends.

We arrived at Khartoum twenty-four hours after leaving Abu Hamed and, after sleeping the remainder of the night on a bench on the station platform, I set off to find somewhere to stay while I obtained information on travel through the remainder of the Sudan.

The city of Khartoum was founded in 1822 by the Egyptian Mehemet Ali, but it was in 1885 that the city became more notably famous when the British soldier, General Charles Gordon, who had opened up equatorial Sudan, was killed during the siege of Khartoum by the Mahdists, the followers of the fanatical, self-appointed Moslem leader, Mohammed Ahmed, the Mahdi. When Kitchener, fresh from his railway-building exercise, crushed the Mahdists at the Battle of Omdurman in 1898, the Mahdi was already dead. It is said that he died of unknown causes but, since it is also said that he was surrounded by the ladies of his harem when he died, it's not difficult to guess the causes of his death – which would appear to have been considerably more pleasant than either Gordon's or Kitchener's.

It seems likely that if it was possible to stage a

posthumous reunion party in Khartoum for Mehemet Ali, the Mahdi, Gordon and Kitchener, they would notice little change between the Khartoum of today and the city that they knew. There are occasional tarmac roads now, though most of these are well camouflaged by sand, but the buildings, despite the fact that many of them are comparatively modern, have been efficiently sand-blasted by the forces of nature, leaving them with an unkempt, lustreless apapearance. The land is parched and littered with all manner of refuse, from empty soft drink bottles to the decaying corpses of dogs, goats and donkeys. Beside the roads, the sand piling up at their bases, lie derelict pieces of machinery and vehicles. The chassis of Land Rovers – given no doubt as well-meant Foreign Aid – are a common sight, stripped to the bone. If a vehicle breaks down in the Sudan it is usually 'By the will of Allah', and if Allah does not will that it should start again then it remains where it is, the movable parts gradually disappearing to re-emerge on the stalls of the native markets.

Khartoum was hot, dusty and prohibitively expensive, and thirty-six hours after my arrival, I was cycling on one of Sudan's few tarmac roads, beneath the light of a full moon, towards Wad Medani, a little over a hundred miles to the south of the capital. The road followed the course of the Blue Nile flowing from the mountains of Ethiopia, but from Wad Medani I continued to Senna where I turned west to reach the White Nile at Kosti. To cycle in central Sudan was, compared with Egypt, almost like cycling in Paradise. With a population of only twenty million in this enormous country the villages were few and far between and though when passing through some of the villages my average speed was increased considerably by the packs of semi-wild dogs that seemed to see me as a tasty piece of steak, I had no difficulties. From Kosti, I had decided to take the river-boat for a thousand miles up-river to Juba in the south of Sudan, for the area through which I would sail is known as the Sudd, the clay plains which for most of the year are a vast swamp presenting a major physical barrier between the north and the south of the country and making travel even by four-wheeled drive vehicle slow and laborious. With only a one-wheel drive vehicle, lack of time again forced me to take public transport and I arrived at the ferry terminal at Kosti where I was assured the next weekly ferry for Juba would leave 'To-morrow'.

Inevitably it was actually two days before we set sail on the voyage which I was told could take anything from nine days to three weeks to complete. The boat, a shallow draft, stern-wheel paddle steamer, was similar to the one on which I had crossed Lake Nasser. It was actually six boats, each perhaps forty feet in length, chained together. There were three side by side in front and three behind, the middle of the three rear boats being the paddle steamer. At least the intention was that they should all be chained together. Unfortunately each member of the crew must have left it to a colleague to chain the four outside boats to the two at the bank, for when at last the crowds of passengers were packed on board, the paddle began to turn and the ropes securing the various sections of the boat to the bank were cast off, the two-thirds of the boat nearest to the middle of the river slid gracefully away upstream while the two remaining sections stayed exactly where they were by the bank. Great consternation had developed among the passengers on the boat which had sailed, exceeded only by the consternation which had developed among the passengers on the boat which had not sailed. None were more anxious than I. I had left my bicycle on one section of the ferry while I looked for suitable deck space on which to sleep on another section. Hearing excited uproar, I looked back to find the majority of the ferry, the bicycle leaning where I had left it against a deck rail, disappearing upstream in the direction of Juba. It took several hours for the two parts of the boat to be reunited and securely fastened together. The delay had extended the lateness of departure to two days behind schedule but, as one of the crew later observed to me with typical African philosophy, 'What is two days in a man's lifetime?'

The boat on which I was to spend the next twelve days as we journeyed up the Nile to Juba, was similar to that on Lake Nasser not least with its memories of past glories: fans that no longer turned, bulbless light sockets, a room with 'Saloon' engraved above the door, but now standing disused, cabins where mosquito-mesh still stretched across the windows, but so full of gaping holes that it would not have kept out one of the hens that wandered the decks far less a tiny mosquito. The three rear boats constituted First and Second Class. For reasons of economy I had opted to sail Third Class and, as at Aswan, I claimed a section of deck and scowled unsociably at anyone who came near. I was joined by two French hitch-hikers who were travelling as far as Malakal, half way to Juba, and we carefully guarded our claimed portion until the dozens of Arabs and Bantu Africans had settled down. We spread our sleeping bags and I chained the bicycle to a post aware that for the whole of the voyage I would be obliged to keep a careful eye on my bags and panniers. The boats each possessed two decks, the upper deck being roofed-in and having large, glassless windows. I had chosen one of these upper decks on which to sleep, realizing that it would be cooler. We were now leaving the hot winter of Northern Sudan and entering the even hotter summer season of the south where any flow of air, day or night, would be welcome.

The upper decks of Third Class were covered with prostrate bodies untroubled by goats wandering across them or by other people moving between them. Groups of men sat and played cards or dice, and practised spitting, which appeared to be popular in Central Sudan. I have never noticed this pastime in any other part of Africa, but it was as common on the boat and in the areas through which the boat sailed as sniffling is in England on a cold winter's day. This was not a coarse hawking retch, however. The Sudanese spitting action is far more refined, so much so that in the early hours of my river voyage when I had not learned the wisdom of positioning myself up-wind of nearby exponents of the art, I thought that I was being gently showered by a fine spray churned up by the paddles. The Sudanese spit is performed with teeth together and through slightly parted lips. It shoots in a thin stream with remarkable speed across an enormous distance and is accompanied by a slight hiss as it is propelled from the mouth. The traveller must move with extreme care, for the Sudanese does not look before he lets fly and to walk near to a group of these artists is like passing through a burst of intermittent fire from a water-pistol. Throughout the twelve days of the voyage the air seemed to be full of the hissing sound as tiny jets of excess saliva shot from between the teeth of the Sudanese passengers. Part way through the voyage two old Sudanese women moved into the space next to me. They were each in the habit of smoking a pipe from which belched thick smoke that reminded me of a Manchester fog. Nevertheless, for the brief duration of their stay in that spot I was glad when they smoked their pipes for when they were not doing so unlady-like emissions were constantly being discharged from their mouths accompanied by the familiar hiss. On the occasion that I returned to my sleeping bag to find that one of the ladies had been inadvertently facing towards it and that it was stained with long, thin damp patches, they were persuaded by my furious gesticulation to gather their belongings quickly and return to a neighbouring deck where most of the women, the majority of whom were Moslems, were crowded together talking and laughing in their high-pitched voices and spitting contentedly.

Third Class passengers were not officially allowed on to the First and Second Class boats, but the Sudanese ticket inspector naturally assumed that Europeans would not travel Third Class and I was able to wander freely on the more spacious decks of the three rear boats. There was a cold shower there, the water being pumped through straight from the river, and it was a relief to be able to stand beneath that several times a day. There was also a toilet which became blocked only periodically, in contrast to the toilets in the Third Class area which overflowed by the second day providing the majority of the Third Class passengers with the excuse to adopt what they viewed as the much simpler and therefore more logical method of relieving themselves on the nearest available piece of deck. The more expensive accommodation provided tiny cabins, shared with either one other person (First Class) or shared with three passengers (Second Class). These cabins contained bunk-beds, but even with a small fan in each room they were stifling. From the First and Second Class Section it was possible to climb on to the roof of the rear boats' upper deck and this was the perfect place to travel, giving reprieve from the noise, smell, and flying spit and providing an excellent view of what became rather monotonous scenery. It was also the ideal place to spend the nights. Unless navigation was likely to be particularly straightforward, the boat would stop when darkness fell, and the limited air circulation on the partially enclosed decks would cease. The other Europeans spent the nights in the fresh air on the roof of the First/Second Class section, but it would not have been possible to get the bicycle on to the roof, and having no wish to return to the deck one morning to find a mere skeleton of my former possessions remaining, I lay each night bathed in sweat in the humidity of a Third Class deck.

The first five days of the voyage were through areas of beautiful African bush. Savanna land stretched away to each side of the river, a region of level ground, long dry grass, trees and rock kopjes. It was peaceful, serene, and under-populated though over-grazed. At first the lands were those of the Arabic Baggara tribes, then of the Nilotics followed by the Shilluk, the far-spread Dinka and the war-like Nuer. The banks of the second longest river in the world attract them and they live nomadic lives, wandering from place to place with their animals, following a life-style of generations with no worries and unaware that they jeopardize their own future as they cut down trees and as their goats tear up the grass and ruin the land. The people now were a direct contrast to those in the north of the country, rushing from their mud or grass huts to dance on the river banks in excitement as the boat passed, clutching their knives and spears, displaying their nakedness in a way which, several hundred miles to the north, would have had Imams calling for a Holy War against them. The river was a slow-moving muddy flow, interspersed with small islands of papyrus brought down from the Sudd. Soon after leaving the town of Malakal, where I had been joined on the boat by one American and two English hitch-hikers, the scenery became almost non-existent as we entered the Sudd. From here to Juba, high reeds stretched on each side, broken only by occasional stretches of firm land. From the lower deck only the reeds could be seen, and since the Sudd extends for two hundred and fifty miles from east to west, the view from the roof was little better. The papyrus, reeds and other swamp vegetation, encroaches upon the river and its tributaries, often hiding the channels. Navigating the river-boat would have been impossible for anyone without experience of the river, as to the inexpert eye there was no way of knowing which channels would end in a wall of reeds.

On the afternoon of the twelfth day since leaving Kosti we arrived in Juba. I was thankful to step from the boat. A cruise up the River Nile suggests a luxurious twelve days in the sun, but in such conditions of accumulated filth, tepid, brown drinking water, and little food apart from mangoes, stale bread, and sticks of sugar-cane to chew on,

I would have been almost happy spending the time in the Nubian Desert! I was also concerned that there had been little by way of activity for twelve days and I could not afford to lose fitness with the difficult section from Juba to the Kenyan border still to negotiate.

9

When I had first planned my journey from the Sudan to Kenya I had hoped to travel from Juba southwards into Uganda and on to Nairobi. From the Ugandan border almost my whole route would have been on tarmac roads, but now Uganda was at war with Tanzania and Idi Amin had declared himself Conqueror of the British Empire. Stories circulated widely throughout Africa from travellers who had never been to Uganda but who could dictate with relish chill stories of the ills that befell those Europeans who had been so unwise as to enter that country. I was prepared to ignore the words of warning that crowded upon my ears from fellow travellers in Juba against attempting to cycle through Uganda. I had visited the country in 1975 and in 1976 when similar hair-raising stories had been abundant, and I had found the Ugandans to be among the most friendly people of Africa. The route was out of the question, however. Amin had closed the borders between Uganda and Sudan to all tourists, making entry impossible. The only alternative route to Nairobi by road was to enter Kenya in the north-west of the country. From previous experience of the Kenyan administration I knew that, once I reached the Kenyan border town of Lokichokio, the road surface, though untarred, would be firm and reasonably smooth. It was the two hundred and fifty miles to the border that worried me. In Juba I was unable to obtain information on the road to Kenya, other than that it was rarely used and that few people lived in the dry, dusty region. The only water-points would be at occasional villages and for the last eighty miles to Lokichokio there would be no water available – not a great distance under normal circumstances but I could be sure of covering no more than twenty miles each day. There were a number of other travellers in Juba, all hitch-hikers, some waiting for the boat to leave from Khartoum, others attempting to reach Kenya. Most of the latter group had decided to travel on an aeroplane which was leaving the following day for Nairobi for, though this was expensive, they had reached the conclusion, having arrived in Juba on the ferry from Khartoum a week before, that they could find themselves waiting for months for a lift by road to Kenya.

I spent the day following my arrival in Juba buying sufficient bread and fruit to last me to the next town, Torit, eighty-five miles to the south-east. To flavour the bread I took some of the local 'tarnheet', a paste that resembles peanut butter and, being made from sesame seeds, is highly nutritious. With the additional food and two gallons of water the bicycle was carrying a tremendous weight and as I rode away from Juba at four o'clock that afternoon, the bicycle bumping on the pot-holed road, I was again conscious of the strain that the wheels were being required to bear. Even so late in the afternoon, the heat was searing and I perspired freely, stopping regularly to replace the sweat by drinking the lukewarm water that I carried. After three hours, when it had become too dark to continue, I was pleased to find that I had covered approximately twenty-four miles along a track which had alternated between soft sand through which I often had to push the bike, and loose rocks across which the bicycle bounced and slithered, and where the only merit was that the going was flat.

The warmth of the night made it unnecessary to erect the tent, and after eating bread and mangoes I lay on my sleeping bag beside the bicycle and slept until dawn. At five o'clock, as the first grey light appeared in the sky, I set off again towards Torit, pushing, riding, pushing, riding, wishing that the cool of the early morning could stay throughout the day.

After an hour the sun arose over the horizon, a beautiful, unforgettable sight, a huge, flaming ball appearing like a bush fire between the long grass and stunted trees. It was nearly 8 am when I first saw the creature that I feared more than any other during my journey. I had cycled through the areas of the wild dogs of the Middle East, and now I was cheerfully camping without even the protection of a tent in country where lion, leopard and hyena roamed, but I had no fear of them as I knew that, for all their ferocity, these animals are afraid of humans and will do their utmost to avoid any contact. There was only one creature that would not have the intelligence to keep to itself and that was the fly. Flies are only irritants and cannot cause pain – unless they are tsetse flies. I had encountered tsetse flies some years before and I knew that their bite is similar to a red-hot needle being pushed slowly into the flesh. On previous occasions I had been in a vehicle and, by driving with windows and air-vents closed, had been able to restrict their attacks. On a bicycle I had no such protection. The only means of preventing the bites of the flies would be to follow the habit that I had adopted in the Nubian Desert of covering exposed skin. A thin cotton shirt would not prevent a bite from a tsetse fly as it had done the tickling of the house-fly, however.

The tsetse fly requires an environment of trees and shrubs for breeding purposes, so when I observed the first arrival perched jauntily on my handlebar bag, unmistakable with its grey thorax and wings folded neatly down its back to give the appearance of a single wing, I knew that this would only be the first of many such flies that I would encounter as I moved through East Africa. There are approximately twenty-one species of tsetse fly on the African Continent, and they are all blood-suckers. Word was obviously passed quickly through the bush that a tasty morsel of Rhesus Positive was travelling slowly through the area on a bicycle, and the tsetses came to dine. I felt the first stinging pain in my neck and reflex-action sent my hand flying to the spot with such suddenness that I almost over-balanced from the bicycle. The tsetse may be able to inflict pain but he had much to learn from his Nubian cousin concerning a hasty retreat and, a moment later, I held the struggling fly between my fingers. The grip would have crushed any similar sized insect but the tsetse is so robust that even a firm swat will usually only knock it to the ground. I examined the little creature, half an inch long and known as 'the Saviour of Africa' because, by feeding on the blood of cattle, the tsetse has discouraged cultivation and caused large areas of the continent to remain wild. Then I squashed it between my thumb and forefinger. It crunched, there was a pop, and red blood, my blood, burst on to my fingers. I rubbed the bitten point on my neck and knew that, in a moment, it would begin to swell into a small lump that would itch madly for the next few hours. I also knew that despite the rapidly increasing heat of the the sun's rays I had to act quickly and put on thick clothing to prevent further bites. Even as I bent over my panniers to extract more clothes, the flies began to attack in greater numbers and I could hear them buzzing past my ears and feel them landing on my exposed back. A few minutes later, dressed in long trousers, and thick woollen jumper, I was able to continue, the tsetses buzzing angrily around my face and hands. After a few bites on the face I tried fly repellent there, a thick creamy layer that discouraged them from landing on me for a while.

As I cycled slowly on during the day the sweat poured from me saturating the heavy layer of clothing which would have been more appropriate in an arctic winter. The stream of sweat was constantly washing away the fly repellent, making regular, liberal applications necessary, Now and again I would reach a section of smoother ground and would be able to cycle for several yards at perhaps fifteen miles per hour, hoping to leave the tsetses behind. On such occasions, instead of trying to fly at my speed, they would simply sit on the panniers, their wings neatly folded, and wait patiently until the road surface forced me to reduce speed to little more than walking pace, whereupon they would resume circling my face. As I entered the outskirts of Torit in the late afternoon, the flies gradually dispersed, seeking the more familiar targets of Sudanese villagers and I was able to return to my normal cycling clothing of shoes and shorts. After a meal of chunks of meat that looked like beef, tasted like goat, but were probably donkey, at a dilapidated Torit restaurant, I replenished my water supply and followed the track out of town towards Kapoeta, a little over a hundred miles to the east, sleeping for the night on the sandy ground beneath an acacia tree.

When I set off again at first light next morning, I wondered if the tsetses would be waiting with breakfast in mind. To my relief there was no sign of them, but Africa has always an alternative and this time I was accompanied by the tiny, black Mopani flies which seemed to have an obsession with my ears. Their bodies no larger than the head of a pin, they would cluster around my face, diving around my ears and emitting a loud droning sound.

The road surface seemed to deteriorate in proportion to the distance that I moved from Torit, the sand and dust giving way to an earth surface which was filled with ruts and pot-holes, many of them deep with mud. A vehicle would have encountered far greater difficulties than a bicycle for I was usually able to cycle around the obstacles. Later in the day the path deteriorated even more when the region became hilly and the track a mass of loose stones interspersed with 'wadis', the dry river beds which, during the rainy season of June and July, could become raging torrents. Now in January, their steep, stony sides led to a bed of powdery sand sometimes a few hundred yards in width. Cycling over loose rocks often caused the wheels of the bike to skid suddenly from beneath me and I became quite adept at leaping from the saddle and jumping clear as the bike fell on to its side. Such incidents, with the added trials of heat, flies, thirst and isolation, played on my nerves to the extent that I would regularly shout abuse at the bicycle, cursing it for throwing me off, sometimes picking up a piece of rock and hurling it at the bike or delivering it a hefty kick, actions which served only to make me feel more thirsty, to scratch the bike's paintwork, or to leave me with sore toes.

In different circumstances the countryside would have been a beautiful area through which to travel. The blue sky was a background to the multiple colours of the African bush, monkeys playing in the trees, and curiously shaped rock formations and termite mounds. That evening I reached a small village, the huts built of cane and covered with mud, each family's group of huts surrounded by a cane stockade to protect against the wild animals of which so many African villagers live in unnecessary fear. A pride of lionesses entering the village could have had no more spectacular response than that which I received as I cycled to the well in the centre of the village. African women standing at the well gossiping, their metal buckets balanced precariously on their heads, observed my approach with horror. Then with one accord they fled, their piccanninies following them uttering loud high-pitched wails. Buckets were scatterred everywhere and, a moment later, the centre of the village was deserted apart from myself. I helped myself to the cool well-water from one of the buckets left behind and a few moments later faces began to appear around the gateways of the stockades. An elderly African male, braver than the rest, cautiously approached, clapping his hands in the traditional greeting of many rural Africans. Uncertain of how to respond, I did so in the only way that occurred to me; having been drinking from a water bottle when he appeared I held the container towards him to offer him a drink. He accepted, lifted the bottle to his lips, poured a little of the water down his throat and the remainder down his chest and then, grunting his thanks, stowed the water bottle away under his robe. I quickly retrieved the vessel from him, explaining to his uncomprehending ears that he was welcome to drink as much of the water as he wished but that he was not invited to keep the bottle. Gradually his colleagues appeared from their huts to welcome me.

I stayed the night in the village, ate supper with the old man, of 'dorra', a kind of doughy bread and meat, and was shown to a hut where I slept on a cane bed until morning. The next day I reached Kapoeta, the last village in the country which had been a constant source of trials and obstacles ever since I had stepped from the boat at Wadi Halfa. In Kapoeta I met five hitch-hikers, a variety of nationalities, who were faced with the problem of finding transport to Kenya. They had managed to obtain rides from Juba on supply lorries to Kapoeta, but no vehicles were travelling on to Lokichokio and one of them had been stranded in this remote village for almost two weeks with still no prospects of transport. Lokichokio was eighty miles away, with no villages and therefore no known water points between. They had considered buying a donkey from one of the villagers, loading it with their packs and setting out to walk the distance, but a look at the available donkeys had convinced them that the beasts were of little use except for being melted down at a glue factory and that they would probably find themselves having to carry the donkey. Besides, they had insufficient water containers and it would have been courting disaster to set off walking over such terrain and in such temperatures carrying only a few pints of fluid between five people. My water situation was a little better, though far from ideal. I had, each day, been drinking the two gallons that I was able to carry, and still feeling thirst afterwards. It could take four exhaustive days to reach Lokichokio, and four pints of liquid a day would be scarcely enough to moisten my lips.

I had planned to leave Kapoeta the day after my arrival, but my passport, which the police had insisted I hand to them on my arrival at the village, had been locked in a drawer at the police station and the key had vanished. The Kapoeta police force searched in vain throughout the day for the key but to no avail. At last they had to resort to breaking open the drawer, inside which they found not only my passport but also the key. The following day, having loaded the bicycle mercilessly with mangoes and sugar-cane, I waited until the sun began to fall a little in the sky and soon after two o'clock in the afternoon, left my fellow-travellers all of whom were fervently wishing that they had come equipped with bicycles. I felt sorry for them. They could have done as so many others when they had been in Juba and taken the easy way out by flying to Nairobi, but they had had the courage to try to press on. It was some weeks later and quite by chance that I met one of them in a Nairobi street and learned that, after a few more days of waiting, they had all been able to obtain a ride to Lokichokio on a Sudanese Army vehicle.

As I rode from Kapoeta I knew that the last remaining miles in the Sudan would be my most difficult since crossing the Nubian Desert. The heat of the sun was again severe and I had not covered many miles before I came to a series of wadis, the sides sloping down in a mass of loose rock into the sandy, dry river-beds. I had found that the best way of negotiating these was to imagine that I was driving a steam-roller as I descended into the wadi. Sitting astride the bicycle, my feet resting on the ground on each side and my fingers on the brake-levers, I would allow the bike to skid down the slope, bouncing from rock to rock, into the sand at the bottom. There I would dismount, drag the bicycle through the sand, and haul it up the opposite bank. The flatter stretches were little easier, slithering across muddy surfaces, bumping clear as the bicycle began to fall over, cursing and kicking it, heat and thirst making my temper short. The further east I travelled the more parched the ground became, much of the vegetation being thorn bushes, the branches growing over on to the track and the spikes, three inches long and as tough as nails, tearing at my clothing as I passed. When, that night, I calculated that I had covered a quarter of the eighty miles to Lokichokio in one afternoon, I was well satisfied with my progress. As I lay on my sleeping bag by the bicycle, beneath a million stars, eating sugar-cane and mangoes, I would have felt far less contented had I stretched forward a hand and felt the tautness of the spokes on the rear wheel.

The following morning began badly. Arising as usual at first light, to cover as many miles as possible before the sun came up, I discovered that my back tyre was flat. In the midst of changing the inner-tube I then discovered that the front tyre was also flat. By the time I had replaced both inner-tubes the sun had appeared above the horizon and I had lost the opportunity to make progress in the relative cool of the dawn. Without a breath of breeze the heat was tremendous by ten o'clock and I pressed on with as much speed as possible since this was the only way that a cooling air-flow could be created around me. Slithering into the wadis, I forced the wheels to turn through the sand, pulling the bike up the other side, riding over the flatter rocks and the ruts, the salt stinging in my eyes as the sweat rolled from my forehead.

It was shortly before midday that disaster struck. The back wheel, which had for so long suffered such abuse in bearing a heavy load over appalling terrain, could stand it no more. Seeing a patch of sand on the track ahead, I rode hard into it, hoping that, as had happened many times before, the momentum would carry me through. The bicycle swayed from side to side and skidded to a sudden stop, almost throwing me over the handlebars. I looked down and saw that the rear wheel had collapsed. It had folded like a piece of paper, spokes hanging loosely like pieces of string. I dropped the bicycle into the dust and crossed to the bit of shade afforded by a straggling thorn tree where I threw myself down and closed my eyes. After a few minutes I decided that I had better do something useful, took the buckled wheel from the rear forks and, using the spoke key that I had never even handled before, tried to straighten the wheel. I may as well have used my teeth for all the success that I achieved with the spoke key. In fact, had I used my teeth, I would probably have done less damage for, after two hours of tightening and loosening spokes at random, the wheel looked as if it had been run over by a combine-harvester. I stopped work to examine the map. I calculated that I had covered thirty-five miles since leaving Kapoeta. Forty-five to Lokichokio. My only alternative would be to push the bicycle from here and hope that I would have sufficient water. Thirty-five miles back to the nearest water at Kapoeta or forty-five on to Lokichokio? I decided that no matter how serious the water situation, there was no going back. I would go on to Kenya. Nevertheless, my water supply was not encouraging. I had drunk about a gallon, half of what I had been carrying. The remainder was tepid and about as thirst-quenching as sea-water. And I was thirsty. My throat felt as though I had been swallowing mouthfuls of dust instead of water, and I could comfortably have drunk my remaining gallon and still wanted more. I jammed the twisted wheel back into the rear forks, finding that, even with force, it would not revolve. Somehow the wheel must be made to turn or the alternative would be to leave the bike and concentrate on getting myself to the next water supply. I removed the wheel again and dismantled the gears then, putting the front wheel in place of the rear, I pushed the deformed back wheel into the front forks. To my relief I found that, with sufficient persuasion, the new front wheel could be made to turn. By this time it was mid-afternoon, so I returned to the thorn bushes to find what little shade I could until evening, when I took another drink from my rapidly dwindling water supply and set out again. Pushing the bicycle was a nightmare. The twisted wheel could not turn freely. With each revolution it would become fast between the front forks and would require particularly forceful pressure to free it. Besides this, the shape of the wheel caused it to wobble with each revolution, the whole bicycle swaying, and this on a surface that was so uneven that pushing a bicycle with immaculately trued wheels would have been difficult enough. Darkness closed in, but though the sun had gone, the air was still hot and dry, and the sweat still streamed from me.

Forty-five miles to Lokichokio. At least twenty-one hours of pushing. Now only seven pints of water remaining. One pint every three hours. The possibility of dying of thirst was negligible. The possibility of serious de-hydration was likely. I knew now what it meant to be thirsty. I tried the textbook methods of combatting thirst; dipping a pebble into my water supply and then sucking it, running my tongue over my teeth to draw moisture from my gums, but there seemed to be no moisture in my gums. My whole mouth and throat were totally dry and occasional, small quantities of the tepid water in my bottles made my craving for drink all the greater. My whole body felt exhausted and I had to rest every few minutes, aware that each stationary period extended the time before I reached water.

I had been travelling for three hours and covered perhaps six miles when I became aware of a noise in the bush. Any form of life meant that there must be water somewhere near, and I listened carefully. The noise increased and I heard the lowing of cattle and, presently, a herd of cows wandered from the trees across the road. I could hear the shouts of men and it was not long before a human form, wrapped in a blanket and carrying the spear with which most people in the bush of southern Sudan are equipped, emerged on to the track. Alone in the bush among the primitive Toposa tribe, the Sudanese cousins of the Turkana of north-western Kenya, I was not anxious to reveal that I was in difficulties and, acting as though it was an everyday occurrence to push a bicycle with a distorted wheel around southern Sudan, I concealed my relief and greeted him formally, before displaying an empty bottle and asking for water. He held up his hands to indicate that he carried nothing but his spear, and my spirits dropped to the level of the dusty track as I remembered that these people travel like their cattle from one water-hole to the next. They can navigate their way through miles of identical bush to a water-hole, with the ease with which a European would find his way to his own bathroom tap. Like the cattle, they drink their fill at one water-hole and then do not drink again until they reach the next. Seeing a human I had naturally assumed that he would carry water. Now I realized that he had none to give me. 'Moya!' I urged, pointing to the empty bottle. 'Moya!' After several minutes of gesticulations from the tribesman, none of which I understood, he motioned for me to follow him and set off at a fast stride in the direction of Lokichokio. I pushed the bike after him, my pace increased in a desperate effort not to lose him, the wheel rasping against the forks with each revolution. He travelled rather like a sheepdog, disappearing ahead at his own speed and, just as I was thinking that I would never catch him, I would see him ahead, squatting and waiting for me. I could have almost imagined him wagging a tail beneath his blanket, except that I could no longer imagine anything except the sight of water. After half an hour we reached a dry river-bed. I skidded down the side, unsure whether I was now supporting the bicycle or it supporting me. I found out when I reached the soft sand in the bottom and had to drag the bike across to the far bank, the African sitting patiently on a rock, watching. He then led me a little way up the wadi to where a ring of thorny branches had been placed. Inside the ring a hole had been dug, four feet deep and six feet across, and in the hole was water. It was almost black, covered in floating weed and, as I stumbled towards it, there were numerous 'plops' as small frogs and lizards leapt to the safety that the water offered. But it was wet. I filled my containers, emptied into them generous quantities of sterilizing tablets, and then drunk until I could drink no more. Still the thirst persisted, and for an hour I sat by the water-hole filling, sterilizing, drinking. My Toposa friend, as if anxious that I was going to consume all the water in his hole, watched for a while then, without drinking, set off back the way we had come. I spent the next two weeks wondering why the African had not drunk when he had been with me at the hole. It was only in Nairobi that I found out.

My water containers filled, I continued towards Lokichokio. By midnight I could push no further, but I knew that though I was still going to be very thirsty, provided I carefully rationed my water I could cover the remaining thirty-three miles to Lokichokio without the risk of serious dehydration. Only one thing seemed to matter now – reaching the border and knowing that I had crossed the Sudan. I had been fighting almost every inch of each mile that I had covered with the bicycle in this country. It seemed to have been a personal duel from the start and only one of us could win. I would reach Kenya with the bicycle, alone and unaided, but only if this vast wasteland could not prevent me from doing so. Now I had almost won the battle, for the Sudan/Kenya border lay some thirty miles north-west of Lokichokio. I estimated that I had travelled approximately forty-seven miles since leaving Kapoeta, which meant that little more than three miles would see me in Kenya. After five hours deep sleep beside the track, my head resting on the saddlebag, I set off again. The buckle in the wheel appeared to be worsening and progress became continually more difficult. The sun came up, Mopani flies appeared, and the thorns on the trees clutched at my clothing. Occasionally I would hear from the bush the sounds of cattle and human voices. Once I came to a large water-hole, the cows trampling in the mud around the edges or bathing, waist-deep, in the pool, and the two dozen tribesmen gathered there gave me curious looks as I laboured past.

In five hours that morning I estimated that I had covered a minimum of seven miles and I stopped beneath a tree to await the lower temperatures of late afternoon. As I sat in the shade, wrestling again with the spoke key and wheel, I heard a different sound in the distance. I leapt to my feet as I realized that a vehicle was approaching from the direction of Kapoeta. A Land Rover appeared over the banking of a nearby wadi and two men and a woman stepped from it and greeted me. They were Germans, who had driven through from central Africa, and they were happy to supply me with two gallons of fresh, relatively cool, water. After a while they drove away, but returned a few minutes later to enquire whether I would like to put the bicycle in the Land Rover and travel with them to Lokichokio. I thought for a moment. There seemed only one important consideration; 'Which country are we in?' I asked. 'Kenya,' was the reply. So I accepted the lift. With a trace of sadness I realized that my battle with the Sudan was over, but I was content to know that I had emerged the eventual victor, if somewhat battle-scarred.

Lokichokio proved to be a tiny military outpost and, with no hope of finding anyone there to repair my wheel, I travelled with the Germans to Lodwar, the first main town in north-west Kenya. Lodwar, however, situated in an area of semi-desert and with sandy streets, was not a town for cyclists, and I was forced to take a lift on a lorry to the town of Kitale, where I was able to find a wheel-builder who, after much clucking and head-shaking, was able to straighten the wheel. Village wheel-builders in Africa, unfortunately, do not worry over much about the theory of wheel-balancing. The fact that all spokes should be of even tension when the work is completed does not concern them. Their object is that the wheels spins evenly and if when they have finished some spokes are too tight, some too loose, but the wheel does not wobble too much, they consider their job well done. Consequently, spoke-breaking was to become almost a habit with me during the next few weeks.

Leaving Kitala, it was pleasant to cycle through Kenya's green, fertile countryside, though adjusting to riding on the left of the road for the first time since leaving England was not easy and nearly had unpleasant repercussions on a number of occasions. My exertions in the Sudan were added to as I cycled towards Nairobi, extending the distance to more than four hundred miles since I had agreed to address Rotary Club dinners at Eldoret and at Kenya's third largest town of Kisumu, as well as to visit two private schools. I was cycling between altitudes of under four thousand feet beside Lake Victoria and more than nine thousand feet at Timboroa, and life was not made easier as I had reached Kenya at the commencement of the annual rainy season. Each day I was soaked by the heavy downpours as I sweated up the spectacular but exhausting escarpments of the Great Rift Valley and shivered my way down. By the time I reached Nairobi in mid-February, with nearly six thousand miles cycled, I had to admit that I did not feel as healthy as my recent exercise suggested that I should. Nevertheless, as I relaxed with a cold beer in the room of a top Nairobi hotel provided for me by the tyre company who were sponsoring my journey I congratulated myself that the difficult sections of the journey were now behind me. I did not know how wrong I was. With the border between Kenya and Tanzania, the only route south from Kenya, closed, and a state of war developing between Zambia and Rhodesia, in some respects my problems were just beginning.

10

Fish and chips. Nowhere south of the English Channel do they make them like they do in Nairobi. That was the way it seemed anyway as, at noon of my first full day in Nairoi, the Indian shop assistant poured on generous quantities of salt and vinegar, and wrapped it all up in a copy of the East African Standard. Not that I needed to eat from a fish and chip shop. Accommodation with full board had been provided for me during my stay, but twenty-pound-a-day hotels do not serve chips wrapped in newspaper for their guests to eat with their fingers. After a double helping of fish and chips I returned to the hotel just in time for lunch, slept for the remainder of the afternoon, woke up, vomited, then hurried back to the dining room for evening meal.

The following day I felt ill. For a few days previously I had felt initial symptoms of what seemed to be a cold and had connected it with the recent soaking as I pedalled towards Nairobi. It soon became obvious that it was more than just a cold, however. I felt completely exhausted. Every muscle ached and every joint was stiff. It required a great effort to get out of bed in the morning and to go in to breakfast. It occurred to me that the lack of adequate food during the last few weeks, coupled with my recent exertions, had perhaps taken out of my body so much more than had been going in. It was simply a matter of eating plenty of nutritious food during the week that I intended to stay in Nairobi, I decided. Besides, I had too much to do to stay in bed. The first thing was to try to obtain the necessary permit to enter Tanzania. The borders between Kenya and Tanzania had been closed more than a year earlier by the Tanzanians as the final nail in the coffin of the tripartite East African Community in which Uganda had also been involved. Tanzania had never specified the reasons for closing the borders but it was certain that both jealousy and economics were involved. Kenya attracts more tourists than any other African country, about four hundred thousand annually. Many of them would leave the comforts of Nairobi for the short drive into the magnificent game reserves of northern Tanzania, returning to the luxuries of Kenya as soon as they had had their fill of taking photographs of game. Socialist Tanzania, with equally as much to offer the tourist as Kenya, had sat back and watched her capitalist northern neighbour develop a prosperous tourist trade, while she had regarded visitors with suspicion. Only the most dedicated masochist would seriously consider basing his holiday in Tanzania when he could stay in Kenya but cross in and out of Tanzania at leisure. It was no coincidence that the instruction from Dar es Salaam to seal the borders prevented these brief excursions by tourists based in Kenya and meant that foreigners who wished to visit Tanzanian game parks would have to stay at Tanzanian hotels. Stories abounded amongst other travellers whom I met in Nairobi. Some had been to the border to try to enter Tanzania, had been allowed through the Kenyan post, but had then been turned back by the Tanzanian Immigration. Others had heard of people who had arrived at the border and been allowed through, but no-one had actually seen that happen at first hand. It was technically possible for travellers wishing to pass straight through Tanzania to obtain a special permit, but since there was now no Tanzanian representation in Nairobi, the only way to obtain this permit was by post from Dar es Salaam. This was reputed to be a lengthy undertaking since, not only did applications tend to become lost in the bureaucracy of the Dar es Salaam Immigration Headquarters, but there was no longer even a direct postal service between Kenya and Tanzania. One American hitch-hiker had presented himself at the Tanzanian border where he was told that he could not enter the country without the special permit. When he asked how he could obtain the special permit he was told that he must go to Dar es Salaam for it. Finally he had given up trying to explain to the border guards the illogic of the situation and took the route that most of the south-bound hitch-hikers had to settle for, by flying to Johannesburg.

I sent an application to Dar es Salaam for the permit, by way of representatives of the tyre company who were sponsoring my journey. No more was heard of it. I was aware that my chances of entering Tanzania were somewhat limited anyway for, five years earlier, I had been made a 'prohibited immigrant'. Jeff and I had arrived in Dar es Salaam in our Land Rover where we were promptly arrested on charges of poaching ivory. Earlier in the journey, in Cameroun, we had obtained from a market place a huge pair of cow horns. They measured six feet from tip to tip and rose three feet high from the base. As the cattle were slaughtered for their beef, the horns were discarded. We had selected the largest from the pile and we tied them to the front of the Land Rover's roof rack. They made an impressive sight and we carried them there for the remainder of the three year journey. Three months after we had fastened the horns on to the Land Rover, in Dar es Salaam Police Station, we were informed that because we had these horns we must be smuggling ivory. Our vehicle was searched but, hardly surprisingly, no ivory was found. This did not deter the Tanzanian police, however, for they had now discovered that Jeff and I were not innocent travellers but were actually Ugandan mercenaries sent by the hated Idi Amin to spy on Tanzania. We were completely taken aback by this new accusation, until the reasoning was explained to us. The registration letters on our vehicle were 'UYX'. All vehicles registered in Uganda began with the letter 'U'. Therefore our vehicle was registered in Uganda. Therefore we were spies. We patiently explained that, if we were mercenaries from Uganda, we would be unlikely to come to Tanzania in a Ugandan-registered vehicle. But the police were too clever for us. They had already thought of that one. We were double-thinking, it was explained. We had deliberately come in a Ugandan-registered vehicle, hoping that the Tanzanians would think that because it was a Ugandan-registered vehicle we were not Ugandans. Jeff and I were finding all this rather confusing and we were kept in Dar es Salaam for six days before the police decided that we were not Ugandan spies. We were white. Therefore we were South African spies. We were given twenty-four hours to leave the country and barred from ever returning.

As I waited in Nairobi for permission to cycle through Tanzania, I was aware that it was unlikely that the Tanzanian filing system would ever unearth that I had been made a 'prohibited immigrant' five years before. I also realized, however, that, in the unlikely event of the fact coming to light, the consequences could be unpleasant if I did succeed in entering Tanzania and it was discovered, while I was in the country, that I had previously been barred from returning.

I tried shipping companies to ask if I could be transported on a cargo boat from Kenya to Tanzania, but was told that no-one was being allowed to leave ships that entered Tanzanian ports from Kenya. The manager of the tyre firm offered to fly me and the bicycle to Zambia, and it began to seem that this might be the only alternative way of moving south. I decided that I would first cycle the four hundred miles to the border, and see if there was any possibility of being allowed to cross. Before I left Nairobi, however, I had some work to do on the bicycle.

The last few days before reaching Nairobi, the bicycle had been emitting strange sounds. I was not unaccustomed to this, but I had found on previous occasions that the noises would stop if I sprayed enough oil around or if I kicked the offending area hard enough. Failing both these alternatives, I had found that if I just kept riding the noise would either go away of its own accord or a piece would drop from the bicycle whereupon, it having diagnosed its own fault, I was usually able to replace and readjust the part correctly. As I approached Nairobi, however, these methods were not succeeding. A horrible grating sound was emanating from the chain with each revolution of the pedal. Since the chain was coated in a generous layer of rust this was hardly surprising but a cleaning and re-oiling in Nairobi made no difference. I thought that perhaps the chain needed replacing and enquired from the Asian manager of one of Nairobi's main cycle dealers, who assured me that the chain was still in good condition. He could not suggest what was causing the painful sound. Eventually I bought a replacement chain and found that the new part solved the problem – but it also gave me a new one. Now, as I pedalled, the chain would slip when certain gear sprockets were engaged. It only occurred on the smaller sprockets and when I was applying significant pressure on the pedals, such as when going up a hill. I consulted the Asian cycle dealer again but he was unsure and suggested that the new chain needed oiling. I tried that but it did not alleviate the problem. I returned to the cycle dealer. The manager was out, but his brother was there and, although puzzled, guessed that it may be because I had put oil on the new chain! Had I possessed the tiniest grain of cycling initiative I would have realized that when the chain was replaced the sprockets of the freewheel mechanism should have been as well. The teeth of the sprockets become worn to accommodate a particular chain and a new chain should have meant new sprockets. I should have known, the so-called cycle dealer should have known. The fact that neither of us did made cycling considerably more difficult for the next two and a half thousand miles, as it restricted the use of certain sprockets and so reduced the number of gears at my disposal. One other problem with the bicycle that it was essential that I take care of while in civilized Nairobi, was the rear wheel. Before it had buckled in southern Sudan I had not broken any spokes. Since it had been repaired in north-western Kenya I had broken two, despite the fact that I had only been cycling on reasonably smooth tarmac since then. I suggested to the Asian cycle dealer that all the spokes may have been strained when the wheel buckled and that perhaps they should all be replaced. He felt that this was unnecessary and, after checking the wheel, assured me that I would have no more broken spokes. Like a dolt I again listened to him. But I did have the excuse that I was not feeling too well!

February 1979. Nairobi. Six months out from England. Miles cycled, five and three quarter thousand. Miles yet to cycle, four and a quarter thousand approximately.

I didn't just feel ill. I wanted to die. I lay on my bed and wished that an angel would come down from the sky on a great golden bicycle, sit me astride the cross-bar, and pedal me back to wherever cyclists go when they die. On second thoughts I would rather he took me to a place where cyclists didn't go when they died. That way, with any luck, I would never see another bicycle again – ever!

Hepatitis is a viral infection of the liver leading to inflammation of the tissue. It is liable to be contracted through water, the symptoms showing between three and five weeks later. I didn't have to think too hard to recall which of my particular supplies of water that I had drunk over the last few weeks may have been infected. Perhaps that was why my Toposo friend had declined to drink from the water to which he had led me three weeks before, although, to him, that water-hole would surely have been as pure as the water of a mountain stream. In the circumstances, even had I known that the water was so contaminated, I would have had little choice but to drink. I had been fortunate that there had been any water at all, and I was doubly fortunate in that, before leaving England, I had been given the gamma globulin vaccination against hepatitis. The vaccination lasts for approximately six months. It was seven months since I had received it. There would have been enough anti-bodies remaining to ensure that my dose of hepatitis was a comparatively mild one. As I shakily cycled away from Nairobi, in the direction of the Indian Ocean port of Mombasa, after nine days in the Kenyan capital, I mentally extended sympathies to anyone suffering a severe dose of hepatitis. My complexion had turned a sickly pale, the whites of my eyes had become yellow. I was constantly thirsty but as soon as I tried to drink I was sick. I was unable to digest food and every movement seemed to require strenous effort. My faeces were almost white and my urine was an orange-brown colour. 'You look worse now than when you arrived in Nairobi,' commented the manager of the tyre company as I said good-bye to him.

The week in the hotel had been intended to prepare me for the last stage of the journey, so that I would be bursting with energy and brimming with enthusiasm as I rode from Nairobi. Instead it seemed unlikely that I would prove capable of pedalling as far as the end of the street and, as I cycled from Nairobi, I felt that a few weeks in bed may have been more appropriate. Instead I had a lot of pedalling before me. In just two months I was due to start work in Rhodesia, and I still had two and a half thousand miles to cover, even assuming that I was able to enter Tanzania. I reflected that I had still not managed to clean Rover and that it looked now as though it would have to wait until I reached Rhodesia. First, I set my mind on reaching Mombasa. It seemed ironic that this had been one of the few stretches of cycling to which I had looked forward when planning the expedition. More than half way through the journey, the high living standards of Kenya, a good tarmac road surface, and a descent over the three hundred mile distance, from five thousand feet to sea-level.

It was worrying. The Royal Geographical Society ought to be informed. Nairobi was not situated at an altitude of five thousand feet. It was actually some way below sea level. Otherwise why would it be necessary to cycle up hills when travelling to the coast? On the day that I left Nairobi I cycled twenty-seven miles. I had never tried pedalling a double-decker bus before but that was what it felt like I was doing. That night I pitched the tent in a clearing amongst the grassy bushland that stretched endlessly on each side, and spent the night alternating between sleeping inside the tent and being sick outside it. I had eaten very little recently and was rapidly drawing the conclusion that during the last week I must have regurgitated everything that I had eaten during the previous twenty-eight years.

The following day was better and I covered more than sixty miles, eating a meal of rice and beef which actually stayed in my stomach (at least until that night) from one of the small African restaurants. As I left Nairobi it became noticeable that the temperature was increasing. It was the hottest time of the year along the East African coast, and that meant *hot*! The heat did not seem to unduly concern the game, however, and herds of Thomson's Gazelle and wildebeeste and an occasional giraffe, watched me curiously, while in the distance the snow-capped peak of Kilimanjaro looked tantalisingly cool.

At one point I passed the place where, four years

earlier, I had had an unpleasant encounter with a puff-adder. Unpleasant for the puff-adder as things had turned out, but it could equally have been my misfortune instead of that of the snake. Jeff and I had driven until late into the night on our way from Mombasa towards Nairobi. Stopping for the night, we drove the Land Rover from the road into a clearing in the bush and I stepped from the vehicle, shining the torch in front of me. Most snakes would have been alerted by the vibration of the Land Rover and determined to put as much distance between themselves and the intruder as possible. But a puff-adder has gained the reputation for killing more people in Africa than any other snake for the simple reason that it is not a particularly excitable creature. If disturbed, it sometimes rouses itself to a supreme effort and wriggles lethargically away. If, however, before it has left the scene, someone happens to step on it, the snake is liable to express its displeasure by sinking its poisonous fangs into them. This particular snake being a puff-adder, it had shown no inclination to terminate its nocturnal excursion merely because a Land Rover had arrived. Had I not been shining the torch in front of me I would have undoubtedly stepped right on to it, but when the light flashed on to four feet of poisonous snake I returned to the Land Rover considerably quicker than I had left it, slamming shut the door, windows and even the air vents in double-quick time. Eventually Jeff and I goaded one another out of the vehicle and, armed with the heavy iron bar that we used to give leverage to the wheel-brace when unscrewing over-tight wheel nuts, I killed the snake.

Somehow one becomes rather attached to a snake that one has almost been bitten by and the skin can make an excellent souvenir. So, in the light of the vehicle head-lamps, I made my first attempt at removing the skin of a snake from its body. As an initial precaution I cut off its head. I did not relish the thought that, even though dead, it might have sunk its fangs into me by nervous reaction.

Indeed, this one must have been of a highly nervous disposition for even with its head removed one of the chief difficulties in slicing open the stomach down the length of its body was in keeping the creature still. Slitting the body of a snake is rather like opening out a sausage to put on a sandwich (except that sausages do not bleed!). Once it has been opened out flat over the entire length, patience is required for the next step. At one end of the body the thumb-nail should be inserted between the flesh of the snake and the skin, rather like separating the inner wrapper from the silver paper on a chocolate biscuit wrapping (except that snakes do not melt!). Once a small corner of skin and flesh have been separated the rest is easy. It is simply a matter of holding the skin in one hand and the flesh in the other and pulling apart, rather like peeling a banana (except that bananas do not wriggle during the process!). If, up to that point, the operator's stomach has not started to churn, it probably soon will, for if the snake was not long dead he may well find that the headless, bloody, rope-like piece of flesh in his hand, continues to squirm as if it was the complete, live snake. When I had skinned the puff-adder I threw the remains of the body into the bush. It lay moving and twisting and, an hour later, when I shone the torch on to it, the headless skinless corpse was still writhing vigorously. To preserve the skin I pinned it out on to a piece of cardboard, rubbed it with salt and allowed it to dry in the sun for a few days. I still have it as a souvenir, together with that of a tree snake that I later killed in Ethiopia, an eight-and-a-half-foot black and white cobra that Jeff ran over in the Land Rover in Ghana, and another puff-adder that seemed to have designs on bringing my bicycle journey to a premature end just short of the Cape of Good Hope.

I followed the road between vast expanses of long grass and with huge trunked baobab trees to each side. Cycling was made no easier by the fact that I was unable to use my highest gear. When it was engaged a harsh grating sound resulted and the chain slipped over the teeth of the sprocket without gripping. I had tried consulting the bicycle repair book that I carried with me but, like all good manuals, it told me everything except what I wanted to know. I had covered half of the distance to Mombasa when I heard an unmistakable 'ping' from the back wheel and quickly confirmed that another spoke had broken. I did not have a lot of energy but, in a burst of frustration, summoned up sufficient strength to deliver the bicycle a kick that sent one of the panniers sailing into the bush and left me rolling in the road clutching my toe. The wheel that, in Nairobi, I had been assured was strong enough to carry me to South Africa on its present spokes, had brought me only one hundred and fifty miles – and that on some of the smoothest tarmac that I could hope to encounter. While I would be able to have a new spoke inserted and the wheel balanced in any Kenyan town, the prospects would be rather more bleak in Tanzania or Zambia. And I had already learned what would be liable to happen to any wheel that I tried to balance myself.

In the next town that I came to I located the bicycle 'fundi' who quickly disproved the commonly held theory that all African village artisans are experts at their trade. I gave him one of my dwindling supply of spare spokes and watched in surprise as he set about replacing the spoke with the bicycle on its side, the wheel still in the forks, and with only a small section of tyre and inner tube removed from the wheel. He fitted the new spoke, returned the inner tube and tyre which he then inflated, and proudly sat back, awaiting my compliments and money. I turned the bike upside down and rotated the wheel. It spun with the precision of a Yorkshire miner performing a pirouette. I explained to the mechanic that the wheel was not balanced and I watched him in wonder as he tried to rectify the fault by unscrewing the wheel nuts and altering the position of the wheel in the forks. It didn't work! I removed the tyre and inner tube and rim tape from the wheel and handed it to him and this time he placed the wheel in a wooden frame and balanced it more accurately.

More than a hundred miles of the ride to Mombasa was in, or alongside, the vast Tsavo National Park, Kenya's main elephant reserve. I did not really feel quite up to riding at top speed away from charging rogue elephants and was not encouraged by roadside signposts warning that elephants may be crossing the road. I began to wish that I was wearing a crash helmet! As if concerned that the erection of a signpost in their honour invoked a responsibility to put in an appearance, a herd of perhaps thirty elephants was feeding nonchalantly nearby, about fifty yards from the roadside. I stopped the bicycle, quietly took out my cine camera and began to photograph them. The atmosphere had been completely still up to that point, but I became aware of a flicker of air on my back as a slight breeze suddenly arose drifting towards the herd. I was now upwind of them and with three days' supply of congealed sweat stuck to my body, the elephants could hardly have been expected not to notice me. Their trunks rose into the air like periscopes, their ears began to flap, they stamped their feet and swayed backwards and forwards, and one of them let out a fearsome bellow. I was not very sure what elephants did when they became angry, but I gathered that this herd was not particularly happy. I decided that I had taken enough film for the time being and moved on rather quickly, casting nervous glances over my shoulder for some minutes afterwards.

The scenery had now become more monotonous than ever before. Long grass rose up on each side. Even in the desert there had been something to look at, if only the emptiness of the place. Here the view was totally obscured, apart from the strip of tarmac stretching on and on. As the tropical night closed rapidly in I looked in vain for a clearing large enough to pitch the tent, but I finally reluctantly decided that I would have to ride on to Voi, the next town, twelve miles away, and find a place to sleep there. The batteries in my front and rear lamps were so exhausted that the glimmer of light that they emitted would not have done credit to an undernourished glow-worm and the night was so black that I could not even see the handlebars in front of me.

After a while I was overtaken by a police patrol car which stopped, and two constables waved me to the roadside. Did I not know that my lights were quiet? I was asked. And did I not know that there were animals in the grass and that they were hungry? I apologized and smiled and apologized some more, and the officers' faces were soon wreathed in delighted grins as they asked if it was possible for someone to travel all the way from Nairobi on a bicycle. Setting off again, the police car followed close behind, its headlamps lighting the way for me and half an hour later, as I reached the outskirts of Voi, a beaming constable leaned out of the car window and informed me that I would be able to take a train the remainder of the way to Mombasa. I pitched the tent on a quiet patch behind a garage, reflecting that travel in Africa would be much easier if all the police forces were like that of Kenya. I remembered the occasion when Jeff and I, returning northwards, had driven into Kenya from Tanzania. Before we left Tanzania the Land Rover had been virtually taken apart by an officious constable who had insisted that we completely empty it for his inspection. Shortly afterwards we entered Kenya where the border-post was manned by two Kenyan policemen one of whom was seated on a chair. He leapt up as we approached, insisted that one of us sit on his chair, and asked his colleagues to bring another seat at once. 'These people are visitors to our country. We want them to know that they are welcome,' he had said to his friend. Such attitudes naturally influence one's opinions of a country.

'The road is not heavy. It is almost sleeping,' I was told of the way ahead as I left Voi; which I took to mean that it was flat. In fact it was anything but flat and, inevitably, the wind was in my face. But it was the sun that was crucifying and by mid-afternoon I was pedalling almost in a daze. The scenery changed from grassland to thorn-bushes; twisted, dehydrated trees, that were the only life able to survive in the parched soil and offering virtually no shade when I stopped to rest. The bushes were not alone in their state of dehydration. I was still finding it almost impossible to drink water. It seemed to taste like sour milk in my mouth and if I forced myself to swallow it I was immediately sick. The only drink that I was able to take was Coca Cola, and then only if it was chilled and in small quantities. The will to cycle was maintained only by the thought of a cold drink in the next village, but each time I reached one of the occasional, small roadside villages, the pile of empty Coca Cola crates outside the general store told its own story. The cupboard was bare as far as Coca Cola or any other soft drink was concerned, until the next delivery which could be the following day or the following week. With just a few miles to go before the next relatively large town of Samburu I reached the point that was, perhaps, physically the lowest of the journey. The road rolled on ahead in a line of endless undulations, the wind blew towards me, the scenery was a monotony of mile after mile of thorn-bush, and the sun was merciless. I dropped the bike on to the road, then fell into the dust in the partial shade of a bush. Somewhere close at hand I could hear a voice muttering curses and blasphemies. I listened and recognized the voice. It was my own! I lay for a while and forgot about cycling. Forgot about hills and wind and heat and hepatitis and, after a time, I returned to the bike and rode on to Samburu where I drank three bottles of cold Coca Cola. It had been probably the only time during the journey that I was literally unable to continue another inch until I had had some kind of brief rest.

Five days after setting out from Nairobi I rode into Mombasa where I spent eight days. Some of the time I spent in contacting shipping companies to try to arrange a passage on a cargo boat to Dar es Salaam should I not be allowed to cross the land border into Tanzania, but the story was always the same, that ships from Kenya were not being permitted to land passengers on Tanzanian soil. I met travellers, hitch-hikers mainly, who were stranded in Kenya being unable to continue southwards due to the closed Tanzanian border. I broke another spoke in my back wheel, again on a perfectly good tarmac road, and consequently had the complete wheel respoked. But most of the time I spent to the north of the town on the beaches. Swimming in the warm crystal clear waters of the Indian Ocean, sleeping on the silvery white sands beneath the palm trees, walking or running for miles along the shore at the edge of the surf, and drinking the milk from coconuts that lay in the thick foliage beside the beach. A week of living off coconuts is sure to remedy any complaints of the liver and gradually my strength and fitness returned and I knew that I could cycle on. The only problem was that sixty miles to the south was Lunga Lunga, the border with Tanzania, and the prospects of being allowed to cross did not look promising. I had tried every other possibility. Now there was only one more alternative. To go to the border and hope that the novelty of the bicycle would influence the Tanzanians into letting me enter.

I had decided to cycle to the border at night when it would be cooler. Mostly I preferred to travel by daylight since, in the African bush almost everything of interest to the traveller tends to disappear during the hours of darkness. Added to this was the fact that the average bicycle lamp is about as useful as the average candle in illuminating the way ahead and only serves to make the darkness blacker. The glass had fallen out of my front lamp in Turkey and the reflector was coated in rust, which made the light even less useful than the average candle. On the particular night that I had chosen, however, there was a full moon and I knew that in the clear atmosphere by midnight there would still be enough light to read a newspaper.

I left Mombasa at 6 in the evening. The ride was quite pleasant with a flat road, no wind, and the air warm enough to keep me damp with sweat while not so hot as to be uncomfortable. Two Africans in a car drew level with me at one point and I chatted with the passenger through his open window as we travelled along by our separate means. With the eternal optimism of the African, who prefers to say what he thinks the listener would like to hear rather than what he actually believes, he assured me that I would be allowed to enter Tanzania and, with the only alternative being to accept the offer of the tyre company and fly to Zambia, I hoped he was right though I did not share his confidence. After a while the car accelerated away, though before it did the passenger handed me a bottle of Pepsi Cola, 'to drink on your long way'.

I could not help feeling somewhat disappointed by the gloom of the night. The moon was not casting off the light that I had hoped for and by 10 pm it was distinctly murky. I glanced up at the full moon expecting to see it enveloped in cloud, but it was plainly visible – or what was left of it was. Someone appeared to have removed a large piece of it. That explained why there had been great excitement and festivity in some of the villages through which I had cycled. An eclipse was taking place. The villagers may have found it cause for celebration but I did not. I had hand-picked this particular night because of the full moon, and now the light was being blotted out.

By midnight the shadow was covering seven-eighths of the moon and there was just enough light to sit by the roadside and make some jam sandwiches while I awaited the course of nature. As the eclipse passed I was able to continue, and camped in the bush at 2 am just two miles short of the Kenyan frontier.

When I arrived at the Kenyan border-post the following morning, a shock awaited me. A directive had just been received from Nairobi to the effect that Kenya had retaliated against the Tanzanians by closing their own side of the common boundaries. Not only could I not enter Tanzania, I could not even leave Kenya! For two hours I coaxed, cajoled, wheedled and persuaded the Chief Immigration Officer, but he was adamant that I was not to be allowed to pass the barrier which would take me into No Man's Land. 'Return to Mombasa,' I was told. 'Mombasa is a nice place. Why do you want to leave Kenya? Do you not like it here?' I consulted the map. There were three miles of neutral territory between the Kenyan and Tanzanian border posts. There were a number of hills but I estimated that I could reach the Tanzanian border in fifteen minutes, – providing that no-one saw me cycling around the barrier! I left the Immigration Officers to their game of cards and, when nobody was nearby, quietly mounted the bicycle and crossed into No Man's Land. The idea was not really a very good one anyway, since the Tanzanians were almost certain to check that my passport had been stamped when I left Kenya even if I had reached Tanzanian territory. Ten minutes after leaving Kenya I heard a vehicle behind me and was quickly overtaken by a Land Rover of the Kenyan Police. In view of the fact that I had committed a blatant offence the two officers were very nice about the matter and I was politely requested to cycle back to the frontier post. Although my attempt had never been likely to meet with success it seemed to have the effect of causing the Chief Immigration Officer to realize how determined I was to reach Tanzania and he informed me that he would contact his superior in Mombasa. His superior in Mombasa had to contact his superior's superior in Nairobi, and it was late afternoon when word from Nairobi travelled via Mombasa to the lowly border-post of Lunga Lunga, that I was to be allowed to cross to the Tanzanian side. However, I was advised that there was one condition.

Whether or not the Tanzanians allowed me to enter their country I would not be permitted to re-enter Kenya. I assumed at first that the officer must be joking, but he was completely serious as he told me that if I could not enter Tanzania I would have to remain in No Man's Land. The Kenyan frontier was closed, he informed me. I would not be permitted to re-enter. As I rode for the second time towards Tanzania, I could not help smiling at visions of being refused entry to Tanzania and then meeting with a similar refusal when I tried to re-enter Kenya. In theory I could be doomed to spend years in a three-mile strip of unoccupied, unclaimed land. It would be like 'Desert Island Discs' without the records!

The Immigration Officer glared at me in a way that I had seen before from Tanzanian officials. It seems that the stony leer must be an integral part of the training. At this border-post it seemed to be the *only* training necessary, as Immigration, Customs and Police wandered aimlessly around. 'Go back to Kenya,' I was told. 'I can't,' I replied. 'They won't let me.' For three hours I waited at the border-post, adopting the same approach to getting into Tanzania as I had used to get out of Kenya. This time, however, it was meeting with less success. I maintained a friendly grin fixed on my face and chatted as pleasantly as the officials would allow. They were not exactly eager to communicate but after I told them, with tongue in cheek, what hospitable people the Tanzanians are, they cheered up a bit and became rather more co-operative. I stressed what a beautiful country Tanzania is and how I had cycled all the way from England partly so that I could visit their country. I emphasized how important it was that I reach Zambia within a month, explaining that I was due to commence work there on a certain date and spicing my story by saying that I had a dying relative in England who wanted to hear that I had reached there before he passed away. I let them prod and poke at the bicycle as they searched for the motor that they were sure I must have concealed somewhere, and watched with raised spirits as they agreed that I had indeed pedalled from England, upon which they collapsed with merriment, rolling on the floor and clutching their sides in uncontrollable mirth. The barriers had been broken down; now was the time to press home the advantage. 'So you see how important it is that I enter Tanzania?' I asked the Chief Immigration Officer. 'Indeed yes,' he replied, wiping a tear of laughter from the side of his face. 'Now I understand.' 'So I can enter?' I urged. 'No,' he answered soberly, 'Go back to Kenya.'

When the Immigration Officers left the post to return home for the night I retreated a few hundred yards into No Man's Land and pitched my tent. The ground was hard as rock and the tent-pegs just bent up when I tried to push them in. Eventually I gave up trying and went to bed leaving the poles delicately balanced. The sky was clear and I knew that it would not rain. It did! During the night the heavens opened and the tent collapsed on top of me covering everything with clammy, saturated nylon. The following morning I was awoken by a Tanzanian policeman to whom I had chatted the previous day. He started to smile, then remembered himself and scowled instead. 'I have come to look at your house,' he said, then asked me if I was on my way to Mombasa. I stretched my sleeping-bag out in the sun to dry then made my way back to the post. The Immigration Officer eventually agreed to telephone his superior and, after a long and involved discussion in Swahili, he asked for my passport. After studying the document in detail, probably to ensure that I had never been to Rhodesia or South Africa, he asked for evidence that I was taking up employment in Zambia. Fortunately I had with me a letter from a Zambian Rotary, inviting me to speak at a meeting on my way through the country. By a mixture of the appalling writing of the Rotary Club's Secretary, the Immigration Officer's limited ability to read English, and some garbled explanations, I managed to convince him that the letter was an offer of employment. I was handed an immigration form to complete and sign, but not until my passport was stamped, the bicycle packed and I had cycled under the barrier and into Tanzania, did I breathe a sigh of relief.

The road from the border to the first main town of Tanga was dirt track, badly rutted and corrugated in parts and I was thankful that I had had the back wheel respoked after all. Soon after crossing the border I stopped for a breakfast of jam sandwiches. I was beginning to acquire a taste for these, which was fortunate because my supplies of dehydrated food had expired somewhere in the Sudan. Now, with long distances of unpopulated country to pass through in Tanzania, Zambia and Botswana, and with no time to spare in preparing laboriously cooked meals, over the following weeks I was to become grateful to the Earl of Sandwich.

Dar es Salaam was my next target. I was to visit an English friend who was working there – something to look forward to as I pedalled south from the border. The bicycle continued to be, as it had throughout the Middle East and Africa, a great source of interest and amusement as I cycled through the villages of north-east Tanzania. Children would rush from the rectangular-shaped mud huts that were their homes, shouting excitedly. Women stopped their work, tilling the land, carrying water, preparing food or washing clothes, to stand open-mouthed, their babies strapped in slings to their backs, while the men of the village roused themselves from their restful postures under the shade of the trees, to amble forward and greet me. Occasionally, from the outskirts of villages, a pack of lean, rabid-looking dogs would burst forth towards me, greatly increasing my speed. I was still adjusting to the problem of being unable to use the highest gear on the bicycle due to the worn chain. It meant that my legs had to revolve more quickly than should have been necessary when pedalling downhill. Periodically I would follow the natural inclination to engage the highest gear, and a lurid grinding sound would result from the gear mechanism. On such occasions I could sense the villagers glancing at each other and shaking their heads sadly, no doubt feeling thankful that donkeys did not need to be pedalled and muttering words of gratitude to their ancestral spirits that goats and cattle were not created with such contrivances as chain-wheels, cottered cranks, and derailleur arms.

The rains that I had encountered before Nairobi seemed to have located me again, as did the tsetse flies which had not troubled me since southern Sudan. Since entering Tanzania the areas through which the road ran had been quite heavily populated by African standards, but a little over half way to Dar es Salaam there was a sudden absence of huts and people. It had to mean a tsetse-infested area and I cycled along awaiting the inevitable. It came as if a red-hot needle had been jabbed into my back and I jumped so violently that I almost fell off the bicycle. I put on my pullover which seemed to discourage them a little, perhaps because it had not been washed since before I left England, but they gradually increased in numbers, sitting on the panniers or circling round my head as if making a reconnaissance before attacking. I could do nothing but keep pedalling and, as the tsetses massed, it seemed as if they were awaiting a command to attack in unison. The shades of a heavy black cloud drifted across the sun and the hot, still air was suddenly cooled as a breeze drifted towards me. Soon heavy spots of rain began to fall, and then the water was cascading down, huge droplets bouncing off the tarmac which moments before had been too hot to walk upon barefoot and which now steamed in apparent protest. The tsetses were clearly not impressed by this meteorological phenomenon and beat a hasty retreat in search of shelter. I was not exactly enamoured of the weather either, but the long grass and occasional banana or palm tree that represented the scenery, did not offer much in the way of cosy refuge and I decided to keep pedalling. At least I could feel thankful that the rain had deterred the tsetse, though occasional ones still made periodic passes around my ears as if keeping a bearing on my progress, despite the fact that the rain continued throughout the afternoon and virtually until darkness. Indeed the tsetse scouts had performed their mission well, for when I emerged from the tent the following morning after camping in a clearing in the long grass the flies were already hovering expectantly. A few more miles of cycling, however, took me out of the tsetse area and back to the roadside villages.

By the time I reached Dar es Salaam all my possessions were saturated. The annual rains had apparently entered Tanzania at approximately the same time as I had, though probably with considerably less difficulty, and previous afternoons had seen constant downpours. Still conscious that time was an important factor, I had been forced to keep cycling rather than waste countless hours in sheltering. Fortunately I was able to spend a few days in Dar es Salaam before again continuing south towards the Zambian border. The 'Haven of Peace', as the Tanzanian capital is rather paradoxically named, reminded me of the towns of Eastern Europe. The country, which was once one of the world's foremost suppliers of sisal, cashew nuts, cloves, cotton, pyrethrum, tobacco, and a large exporter of diamonds, was now devoid of foreign currency and heavily in debt. Shops in the modern capital were sparsely stocked, dark and dusty, apparently intent upon deterring prospective customers from buying. Merchandise was tipped carelessly on to rows of shelves, food tins coated with rust, and, in the state-owned shops, the staff unconcerned as to whether anyone buys there or not. The staple food of rice was practically unobtainable throughout the country as were a great many items ranging from sugar to bicycle spare parts. I tried to have a lost filling replaced while in Dar es Salaam, only to be told by the dentist that it would not be possible as there were no fillings in the country.

Fifty miles per day for the next five weeks was my schedule as I left Dar es Salaam, in order to arrive in Rhodesia to commence work on May 1. By the standards of travelling by bicycle in England it did not seem far, but I was still carrying a lot of equipment and had a couple of mountain ranges to cross. With the weather alternating between extreme heat and heavy rain, and the likelihood of bad roads in Botswana, I could not afford to take a break from cycling and so risk falling behind on my average. At least I knew that for the next few hundred miles the scenery would improve, with the Mikumi Game Reserve to cycle through, and two mountain ranges to cross before I reached Zambia. And the rain could at least be given credit for being predictable. The mornings would usually start cold and overcast and I would pack the wet tent and push the bicycle through the long grass which invariably lined the roadside, back to the tarmac. By mid-morning the sun would have broken through, the cloud dispersed and the temperature be rapidly increasing. Early afternoon would bring the cloud and then the rain which would persist until evening and often well into the night.

I timed my arrival near Mikumi so that I would camp just before entering the reserve and have left before nightfall. A signpost warned 'Danger. Wild Animals' and during that day I cycled close to most of the animals of the African plains excluding rhinoceros and cats, neither of which I was particularly anxious to see. Even so, it being the wet season, the grass was so long that a lion could have stood beside the road waving to me and I would not have seen it. Giraffes were particularly numerous. One pair ran through the bush almost alongside me as I cycled on the road, then changed direction and ran across the road in front of me. One of the most dangerous animals of the plains is reputed to be the lone buffalo. I spotted one feeding close to the road and, it having its back to me, I carefully took out my cine camera and sat astride the bicycle filming it. As I watched through the viewfinder the buffalo began to move away and I continued filming until I realized that it was not walking away but was turning in a semi-circle and heading back towards me. Marie Antoinette's hair is reputed to have turned white overnight. Mine must have become a few shades lighter in a matter of seconds. I dropped the camera into one of my front bags and pedalled, and only a little cloud of dust and the smell of scorched tyre showed where I had been moments before.

As I left the game park in the afternoon, the road climbed steeply before dropping down to run parallel to the Great Ruaha River. The scenery was magnificent with the brown, swollen river running beside the road, mountains stretching away into the distance, and the vegetation lush and green, interspersed with giant baobab trees. There were few people, and vehicles were scarce, for Tanzania had little to transport any more. The rain held off and even the breeze was behind me and I realized that, for the first time since perhaps leaving the Middle East, I was again enjoying cycling. That evening, having cycled more than seventy miles for the second consecutive day, I pitched the tent in the valley of the river, and stood near the tent looking across the green hillside. It was the kind of still, peaceful evening when you can be completely alone but never know loneliness, and when I was able to realize how fortunate I was to have come so far and to places like this. Even finding that I had inadvertently kept my bread supply wrapped in a plastic bag and that it had gone mouldy could not spoil the evening. It simply made the bread taste twice as good when I had scraped off the mould and added the jam.

Next day I crossed the river by way of a large bridge. The Tanzanian phobia of spies and sabotage to essential lines of communication was inevitably active and two soldiers on guard duty leaned tiredly against the bridge chatting to each other and looking like unwanted spare parts. If a log is laid across a ditch on a Tanzanian footpath, a soldier is likely to be called on to guard it.

I was usually able to obtain a reasonable meal once a day from one of the village restaurants. I would prop the bicycle against the side of the mud-brick building and sit close to the open doorway where I could keep at least one eye on it all the time. Word would quickly spread round the village that a 'muzungu' (white man) had arrived on a bicycle with a hidden motor, and crowds of children would appear, positioning themselves so that they could look at both the bicycle and me at the same time, and watching every movement that I made, amazed to see me eat and drink as they did. If I scratched my head or swatted a fly a gasp of awe would spread amongst the watchers, and when once I sneezed, the incredulity could not have been surpassed had I pulled a rabbit from a hat. Generally the meal would be quite satisfying even though I was often not sure what it was. Usually it was a kind of beef stew, though on one occasion the chunks of meat were obviously goat. I could tell by the fact that some of its fur still clung to the meat.

Before the town of Iringa I came to the next steep climb, an escarpment that climbed up to around six thousand feet. 'I find it difficult on my motorbike,' a Tanzanian with whom I had been talking earlier had joked, and once again sweat rolled from me, dripping continuously on to the road, as I climbed. It occurred to me that my liquid turnover during the entire journey must have been incredible and that it would have been fascinating to collect and measure all my sweat.

My progress to the Zambian border was well above the average for which I was aiming and I reached there ten days after leaving Dar es Salaam. Despite the adverse weather conditions which, as so often in Africa, varied from one extreme to the other, I had enjoyed the ride through southern Tanzania and now felt probably fitter than at any time during the journey. I had enjoyed meeting the Tanzanians too – at least the ones not in uniform. They were simple, unassuming people, who wanted nothing more out of life than to earn sufficient money to buy food and beer and to watch their children grow up so that they could earn sufficient money to provide their parents with food and beer. The politics of Tanzanian Socialism was beyond the understanding of most of the people, who had little love for a system which dictated both what they should do and say and gave them few visible benefits.

At one stage of my journey through Tanzania I heard a shout from behind and looked round to see an African pedalling his rusty old Chinese bicycle towards me for all he was worth. It heartened me to see a bicycle in such awful condition as, with each revolution of the cranks, it was making even louder grating sounds than my own. The cyclist was travelling to the next village ten miles further on, and we rode together, talking as we pedalled. He spoke good English and his personality was typically African in that everything he said he regarded as highly amusing. He laughed infectiously and chattered non-stop, the type of person who could sell a pork chop to an Ayatollah. When I mentioned President Nyerere he almost fell off his bike with laughter and, lifting back his head he noisily cleared his throat then spat forcefully into the air ahead of us to indicate his feelings towards his President. He obviously did not like Nyerere. Equally obvious was that he did not know that there is more to cycling than balancing astride a frame and two wheels, for his lump of phlegm, after performing a graceful arc in the air, was carried back by the breeze to land in an unsightly mound on the front of his shirt.

In the villages the people were invariably friendly and courteous and, if they often appeared rude and could be irritating because of their tendency to stare, they could be forgiven when it is considered that the arrival of a 'muzungu' on a bicycle to them was perhaps comparable to a Martian craft landing in an English village. I encountered very little of the begging which is often common in the larger African towns, though there was an occasional, 'give me smoking' or 'bring me money,' for to the African villager a white man is a rich man, whether he travels by bicycle or by Range Rover. It is regrettable that in a country where most of the people offer a simple, open welcome, that many of the officials suffer from paranoia. They cannot accept that a person travels simply for pleasure and with no devious political reasons. In the eyes of the authorities, if a European wishes to move from country A to country B he does so by air and if he chooses a more mundane form of transport then he has an ulterior motive. Travelling by bicycle I could not have been placing myself under greater suspicion had I been moving through Africa in a Chieftain tank, and the nearer to the 'White South' that I moved the more suspicious any official, from a private upwards, became of me.

A hundred and fifty miles before the Zambian border I was having a brief rest, sitting astride the bicycle at the roadside. It was lunch time and, having carelessly allowed my bread supply to become too low, I had run out of food the previous evening and had not eaten for the last eighteen hours. The rain had started early that day and I was already thoroughly wet, besides being rather hungry, when a police Land Rover came from behind and stopped in front of me. Four policemen informed me that they had been sent by 'our bosses' to take me back to the last village through which I had cycled, five miles away, 'for further interrogation.' I asked if they would be prepared to bring me back to this same spot afterwards or if I would be expected to cycle the five mile distance a second time and was told, 'that will be for our bosses to decide.' I was contemplating the value of a discussion on the role of 'bosses' in a peoples' republic when, forgetting that they had just informed me that I was to be taken back to the village, they asked to see my passport. They looked at this from various angles, obviously not too sure which way up the document was meant to be, and then told me that they wished to see everything that I was carrying. Had I been driving a Bedford truck I could have understood the need for such a search, but it seemed unnecessary with a bicycle. It was typical of most of the checks throughout Tanzania and Zambia and usually, with controlled patience and forced good humour, the underlings could be persuaded to return to their 'bosses' after perhaps half an hour with a few notes of passport details scribbled on a scrap of paper. The absurdity of the checks made one want to shout with irritation, but I usually found that by gripping the saddle of the bicycle with one hand and the handlebars with the other and squeezing both very hard, I could tolerate the checks without showing annoyance or submitting to the temptation to use heavy sarcasm which would undoubtedly have caused difficulties. I remembered the story of an American hitch-hiker who had been stopped by the police in Dar es Salaam and told that they thought that he might be a South African spy. 'Of course I'm a spy!' he had scoffed. 'What else would I be but a South African spy?' He was jailed for twenty-four hours on charges of admitting to being a spy! No matter how trying the situation I was aware that it was advisable to show the same lack of wit displayed by the officials. Consequently, when, as I stood with the rain dripping from me beside my mud-splattered bicycle, one of the officers blankly asked, 'How did you come to this place?', I refrained from replying, 'I just flew in on Concorde,' and answered simply, 'I came on this bicycle.'

The following day I was stopped at a road block which was staffed by a lone woman dressed in army combat uniform. She looked as compatible with her role as an African man would have done tilling the land with a baby strapped to his back and as she waved her automatic rifle at me I fervently hoped that she knew what a safety-catch was. She asked if I had reported to the police in the last town. I pointed out that since entering Tanzania I had cycled through more than fifty towns and that if I had called at the police station in each town I would still be somewhere north of Dar es Salaam. After making me wait unnecessarily for a few minutes she allowed me to pass through the barrier. The same day I was stopped three times in one town and taken 'under suspicion' to the police station each time. Finally the desk sergeant must have become tired of seeing me and stamped my passport so that I could just show that to the next person who wished to arrest me.

As I rode towards the Tanzanian border town of Tunduma at the crossing point to Zambia, I was given a final memory of Tanzania's rainy season. I was cycling slowly up a steep hill and a number of Africans were walking along the roadside towards the town. Suddenly one of them shouted and pointed to his left, across the mountains. The other Africans began to run in the direction of Tunduma. I looked across to where he had pointed to see an amazing sight. A rain cloud, so dense that it seemed like a solid wall of water, was sweeping towards us. The air was warm and still and yet, several miles away but coming closer every second, was this deluge. The Africans gave up trying to reach the town and instead took cover among the rocks beside the road. I knew that if I could only make it to the top of the hill it would take but moments to ride down into the shelter of Tunduma, but the hill seemed to drag on interminably. I pedalled harder, watching as the cloud swept towards the road until it blotted out the sun and it became almost as dark as night. As the first of the wind caused by displaced air hit me, I knew that I was not going to reach Tunduma and, moments later, it seemed that I had been hit by a tidal wave. The wind gusted in all directions forcing me to stop pedalling and then the rain came down almost as a solid mass, stinging and blinding. I could do nothing but wait until it had passed before riding on to the border with a steady stream of water running from both the panniers and myself.

April 1979. Tanzanian-Zambian border. Eight months out from England. Miles cycled, seven and a quarter thousand. Miles yet to cycle, two and three-quarter thousand approximately.

As I left Tanzania and reached the Zambian border-post I congratulated myself. I may have left Tanzania considerably wetter than I entered, but I had successfully negotiated what I was sure must be the biggest obstacle on my route in terms of political controversy. I was ahead of schedule and had now exactly one month in which to cross Zambia and a little of Botswana to reach Rhodesia. It was April 1 and if I thought that I was entering a country of temperance and sobriety, I must have rated as the biggest April Fool of the year. For, as I was entering from the north, Zambia was receiving other visitors. They came from the south. They came to seek out and destroy the Zambian-based terrorists who were infiltrating their country in an attempt to cause anarchy. They were Rhodesian soldiers and they came by vehicle, by rail and by air. In fact they came by any means, except by bicycle. But the Zambian Army wouldn't believe that!

11

I had visited Zambia before and I was not expecting a great deal in terms of honesty or efficiency as I entered the Immigration Offices. What you do not expect you are not disappointed when you do not receive. I had three departments to visit before I could enter Zambia. The first was the officer inspecting health certificates to ensure that I had received the necessary vaccinations prior to my arrival at the border. The second was Immigration, where new arrivals had to fill in an entry form. The final department was the Customs, where currency declaration forms, stating the amount of foreign currency carried, were to be completed. I arrived at the medical desk with my three standard certificates of immunisation: yellow fever, smallpox and cholera. The official glanced at them and then asked, 'What about plague?' A certificate for vaccination against plague was new to me. I knew that there had been a minor outbreak in Kenya at the time I was there, but I had never heard of a vaccination certificate for the disease and was immediately suspicious. Without a certificate, I was told, I could not enter Zambia, and the official informed me that I must go back and obtain one. Where I was meant to go back to he did not specify. Presumably he meant to England and I had to fight hard to refrain from saying, 'Certainly, I'll go and get a certificate at once. You just wait here while I cycle back to England for my plague vaccination and I'll be back in no time.' Instead I managed to wait, until the official told me that he would like to help me if he could. Then I was more than just suspicious. He drew a dollar sign on a piece of paper. 'Do you have any of these?' he asked. 'No,' I replied, 'I only have travellers' cheques.' I knew that these would be of no value to him even if I gave him one. 'Do you have any of these?' he asked and drew a pound sterling sign on the paper. 'No. Only travellers' cheques,' I answered. Realizing that he was not going to receive an unofficial supplement to his salary, he retired gracefully. 'I will allow you to pass anyway,' he told me.

At the next desk was the Immigration Officer. He was looking rather harassed and was surrounded by a group of Africans who were obviously waiting to enter Zambia but were being delayed. The problem was that the Immigration Office had run out of entry forms and no-one was allowed to enter the country without first completing a form. There was an adequate supply of exit forms I was assured, and if I had been wishing to leave Zambia there would have been no problem. A messenger had been sent some time ago to obtain some more forms from the Immigration Post at the railway station but he had not returned. Nor had the second messenger who had been sent to look for him. Finally the Chief Immigration Officer disappeared in the direction of the railway station. While he was away I found an entry form on a desk in the corner of the room, completed it, and was stamped into the country by another Immigration Official while the waiting Africans continued their vigil.

From Immigration I moved on to Customs. The problem here was that the currency declaration forms were locked in a drawer and the officer on duty did not have the key. He was waiting for his colleague to arrive to unlock the drawer. In order to save time, I asked, if he wished to search my bicycle, would he search it while we were waiting for the key? Unfortunately, no. The declaration forms had to be completed before the search was made. It was the rule.

Most of Zambia lies on a plateau, three to five thousand feet above sea-level. Potentially it is one of the richest states on the African Continent being the world's third largest producer of copper, after the United States and the Soviet Union. In reality it has become an economic disaster, totally reliant on its copper to earn foreign exchange so that agriculture, in what is basically a fertile country, has been allowed to stagnate totally. Recently not even the staple crop of maize has been produced to self-sufficiency, but that has never been the fault of Zambian policies. One year it would be too little rain; the next year too much. In 1979 it was the Rhodesians who were responsible for the sad state of the Zambian economy. President Kaunda's advisors seemed to be expert at finding excuses, but not solutions.

The Zambian scenery does not offer a great deal, for the country is mainly bushland, arid, tall, perennial grass, but it was ideal for my purpose since, on the whole, Zambia is flat. It was principally the lack of hills that determined my route from the Zambian border. I had considered turning south-east when I entered the country and cycling into Malawi, the small state between Zambia and Mozambique. From there I could have either cycled beside the lake, or taken a steamer, to the south of the country and re-entered Zambia some way north of the Zambezi Valley before continuing to Botswana. My decision to avoid Malawi resulted partly from the uninviting hills but also from the fact that I had been made a 'prohibited immigrant' from that country too, charged with corrupting the people with Communism. It was the year after Jeff and I had been expelled from Tanzania. We had painted on the side of the Land Rover the names of the countries through which we had driven, being careful to omit the names of Rhodesia and South Africa knowing that these would cause offence in other African countries. We had not catered, however, for the anti-communist views of Malawi where, under President Banda, a dictatorship was in power which would have made Adolf Hitler appear a militant left-winger. On the side of the Land Rover were painted the names of the six Eastern Europe Communist Bloc countries through which we had passed and, of these, the name 'Czechoslovakia' was recognized by a plain clothes police officer. We were taken to the police headquarters in the town of Zomba where we were informed that we were undesirable aliens and we were given six hours to leave the country. Now, on my bicycle, I decided that, having crossed one country which I was theoretically barred from entering, without incident, it would be inadvisable to press my luck too far. Besides, my days of enthusiasm for cycling, when I took unnecessary diversions to Poland and to the Black Sea coast, were over. After almost eight months of cycling I now wanted to reach Rhodesia as soon as possible and spend a while sitting on something more comfortable than a strip of leather.

As I put my head out of the tent door on my first morning in Zambia, I was reminded of a summer's morning in the Lake District, with low cloud forming a mist and causing a fine drizzle. I had eventually crossed the border the previous evening and cycled through the border town of Nakonde before camping in a field of maize. During the morning the drizzle ceased but the cloud remained heavy throughout the day – ideal for cycling. There had been a time when I had enjoyed riding beneath a hot sun, but now it was a relief to have cloud to provide shade and I was never able to really decide whether or not I preferred to cycle in the rain rather than beneath the blazing tropical sun. For the first half of the morning I saw no vehicles and throughout the whole day there were only occasional empty lorries driving towards Tanzania. The lack of traffic on the Great North Road, as the five hundred mile stretch between the Lusaka-Copper Belt turn-off and the Tanzanian border is known, was to become familiar to me over the next few days. Tanzania had seemed short of basic commodities, but it was a sign of the desperate situation in Zambia that the Zambians needed to import supplies from Tanzania and that the people living within reach of the border would cross to Tunduma to do their shopping.

There being very few villages and consequently no reason to stop other than for the occasional rest, I had covered the seventy miles to the next town of Isoka by mid-afternoon. Having no Zambian money I dismounted from the bicycle and pushed it along the street, looking for Asian shopkeepers who I knew would be selling Zambian money at advantageous rates on the black market in exchange for sterling or dollars. I was immediately stopped by a policeman who led me to the local police station for my passport to be examined. I had met some friendly police in Africa but, with odd exceptions, the Zambian police were the most cheerful of all. They forgot all about my passport as they clustered round the bicycle like the flies had been doing earlier in the day, making the strange whistling and sighing sounds that are common to Africans when they are amazed by something. 'To where are you heading?' I was asked, and there were more whistles and gasps as I told them that I was cycling to Botswana. They shook their heads in disbelief that I had cycled all the way from the Tanzanian border. 'It is too far,' they breathed, 'too far,' and they collapsed in gales of merriment, slapping one another on the back and shaking my hand. They begged me to stay the night at the police station, telling me that I would be welcome to spend a few nights on the floor there if I wished. However, hearing that there were Europeans teaching at the local secondary school, I shook hands all round for about the fifth time and set off in that direction. I reached a small estate of neat, corrugated iron roofed bungalows that was obviously the European area and pushed the bicycle along the street with a hopeful kind of expression on my face. A young Dutch woman appeared in a doorway. 'Are you looking for a place to sleep?' she asked. I could hardly believe my luck, but then her husband loomed in the doorway behind her and I came back to earth. I was still made most welcome, however, and quickly had a cold bath before the water went off for the night.

The next morning the Dutch couple gave me the address of a Dutch teacher in Chinsali sixty miles to the south, an ideal distance for a comfortable ride. In actual fact it was far from comfortable. I had recently begun to develop saddle-soreness for the first time since my early days in Europe, and was unable to work out why I should be experiencing discomfort after all this time. Normally, when I took a short rest every hour or so, I would sit down on the roadside, but I was now finding that I preferred to stand. In fact not only did I prefer to stand – it was a distinct pleasure!

The road to Chinsali continued virtually flat, the scenery consisting only of typical African bush during the rainy season, small trees amid long, green grass. Occasionally a mud-hut would come into view in a clearing and sometimes there would be a larger number, grouped into a village and often centred around the primary school which usually took the form of a single-roomed building surrounded by a low wall and with a thatched roof supported on mud-brick pillars. I took the opportunity to visit some of these villages as I stopped for fresh supplies of water and the manners of the people, here more than anywhere else on the continent, amazed me. It was as if I had travelled back in time over thirty years. They would stand by the roadside as I approached, clapping their hands in traditional greeting, a gentle clap which seemed to express genuine feeling, as if they had just witnessed Jack Nicklaus sink a twenty yard putt at Royal Lytham. Many of them still adressed a stranger as 'Sir', which would be frowned upon in Tanzania where one is 'brother' or 'friend'. The handshake takes a little time to become accustomed to unless you have the nimble fingers of an expert piano player, shaking hands, then thumbs, then hands again, all in one flowing movement. I usually ended up with someone's thumb stuck between my fingers, to the delight of the thumb's owner who would attempt to give me instruction in the art. At the same time as the handshake comes a type of curtsy, particularly from the children when greeting an adult. As they lead the visitor into their hut the people are liable to push themselves through the doorway ahead of him. This seemed strange until I was told that it is to show that if they invited you to go first they could be suspected of trying to attack you from behind. Their going first shows that not only do they not intend to attack you, but that they trust you not to attack them. In the hut they may immediately sit down on the floor, leaving you standing, the intention being to show that they consider themselves lower than you. It struck me that we can still learn from the Africans.

For the second consecutive night I had a bed to sleep in and before leaving I was given another address, this time in Mpika, a hundred miles to the south. I decided to cover the distance in two easy days rather than one hurried one, part of the reason being that there was something of a moral obligation to the numerous people who were good enough to provide accommodation, to sit and give a résumé of the journey and answer questions which were invariably of a similar nature. It seemed unfair to arrive at the house of someone who usually did not expect me, had certainly never met me, and who was, I hoped, going to give me food and a bed, and then fall into an exhausted sleep within ten minutes of arriving because I was tired out from cycling so far. Before leaving Chinsali I visited the sparsely stocked market where, knowing that I would probably see no food on sale until I reached Mpika, I bought oranges and sticks of sugar-cane and, bread being unavailable, some biscuits to eat with my Tanzanian jam. That night I slept in the bush and reached Mpika the next day where I stayed the night with the English couple whose address I had been given two days before and who were working in Zambia, like most of the Europeans, as part of a government aid to Zambia scheme. I always received strange looks when I arrived at someone's house and explained that I had just arrived from England on my bicycle. Despite the fact that I often turned up unexpectedly and without direct invitation, the further I had travelled the more lavishly was the fatted calf usually killed. At Mpika I was introduced to a Dutchman and his Zambian wife who invited me to spend the following night at the hospital at which they worked twenty miles further south. Being ahead of my schedule to reach Rhodesia I accepted the offer and, at their house, the couple borrowed my map, took an address book, and set about providing me with addresses of friends of theirs for each night of the remainder of my intended journey through Zambia, even writing an introductory note to each person which I was to present to them on my arrival.

As I travelled further south the weather became drier. I left the rains behind, the cloud dispersed and I was cycling again beneath a clear blue sky and a hot sun. Each village through which I passed presented the same picture of a broken economy, the roadside stores now closed and shuttered because they had nothing to sell. Goods had long since ceased to be delivered from Lusaka despite the fact that the lorries bringing supplies from Tanzania were returning north empty and could have been used to deliver to these villages. Now the only food in the villages was the bare minimum that the residents troubled to produce themselves, and the only goods on sale was the one product which was regularly delivered – crates of beer. From some of the smaller villages I even had difficulty in obtaining water, which appeared to be carried from miles away by the women and children. This was not uncommon in more remote areas of Africa, but some of these villages had been specially constructed as maintenance stations for the Chinese-built Tan-Zam Railway between Dar es Salaam and Lusaka. The Chinese appeared to have thought: 'We've built the railway for them: they can tap their own water,' and consequently no water had been tapped. As I approached one of the villages four children were each carrying a large metal pan on their heads, their knees bending slightly beneath the obvious weight. Three of the pans were full of water, the fourth contained some type of herbs. They looked as if they had walked some distance with their loads, and as I came near they stopped and watched, their faces full of fear. It was obvious what was going to happen and I tried not to draw too close to them but a moment later one of the children turned and fled towards the village holding the pan on his head and showering himself with water as he ran. He looked so funny that I could not help laughing, whereupon the other three, not showing quite the same *sang-froid* as their friend, dropped their pans and followed him. It was interesting how often during the journey the bicycle, presumably because of its strangeness, caused similar reaction amongst people, whereas a car would probably have been accepted as being quite familiar.

As I travelled further south down the Great North Road not only did the amount of sunshine increase but so did the number of police checks and at the larger towns I was usually stopped at some point and politely asked to report to the police station. This normally took only a few minutes and the police constables were often too fascinated with the bicycle to worry about such trivialities as passports and entry permits. The army was a different matter, however, as it so often is in Africa, where there seems to be a sullen hostility towards civilians, an attitude of superiority gained from flaunting their lethal weapons as if they were toys. As I neared the Lusaka-Copper Belt Road junction it was becoming common to see small convoys of military vehicles, most of which ignored me. On one occasion, looking for a turning from the main road to a nearby town, I came to a dirt track and, unsure as to whether or not this was the turn-off that I wanted, I sat by the roadside and waited until a vehicle came so that I could ask the occupants. After about half an hour I heard an engine in the distance and stood beside the road, flagging down the tiny speck which was rapidly approaching. As it came nearer my spirits sagged as I realized that I was waving down an Army Land Rover but having no doubt been spotted I could hardly just stop waving. The vehicle halted in front of me and a dozen soldiers scrambled out waving their rifles around as if they were no more lethal than water pistols. I smiled brightly and asked the way to the town. The soldiers demanded to see my papers. I offered my passport and, still smiling, asked if the turn-off would take me to the town. The soldiers wanted to know where I was going, where I was from, and most details of my life history, and then climbed back into the Land Rover and accelerated away, leaving me still wondering which road I should take to the town.

The traffic increased considerably when I reached the main road linking the Copper Belt and Lusaka, many of the vehicles again belonging to the military. The Rhodesians had recently bombed the training camps of Joshua Nkomo's ZAPU Army throughout Zambia, entering and leaving the country almost at will, while the Zambian leaders seethed with indignation but were so thoroughly disorganized as to be totally incapable of any form of resistance. Army Land Rovers and lorries scurried up and down the highway like ants defending a nest, as troops were moved from place to place, usually arriving two or three days after the Rhodesian raiders had left. Most of the vehicles' occupants left me alone but a few stopped me, apparently with the desperate hope that they might just find some document on me which would prove that I was a Rhodesian infiltrator and that consequently they could for once claim some kind of a victory in the war. One lorry overtook me and stopped and a number of soldiers leapt from the back, forming a circle round me and poking their rifles at me. I could not help smiling as it occurred to me that if I moved suddenly they would probably all start shooting and that, since they would be firing across a circle, they would be liable to shoot not only me but one another as well. My passport was called on for examination so often that it became more convenient to keep it in my pocket rather than in its usual place in a pannier. Two dates were stamped in the passport, the date of expiry, 1988, and, below it, the date of issue, 1978. 'Why is this passport issued in 1988?' one of the soldiers who stopped me wanted to know, and he regarded me suspiciously when I explained, as if trying to fathom out if this was really a flaw in my story.

I arrived in Lusaka ten days after entering Zambia, having averaged more than sixty miles a day since leaving Dar es Salaam. I stayed for two days with an English company director, during which time I looked around the shopping centre of Lusaka (which did not take long), and also found the reason for the saddle-soreness which had been causing me increasing discomfort over the last few days. Before I had left England I rubbed oil into the new leather saddle in order to soften it. The treatment had given the desired effect in the early days, but now the saddle had stretched and sagged so that when I put weight on it I was actually sitting on the two narrow metal support bars which ran below it. It was not surprising that I had found it uncomfortable and, rather than risk the likelihood of turning something the wrong way and the saddle falling irreparably to pieces, I settled on a temporary solution to the problem by folding a shirt and pushing that underneath the saddle between the bars and the leather.

I had now two and a half weeks in which to cycle less than five hundred miles though I knew that the distance was the least of my problems. The Zambians had become obsessed with the idea of Rhodesian spies and even the

Europeans who were working around Lusaka had to be extremely careful as they were under suspicion from every direction. The two national newspapers were largely responsible for the near neurosis among the people as each morning editorial comments appeared on the front pages urging readers to be vigilant in seeking out spies and in reporting anything suspicious. One article informed Africans employed by Europeans that they were in a better position than anyone to notice anything strange in their employers' homes and that they should try to eavesdrop on suspicious conversations and report them.

The most direct route to Rhodesia would have been on the main Lusaka-Salisbury Road crossing the border at Chirundu, but the border post between the two countries had been closed to road traffic for some years and the only alternative was to ride to Livingstone, the most southerly town in Zambia, and then cross the Zambezi on the ferry to the Botswanan town of Kazungula. This involved a ride of only two miles through Botswana before entering Rhodesia. I planned to leave Lusaka on the morning of my third day in the capital – Friday the 13th of April, Good Friday; only it wasn't good, for Zambia, for Joshua Nkomo, or for me.

In the early hours of the Friday morning I was lying in bed being slowly driven to distraction by a mosquito which whined incessantly around my ears. Finally I gave up trying to get back to sleep, stepped out of bed and groped around for the can of fly spray that I knew was there somewhere. Unable to find it, I felt my way to the light switch and pushed it down. Nothing happened. I looked out of the window to where the lights of Lusaka should have been. It was all darkness. The power had been turned off. It could only mean another Rhodesian raid. I silently cursed the Rhodesians for their apparent attempts to make cycling through Zambia as difficult for me as possible. Though I did not know it until the following day, less than a mile away, Joshua Nkomo, the leader of the Zimbabwe African Peoples' Union must have been cursing the Rhodesians with considerably more volume and feeling than I was. In one of their most daring raids yet, the Rhodesian Army had crossed the Zambezi near Chirundu, in Land Rovers painted in the colours of the Zambian Army, then driven almost a hundred miles along the main road to Lusaka. While one group raided Zimbabwe House at the northern end of the city, a second group had attacked and ignited Nkomo's home in what seemed to be almost a practical joke. According to the Rhodesian version, Nkomo had been sitting on the toilet at the time of the raid and had escaped the conflagration only by squeezing his colossal frame through the bathrom window.

The day started badly for me with the news on the radio that the Kazungula ferry on which I had been planning to cross from Zambia to Botswana had been sunk by the Rhodesians at the same time as their early morning raid on Lusaka. I decided that, since there was no other way south, I would have to continue to Livingstone as planned and worry about what to do next from there. Next came the news that the person with whom I had been staying, who had promised to give me some Rhodesian money which had come his way and which was of no use to him, had forgotten to bring it from his office and I would have to go without it. Then, leaving the house, before I had ridden a mile, I had a puncture and spent some time in changing the inner-tube before continuing to the post office in the city centre. There I had some letters which I was anxious to dispose of. They were written to various friends in England and in them I had talked of my plans to work in Rhodesia. I had no desire for any Zambian officials to see the letters since they were an admission that I was going to Rhodesia, and I would normally have been more cautious than to write anything like that, but I knew that I would be posting the letters immediately and not carrying them with me. I only needed to buy the appropriate stamps and the letters would be off my hands. But, of course, it was Good Friday; the post office was closed. I contemplated throwing the letters away, then placed them into a brown paper bag which I put in my saddle bag to post them in Mazabuka the following morning.

The road south was almost bare of traffic. It was the same one on which the Rhodesians had arrived and departed earlier in the day and a series of road blocks had since been hurriedly set up in what seemed to be a rather belated closing of the stable door. At the third check point the police were about to search the bicycle when a constable stepped forward with a huge smile on his face and asked did I remember him from a previous road block some days earlier. I didn't remember him from anywhere but it seemed appropriate to do so and I greeted him like a long lost brother. He quickly assured the other policemen and the soldiers at the road block that I had already been cleared and that I should be allowed to proceed.

The first town that I reached was Kafue, thirty miles south of Lusaka, and I was again stopped by the police and taken to the police station where I was shown into an office and interviewed by a plain clothes officer. After answering a lot of tedious questions I was informed that I appeared to be what I claimed to be. I was thankful to know that but was not so pleased when he continued by saying that he was unable to allow me to proceed south. It may have been a half-hearted attempt to obtain a bribe but, more likely, was simply that he had not seen many cyclists passing that way before and, not being quite sure how to handle the situation, thought that he had better make a token objection. Eventually he took an easier line, saying that because I was travelling south I could continue whereas if I had been going north he would not have been sure. I could not really follow the reasoning in his statement and assumed that, had I been heading north, he would have said the opposite.

After crossing the Kafue Dam I reached the point where the road forked, left for Chirundu and right for Livingstone. Approximately eight hours earlier the Rhodesian assailants would have taken the left fork, which meant that once I had turned right I should be regarded with at least a little less suspicion. I moved into the centre of the road and was about to turn towards Livingstone when an Army lorry overtook me and I was waved to stop. Six soldiers approached. They were reasonably friendly. They checked my passport and then told me that I could proceed. As I mounted the bicycle I heard one of them ask if they shouldn't check my bags and, as I began to slowly pedal away, I was called back. In a way I was really rather unlucky. On the other hand, in the circumstances, I had probably been fortunate to reach as far as the Livingstone turn-off.

The search began in a reasonably organized way, but then another lorry arrived with about fifteen more soldiers and there was not a great deal that I could do as they began to pull everything from the bike. It was quite obvious that a white man heading south on a bicycle had to be a Rhodesian soldier left behind by his colleagues after the previous night's raid and making his own way home. After a while they told me that I was to be taken to answer some questions and I climbed, with the bicycle, into the back of one of the lorries. The lorry headed back northwards before turning off on a dirt track into the bush. The soldiers had not been unfriendly up to that point, but when the lorry stopped in a bush clearing, one of them ran off, obviously to go to a nearby camp to report my presence. I assumed that he would be fetching an officer who would ask the usual questions and then I would be allowed to continue cycling, but there is always the natural inclination to feel uneasy in such a situation when no-one has actually 'seen' you disappear. He must have decided to add a bit of flavour to the message that he was bearing because, a few minutes later, a group of twelve to fifteen soldiers came running from the bush shouting that a Rhodesian soldier had been captured. 'He is one of those who burned Nkomo's house,' shouted one as they approached. They dragged me from the lorry and laid in enthusiastically with fists and boots. Meanwhile others were searching the bicycle bags. With a cry of triumph, one of them held up the empty cartridge case that I had been given by the Syrian Major in Beirut. After scraping off encrusted dirt and emptying sand from inside it he put it to his nose and announced, 'this has just been fired recently'. Another soldier held out a live round of ammunition, obviously his own, and informed everyone that he had found that on the bicycle too. 'I saw this man in Lusaka with the Rhodesians who raided,' one contributed, while another added, 'I saw him two months ago in the north of Zambia. He had a notebook with addresses of people in Rhodesia in it.' A moment later I staggered back as one of them swung his Kalashnikov rifle at me. I didn't even see it coming. It just smashed into my face above my right eyes opening up a deep cut from which blood poured into my eye. The effect on his rifle was even more spectacular than the effect on my face. The wooden stock snapped clean off and fell to the ground, leaving the soldier holding just the barrel. 'Ah, these so-and-so Chinese rifles,' he muttered in disgust. Except that he didn't use the expression 'so-and-so'.

For a time the group diverted their attention back to the search of the bicycle and I waited for them to find the letters that I had written in which I had mentioned being on my way to Rhodesia. So far I had insisted that I was not going to Rhodesia but was on my way to Botswana. If they found the letters it would prove that I was not only lying about my destination but that I was also going to Rhodesia and, as far as they would be concerned, people who went to Rhodesia were not just innocent cyclists. As the searchers neared the point where the letters were packed in my saddle-bag I began to talk again, explaining slowly and carefully that I had reached Zambia from the north not from the south. Attention was switched back to me again and I received a few more blows and kicks before I was told to get back on to the lorry. My equipment was pushed back into the bicycle bags and I breathed a very small sigh of relief that the letters had so far been overlooked.

I was driven some miles to another camp where word had preceded my arrival. A large group of soldiers was waiting and I was immediately pulled from the lorry while they almost fought among themselves to reach me. Question time came then. 'Do you think we are so stupid as to believe that you came all the way from England on this bicycle?' I was asked. 'Why do wild animals not attack you?' The questions came thick and fast, faster than I could answer them and often irrelevant or absurd. 'How did you cross the sea?' 'Why are your tyres not worn out?' If I paused before an answer, they would quickly set to work on me again. Since I would not voluntarily admit to being a Rhodesian spy attempts were made to make me admit to the charge. Besides fists and feet, bayonets were used to carve lines on my back, chest and shoulders. Cigarette lighters and matches were used to burn the backs of my hands and sides of my feet, until it no longer seemed particularly painful. It was as if I was watching a film of what was happening to someone else. 'Admit that you are a Rhodesian spy and we will stop,' was the message. And I knew that to say 'Yes,' would have been to sentence myself to death.

I was taken to two more camps during that afternoon. Both times the treatment was the same, as was the message. At each camp there was no evidence whatever of any form of discipline or authority – each camp was complete anarchy. At each camp the cries were the same, 'Take the muzungu into the bush and shoot him. No-one will ever find the body.' At each camp the bicycle was again searched and, somehow, the letters in the brown paper bag were passed over every time. I realized how similarly lucky I had been when the person with whom I had been staying in Lusaka had forgotten to bring the Rhodesian money for me. If the Zambian Army had found Rhodesian money in my possession I would never have had the opportunity to spend it.

Finally, as night closed in, I was told once more to get back into the lorry. By now I had accepted that I was likely to be shot and would not have put much money, at any odds, on my chances of survival. The thing to do was to not think about it, which was not really very difficult because all I wanted to do was go to sleep. I felt no more than a great sense of disappointment that, after pedalling so far, I would not now reach the Cape.

The lorry turned back on to the tarmac and I knew that while we were on that surface I was safe. After a longer ride than usual I realized that we were in a town and I was taken into a police office. It seemed almost funny when I learned that I was back where I had set out from twelve hours earlier, in Lusaka. The Central Police Station in the Zambian capital is not normally associated with distinguished guests but, compared with the Army treatment, I was looked after like a VIP. First came another search of the bicycle and once more the little brown bag went unnoticed. When everything was taken off the bicycle one policeman had the idea that there might be a bomb inside the frame and I was ordered to throw the machine into the air to see what happened. I was not in the mood to appreciate jokes but the idea of an exploding bicycle did have its lighter side, and the officer seemed more than a little disappointed when Rover jarred to the ground without even the slightest sign of a detonation.

One of the police officers, with whom I was later to become quite friendly, decided that I ought to be taken to hospital and I received some strange looks as I entered the hospital with two armed guards. My clothes were torn. In addition to a variety of cuts and bruises and burns on various parts of my body, the right side of my face was swelling, my right eye was closed, my left eye partly closed, and a line of dried blood ran down my face from the gash over my eye. I was given stitches in the cut over my eye and rather basic treatment for the other cuts and burns. What concerned me rather more was that I had spent what had seemed to be a considerable part of the afternoon on the ground and picked up rather a lot of dirt, but no attempt was made to clean the dirt out of the cuts before they were dressed. It was obvious that this was not a good mixture, so I asked if I could have a wash. 'Of course,' replied the doctor and showed me to a washbasin. 'Where is the soap?' I asked. 'I am sorry, we have no soap in the hospital,' he replied sadly.

After the treatment I was taken back to the police station where the bicycle stood in the main charge office, thankfully looking considerably more healthy than I was, and almost resplendent in its green and white stripes. The colours of the Rhodesian flag in the Lusaka Central Police Station. I had to smile! I was asked to give a statement of the day's events to the desk sergeant who laboriously wrote it down. He could barely write English and the statement read as complete nonsense but when I made an offer to write it out instead of dictating, he wrote that down too thinking that it was part of my statement. I assumed that the very fact that I was still alive was acceptance by the authorities that I was not a spy and I equally assumed that when my statement had been given I would be allowed to go. It came as something of a shock, therefore, when I was taken to the prison warders' office. My name was entered in a large book, prisoner number 2510, and I was taken through to the cells. The door opened. I walked in. The door slammed shut. It was again like watching a film. It was only the smell that made it realistic. The smell of sweat, urine, and, by the looks of the other occupants, fear. The cell measured about twelve feet square and was occupied by seventeen Africans who sat or lay wherever they could squeeze, their legs either twined around other people or hunched up to their chests. They were there for a variety of offences: selling cigarettes on the black market, theft, or traffic offences. Some claimed that they did not know why they were there. Most were awaiting trial. Some had been waiting for several weeks. Accommodation in the cell was not exactly five star, though there was running water (through the roof), electric lighting (all through the night), a WC (a sack over a hole in the floor), and air conditioning (a small grill in the metal door).

It was a long night, made no more comfortable by the glaring light bulb, the heat, and the cramped conditions. By the following morning my right eye was completely closed and my left one was rapidly catching up with it. My ribs felt as though someone had been testing a steam hammer on them and the dirt in the cuts on my feet had caused my ankles to begin to swell. At about 10 am the cell door swung open and the police officer who had suggested the previous night that I be taken to hospital called me out into the warders' office. 'This man is sick,' he told his colleagues. 'He needs to go back to the hospital.'

During the next four days I was able to leave the cell a number of times for visits to the hospital (always accompanied by two armed guards). Also I was taken to one of the upstairs rooms in the police station where I had numerous interviews with police officers. I made the most of these opportunities to delay as much as possible returning to the cell. By becoming friendly with a number of the police, I managed to spend long periods in a comfortable chair in the warders' office. This in itself was an eye-opener as it was the room where new prisoners were taught to 'respect' the police. The two warders responsible for discipline were dressed in blue boiler-suits and apparently hired solely for their sadistic qualities. If a newly arrived prisoner was lucky he would be brought in at a time when these two were occupied in touring the cells. Most prisoners were unlucky and, as a spectator, I learned quite a lot while in the warders' office about the art of inflicting pain without leaving marks. The two wardens obviously enjoyed their jobs. Most of the prisoners that I saw brought in, including old men and, on one occasion, a blind man who had been brought in for breaking the curfew, were given the treatment of open-handed slaps on the bare back, kicks on the feet and legs, elbows in the stomach, and fists on the top of the head. The more victims screamed and begged the more punishment they received as those inflicting it became affected by excitement. One prisoner was brought to the charge office from the cells claiming to feel ill, but the 'treatment' that he received soon persuaded him that he was cured. The saddest part concerned the ordinary policemen on duty in the warders' office. I found them to be very friendly, decent sort of people. Yet once one of the 'sadists' started, the policemen in the room would change and, without exception, become different people, their eyes lighting up wildly, while they jostled to get in for a swipe at the victim. One young policeman, with whom I had just been having quite a detailed discussion, rushed around shouting, 'Where's my hose-pipe? Where's my hose-pipe?' Failing to find it he settled for a truncheon, giving a prisoner who had done nothing to deserve it a blow on the head that would have cracked a rock.

The warders' office was also the place to meet numerous foreigners who were being brought in from the streets of Lusaka and who had to prove their innocence. An Irish missionary, a German expatriate worker, a Dutch volunteer teacher and a Japanese tourist were among my passing acquaintances as I sat in the warders' office. The latter could hardly speak a word of English and was utterly confused by his predicament. 'Why has he been brought in?' I asked one of the policemen. 'He is a suspected Rhodesian spy', was the reply. 'Why do you suspect him?' 'Because he is wearing khaki-coloured trousers the same as Rhodesian soldiers wear.' When I pointed out that this was the colour of the Zambian police uniform and that he, the policeman, was also wearing identical light, khaki trousers, the reply was, 'Ah! But mine have a blue stripe down the outside.' The chair that the young Japanese had been on was barely cold before the German expatriate was brought in. He had been wearing a tiny toy gun on a chain around his neck. 'Is it possible to kill a man with this?' a policeman asked me. The Irish missionary had not been in Zambia long. He was somewhat confused that, having given up all to help the people of Zambia, he had been arrested as a spy.

After four days in prison it was decided that I might not be a Rhodesian soldier after all and I was released, though my passport was held. As I walked outside, the sky was blue, the sun was shining, and I could feel more than ever before the value of freedom. I have always believed in severe sentences and spartan prison conditions for criminals but, as I emerged into the open after four days in prison, I could feel deeply for the hopelessness that someone must feel if they are condemned to fifteen, ten or even five years in detention.

I was thankful to be able to have a bath. My face had begun to return to its original shape and both eyes were partly open. But some of the sores on other parts of my body were beginning to turn septic and my ankles had swollen badly. I was able to check the bicycle and found that although a number of things had been broken, most were at least still there which was quite amazing. My burglar alarm would never work again. To the soldiers it had clearly been a device for radioing coded messages to Rhodesia and they had vented their anger on it when they were unable to make contact with any military bases across the Zambezi. My cine camera too had aroused suspicions and had suffered some damage. For many months after I had my own 'souvenirs' – burn marks on my hands and feet, small scars on my chest and shoulders, and a mark over my right eye to remind me that my head was harder than a Kalashnikov rifle. I would have liked the two broken halves of the rifle but decided that I would have been ill-advised to ask for them. I didn't even get back the Syrian Major's empty cartridge case!

Two days later my passport was returned to me and I was told to put myself and the bicycle on the first available plane to Botswana. I landed in Gaborone with exactly one week in which to reach Salisbury on May 1, and immediately started pedalling again, this time heading north towards the second largest town in Botswana, Francistown, from where I hoped to be able to cycle on into Rhodesia. The road joining the capital with Francistown was marked on the map as a dirt surface, but was actually under reconstruction. In parts it runs close to the borders with both South Africa and Rhodesia and troop movements were again in evidence, though on a far smaller scale than they had been in Zambia. It was a pleasure now to be able to cycle without regular police checks, though I kept a wary eye on Army lorries that passed. One stopped soon after I had left Gaborone, and two soldiers approached – but they were of the friendly variety. When they wanted to know why my face was a rather strange shape I told them I had been attacked by robbers in Zambia, rather than rouse suspicions by saying that I had fallen foul of the Zambian Army. Whereas since my days in Eastern Europe, I had told officials that I was on my way to Zambia and, in Zambia, I had said that I was bound for Botswana, now I told them that I was cycling to Francistown and that from there I would return to Gaborone. 'What is your mission in Botswana?' one soldier asked me. 'I am a tourist,' I replied. 'A terrorist?' he demanded, and I realized that I should be more careful with either my terminology or my pronunciation.

Botswana was a beautiful country in which to cycle, especially since it was the cooler time of year. The road was flat for almost the whole of the two hundred and sixty miles to Francistown and at times there was even a breeze at my back. The new tarmac road had been laid for part of the way but had not yet been completed enough to open it to traffic. To prevent vehicles from being driven along the new surface prematurely, lines of stones had been placed across the road every few hundred yards. For a bicycle this presented no problem and I was able to cycle for many miles on new tarmac, steering between the intermittent lines of stones. The alternative would have been a bone-shaking ride alternating with stretches of pushing the bicycle on the stony, sandy track. Arid bushland stretched away on each side. The sun rose over Rhodesia and sank like a huge red balloon into the fringes of the Kalahari Desert. Botswana does not benefit from a regular rainy season in the same way as do Tanzania and Zambia, and the green of those two countries was now replaced by a multitude of orange, brown, red and yellow shades, like an English woodland in autumn. The evenings were unforgettable: warm, silent, and so still that I was able to sit outside the tent writing my diary by candlelight and the flame did not even flicker. So peaceful that it was difficult to realize that, just a few miles to the east, a war was being fought. None the less, if I heard the sound of a vehicle on the nearby track, I would quickly extinguish the candle until it had passed. I had no wish to be picked up as a Rhodesian soldier making his way back home after an incursion into Botswana. The low-density population of the country meant that I had no difficulty in concealing myself when I camped in the evenings, but I still missed the security of having the burglar alarm attached to the bicycle when I was in the tent at night. A suitable alternative soon became apparent, however. The dry earth meant that there was always an abundance of dead branches, and with a few of these stretched across the bicycle at night a prospective thief would have woken an anaesthetized Rip Van Winkle before he had removed the bike.

In dry, dusty Francistown I called at the police station to register my intention of cycling the fifty remaining miles to Rhodesia, so that if I was stopped by any of the authorities, they would have a record of my passing officially through the town. The police were, as usual, happy, jovial and inefficient. They were horrified that I planned to cycle through an area that was occupied by terrorists. The terrorists would attack and probably murder me. I was surprised to hear them refer to the African Nationalists as 'terrorists', until I realized that, from their point of view, the 'terrorists' were not ZAPU but the Rhodesian Army.

The traffic north of Francistown was virtually non-existent. I again camped the night in the isolated bush, on the way to the border. The following morning I was awakened by a sound outside the tent. It had seemed barely noticeable and I knew that if I had not become conditioned to listening for sounds as I slept, I would not have heard it. It was just beginning to grow light and I strained my ears to catch the sound again. Then it came, a slight snapping of twigs underfoot and a low rumbling sound, as if from deep down in a cavernous throat. I had never heard a leopard before but there was no doubt in my mind that I was listening to one now. It came again, a soft reverberation, almost a purr, that immediately convinced me that the playful tabby cat sound was made by the only African mammal that would attack a human without fear and without provocation. I had my knife in the tent, though I knew that I may as well have offered a saucer of milk for all the good that it would do me. Another twig cracked beside the tent and I lay still, scarcely breathing, in the hope that the animal would leave. I waited, listening for any sound that might suggest its intention and, as the minutes passed, the light increased. Dawn, the time that the predator loves to make its kill. The sounds continued, occasionally and softly. The deep-throated rumble and the crack of a twig. I lay and waited. This seemed to be a rather dithery leopard. Where was the swift, incisive attack, the ball of fur, teeth and claws, ripping into the neck of its prey? I wriggled forward towards the tent door and gently began to slide up the zip a few inches. Pressing my head against the floor I could now see through the opening. Four legs were visible just outside the tent and, as I sighed with relief and pushed up the zip to open the door fully, the cow changed its low rumbling sounds to a bellow of protest and lumbered away into the bush, snapping more twigs beneath its feet as it ran.

The tiny, needle-sharp thorns of the Botswanan bush were expert at seeking out cracks in my tyres. Since the tyres were given to me during the journey I could afford to change them regularly and this undoubtedly restricted my total puncture collection. Throughout the ride I had just seventeen punctures, an average of one puncture to almost six hundred miles. Five of these were in Botswana where the average was one to a little over sixty miles. Two of the punctures came in spectacular fashion as I pedalled to the Botswana-Rhodesia border, blow-outs from the front wheel, accompanied by a loud bang, sending me skidding across the sandy surface of the track.

I was only three miles from the Botswana exit-post when I heard vehicle engines behind and was overtaken by two Army Land Rovers, both full of soldiers. I stopped pedalling as they jumped from the vehicles and they surrounded me, pointing their rifles and with bayonets uncomfortably close. They checked my passport, asked about the marks on my face which I again explained away by saying that I had been attacked by robbers, and searched the bicycle bags, though in a more organized way than it had been done in Zambia. Why was I going to Rhodesia? I explained that I was a geography teacher and wished to visit the Victoria Falls, but assured them that I was returning to Botswana immediately afterwards. They were satisfied then, returning the way they had come, while I continued to the border post. There my panniers were searched for the last time of the journey as an optimistic customs officer searched thoroughly but in vain for the supplies of arms that so many other customs, police and army seemed to have been convinced must be concealed somewhere. I passed through a pair of large metal gates and crossed the five miles of No Man's Land into Rhodesia. It was the afternoon of the 27th of April, three days before I was due in Salisbury.

I stayed the night at the police station at the border town of Plumtree. I had been told before leaving England that cycling through Rhodesia would be out of the question because of the war. In the eight and a half months since I had left England the terrorist attacks had escalated even further and on many of the roads in the country it was necessary to travel in a convoy with a military escort. I decided to cycle where I could but to heed the local advice which was generally both accurate and realistic. Consequently I found myself travelling the sixty miles from Plumtree to Rhodesia's second city, Bulawayo, on the back of an Army lorry, holding a rifle, having been given a quick instruction on where to point it and what to press if the need arose. From Bulawayo I set off to cycle towards Salisbury, two hundred and seventy miles away, until I was stopped by a police road block, given a cup of tea, and told to put the bicycle on the next lorry heading in my direction. When the lorry turned off my route I continued cycling until a similar situation occurred. I eventually arrived in Salisbury on the evening of April 30. The next day I started work!

A few days after my arrival in Salisbury I read in the newspaper that a motorist had been shot at on a section of the Bulawayo-Salisbury road along which I had recently cycled. That finally persuaded me that travelling by bicycle anywhere in rural Rhodesia was asking for trouble and I cheerfully locked Rover away in a shed and forgot about it for a while. I had been posted to teach at the

School of Kariba for a term and I was provided with a house from which there was a fabulous view looking across the Dam towards Zambia. I learned to shoot, to stay the correct distance from the vehicle in front when driving in convoy, to check security fencing, and what to do in the event of a mortar attack from Zambia. Fifteen weeks later I hauled the bicycle out of storage, scraped off the worst of the dirt, splashed around generous quantities of oil and packed my bags muttering promises that I would definitely give the bicycle its well-deserved clean when I reached the Cape. I was sorry to be leaving Rhodesia, or Zimbabwe-Rhodesia as it had become on June 1 1979 in a last attempt by the whites to retain some control over the future of the country. There were undoubtedly faults in the politics of Rhodesia, but there were virtues too that too often went unseen or were misunderstood thousands of miles away in Europe. Having seen the results of 'independence' in more than thirty African countries, I was in no doubt as to where my sympathies lay, and I wonder what the price of a vote in 'Zimbabwe' may yet prove to be.

My enthusiasm for cycling, never very noticeable even at its peak, had by this time reached vanishing point, but I was certainly not going to give up so close to the Cape. Vehicles travelling from Salisbury to the South African border did so in military convoy and I was told that I would not be allowed to cycle even if I wished to. So, I took a lift to South Africa where, after weeks of excessive eating, drinking and inertia, while in Kariba, I resumed pedalling. It was like leaving England all over again!

12

It was nice to be camping again. On my first night back in the tent I was awakened by a tremendous thunderstorm. My tent had never been particularly effective in keeping out water or in staying upright in anything more than a gentle breeze and I lay peacefully, waiting for it to fall down on me, which it eventually did. I extricated myself from the folds of sodden nylon and splashed around in mud and puddles, re-erecting the tent, then tried to go back to sleep. The tent now began to sag inwards on to my sleeping bag, soaking it through to the inside. I unzipped the fly-sheet and looked at the sky. It was obvious that the heavy rain was intent on persisting for a long period, so I again went outside the tent, extracted the mud-caked polythene survival bag from underneath the ground sheet where it was acting as a spare ground sheet, laid it inside the tent and climbed inside it in my sleeping bag. The rain immediately stopped! The following morning there was a sea of mud outside the tent and an ocean of mud on the inside. I lay for a few moments wondering if I had left Rhodesia a day later would I have missed the storm or would the storm have come a day later, then crawled out of the tent, lowered it, screwed everything into a ball which I packed on to the bicycle and set off pedalling.

Mother Nature seemed determined to compensate for the trials of the previous night. The sky soon became an endless sheet of blue and a strong wind sprung up from behind me. At lunchtime I stopped and, while I heated a tin of braised steak on my camping gaz stove, the hot sun dried out the results of the previous night's deluge. Suddenly things did not seem so bad after all. The meal that I was about to eat was one indication of the comparative comfort of cycling in South Africa. Varied and nutritious food was readily available and the small camping gaz stove which I had acquired in Rhodesia was in itself a luxury now that I could buy replacement cylinders. In previous weeks there had been times when I had been thankful to obtain a bunch of bananas as it had been the only alternative to going hungry. Later that day I stopped at a garage to wash off the remaining traces of mud, another sign of the change of life-style for garages in South Africa often had a wash-room and no-one ever objected to me parking the bicycle outside one of these and emerging a few minutes later freshly scrubbed and feeling much refreshed. A wash nearly every day was in direct contrast to the times when I had counted myself fortunate to have one in a week. Moreover, I was now able to throw out my sterilizing tablets, for the water was clear and fresh, unlike the foul-tasting liquid that had often been all that was available and that it had been almost necessary to chew down on occasions.

With the wind at my back for the first few days of cycling in South Africa, and roads that were at first relatively flat and of a smooth tar surface, I was able to cover some encouraging distances, and my leg muscles gradually awoke to the fact that their period of redundancy was temporarily over. I had obtained new gear sprockets while in Rhodesia, which meant that I was now able to use all the range of gears again, and I had succeeded in adjusting the tension of the saddle so that I was sat once again on pure leather and not on the narrow metal support frame. I had decided not to cycle the most direct route to the Cape, south-west across the wastes of the Karoo, but to aim instead for Zululand in the south-east of the country and then to ride west along the

Indian Ocean coast. From the flatness of the Transvaal with its bushland and plantations of cotton, maize, wheat and oranges, I crossed into Natal and the scenery changed to moorland as I reached the foothills of the Drakensberg and rocky kopjes rose to each side.

The 'Trust Territory of Kwazulu' could have come straight out of Hollywood. Green, rolling hills stretch as far as the eye can see, dotted with mud-huts, outside which Zulu women attend to their children or to the cooking pot on the fire. The men now carry the large cow-hide shields, spears and knobkerries only at traditional gatherings but, with their height and graceful movements, it is not difficult to imagine that they must once have made a formidable adversary. I camped a night at Isandhlwana among the gravestones and memorials to the one thousand three hundred and twenty-nine British and African soldiers who had been annihilated by Cetywayo's impis of more than twenty thousand Zulus, one hundred years before. I sat on Isandhlwana Hill, a thousand feet above the battle ground, watching the sun set over the distinctive rise of Rorke's Drift ten miles to the west and thought that, whatever its bloody history, there can surely be few more beautiful places than Isandhlwana. The following day I cycled on to Rorke's Drift, the mission station to which four thousand Zulus had continued after the slaughter at Isandhlwana. One hundred and forty defenders had resisted the attacks throughout the night and it remains an unsolved mystery as to how the Zulus were held off. Perhaps if Cetywayo's men had travelled from Isandhlwana to Rorke's Drift by bicycle instead of running the distance, they may have felt more fit on arrival, but, if the feeling in my legs was anything to go by, I was inclined to doubt it, though I did have the handicap that it is three times further by road.

The spectacular scenery of Zululand meant, as spectacular scenery always did, steep hills up which to pedal. Preferring to stay away from the main roads where possible, I often found myself on dirt roads, some of which, as cycle tracks, left a lot to be desired. The ascents were slow and painful, the wheels skidding on loose rocky surfaces. The descents were frustrating since I had to subdue the desire to let the bicycle run freely and instead had to keep the brakes firmly engaged as I picked a route carefully between the larger stones. Despite my care I broke a spoke which, unknown to me, proceeded to wrap itself neatly around the axle between the wheel and the fork of the frame, pulling gradually tighter. Had I been riding down a hill at thirty miles an hour when the spoke reached its maximum level of tightness around the axle, the bicycle would have stopped considerably quicker than I would have done, but fortunately it chose a moment when I was ascending a hill. Instead of me being damaged it was the hub on the back wheel that suffered, as a section where the spoke entered the hub sheared off. The back wheel subsequently turned with a wobble that caused it to grate on the mudguard with each revolution, but with less than a hundred miles to the city of Durban I decided to ignore the scraping and have the repair carried out professionally.

The winter of 1979 had been a severe one in South Africa with snow falling in areas where it had not been seen for years. The worst of the winter was past by late August, but the nights in the mountains were still very cold. I was not helped by the fact that I now had no door on the inner compartment of my tent. On a previous night I had been awakened by a crawling sensation on my face and, the bulb being broken in my torch, it was by the light of a match that I saw that swarms of ants were streaming into the tent through the small gap where the two zips of the inner compartment met and were marching across the groundsheet with the confidence of a party of bailiffs serving an eviction order. I lit my candle to see better but, finding that thousands of ants had already entered and seemed to regard me as the intruder, I decided to evacuate the tent until daylight. In my hurry to pull out my sleeping-bag before the ants claimed squatting rights in that too, I knocked the candle over on to the nylon door of the tent which promptly glowed alarmingly and frizzled away to almost nothing. I reacted swiftly and foolishly by smothering the glow with my hand, which instantly welded the smouldering nylon to my palm and, while it prevented the fire from spreading to the walls of the tent, left me dancing around the veld trying to remove molten tent door from a rapidly blistering palm.

South African towns on Sundays tend to be as great a source of activity as Nubian Desert railway maintenance stations are on any day of the week. The Sunday on which I left Zululand and re-entered Natal was cold and wet and the Drakensberg to each side were a bleak sight. I was not equipped for cycling in anything less than pleasantly warm weather and, by the time I reached the capital of Natal province, Pietermaritzburg, I felt as if I had spent a winter's night on the Yorkshire moors in only a pair of swimming trunks. When I finally found a shop that sold the nearest thing available to hot coffee I was shivering so much that I had difficulty in drinking from the cup. I was due to visit friends thirty miles south-east of Pietermaritzburg on the road to the coastal city of Durban and, it being already late afternoon, I was only interested in the shortest route. A modern highway now links Pietermaritzburg with Durban and, though it looked suspiciously like a motorway, there was no notice indicating that cycling was forbidden, so I cycled down the slipway and on to the highway. For the first half hour I made good progress despite the chill wind and persistent rain. Then I was overtaken by a police car which pulled in and an Afrikaaner policeman approached. I could tell that he was thoroughbred Afrikaaner as soon as he stepped out of the car. Short, stocky, red-faced and with the inevitable moustache, one might be tempted to think that Afrikaaners are factory-produced. I tried to pacify him with the type of friendly smile that had influenced numerous African policemen during the journey, but it is not for nothing that Afrikaaners are termed 'Rocks' by the British settlers in South Africa and I may as well have smiled at the tarmac. He stood blank-faced while he delivered a heavily accented account of the South African laws relating to cyclists on freeways, which I could barely hear above the uncontrollable chatter of my teeth, and informed me that, if I did not leave the freeway at the next exit, he would 'compound the bicycle.' I didn't want the bicycle to be compounded. I don't know how one compounds a bicycle and I had no desire to find out, though I privately wondered if he meant 'impound'!

I reached the home of the friends with whom I was to stay for several days, after a rather long and unpleasant ride through a maze of unlit, unsignposted country lanes. During the next few days I thought about cleaning the bike, but it hardly seemed worth it with only just over a thousand miles left to cycle and I was a little worried that more pieces might fall off if I began to remove dirt, some of which had been there since Europe. I also considered having the hub replaced in the back wheel in view of the piece having sheared off in Zululand, when my mind was made up for me while cycling on the outskirts of Durban. I had dismounted from the bicycle to ask a direction from two typically mass-produced Afrikaaners. 'How far are you cycling?' they asked. 'Cape of Good Hope,' I replied confidently, placed one foot on a pedal, pushed away from the kerb, lifted the other leg over the saddle, and found myself lying in the gutter looking at the sky, with the bicycle on top of me. The two Afrikaaners looked at me expressionlessly as I struggled to my feet. 'Have a good journey,' said one without a trace of amusement, and I nodded cheerfully to him, in an attempt to salvage some trace of prestige from the incident and give the impression that I had fully intended to prostrate myself at the roadside. A brief examination of the wheel revealed that it had folded in the same way that it had done in southern Sudan, the consolation being that it had chosen a more appropriate place than on the previous occasion. I looked up and down the busy street. There were numerous office blocks but there was only one shop in sight – a *cycle shop*, it seemed like an hallucination! The shop was owned by an Englishman to whom I delivered an account of my journey before informing him that my back wheel needed repairing. He agreed to straighten it without charge, until we looked at it more closely and found that its days of revolving were over. The rim was cracked in two places; I would need a new wheel. For next to nothing the cycle-dealer provided me with a replacement. It was of light steel construction, heavier and of inferior quality to its aluminium predecessor, but as long as it lasted to the Cape the technicalities of its structure did not concern me.

Meteorologists are notorious for being wrong in their forecasts. The evening before I left Durban, a solemn-faced weatherman stood before the television cameras of the South African Broadcasting Corporation and dolefully predicted incessant rain on the following day. I awoke to a clear blue sky and, as I resumed my pedalling, in a south-westerly direction, I did not see even a cloud for the next five days. It made a pleasant change to be cycling in bright sunshine, though the afternoons of the next few days grew uncomfortably warm, especially since numerous river valleys ran at right angles to the road providing a regular supply of downhill runs followed by steep climbs of up to six thousand feet above sea-level. On the second day after leaving Durban I entered the Transkei, the first of South Africa's 'independent homelands. It seemed absurd to have a visa stamped into my passport in order to enter a territory which only South Africa regarded as a separate country and, though the immigration officials may even have agreed with my point of view, it did not prevent them charging me fifty cents for the entry visa. Many of the mud-hut villages were newly built, having become necessary in order to accommodate Africans returned from South Africa itself to the Transkei. An African with whom I had talked while he walked beside me, as I rode slowly up a steep hill, complained that since being sent back to the Transkei, he could find nothing to do to occupy his time. He led me to his village to 'inspect' his rondavels, the round mud-huts with thatched roofs. He possessed two, he explained. The first I saw to contain an assortment of old, wooden furniture and a bed, and was his own house. The second appeared to be on fire but, once inside, I realized that it was full of smoke because a cooking fire was glowing in the middle of the floor. Around the fire were sleeping mats, occasional pieces of dilapidated furniture, his two wives and so many infants that I could not help but observe that for someone who claimed to have nothing to occupy his time he seemed to have been keeping quite busy.

Southern Transkei was considerably flatter than much of the land since northern Transvaal, low green hills undulating into the distance, and the road remained relatively flat as I cycled back into the Republic of South Africa. Outside Grahamstown I received a reminder that I was close to my destination, when I noticed a sign-post pointing west and bearing the words 'Cape Town'. The mileage given was five hundred and fifty-three, though I knew that I yet had a diversion to make to Cape Agulhas, the southernmost tip of Africa. My journey was almost over. In fact if the immigration authorities had had their way, it would have been over sooner than I expected!

September 1979. Port Elizabeth, South Africa. One year and one month out from England. Miles cycled, nine and a half thousand. Miles yet to cycle, five hundred approximately.

The Afrikaans Immigration Officer in his Port Elizabeth office gazed expressionlessly at me from behind his moustache. His face had become several shades redder in the last few minutes and he looked like an over-cooked sausage spitting out hot fat as he played his trump card. 'You have until midnight tonight to get out of South Africa,' he informed me in a welter of exaggerated syllables and over-pronounced t's. I had gone into the Immigration Offices in Port Elizabeth to renew the one-month entry permit which had been stamped into my passport when I entered the country from Rhodesia and which expired at midnight of that day. South Africa has long been a destination for overland travellers from Europe who have had barely sufficient funds to reach the country and have become something of a liability on arriving virtually penniless. The South Africans often had to resort to putting the itinerants on an aeroplane and flying them home in order to be rid of them and, quite understandably, brought in a regulation that travellers arriving at the borders should be able to produce either an air ticket out of the country or evidence of sufficient funds to purchase an onward ticket. I had not been asked to do that when I entered South Africa because the Immigration Officer at the border had been too interested in the bicycle. The Immigration Officer at Port Elizabeth was not in the least interested in it. He also appeared to have an unusual interpretation of the regulation. His impression was not that I should have evidence of money to buy an air ticket out of the country, but that I should deposit the money in a South African bank. This I refused to do on the grounds that I would not be allowed to withdraw the money until I was leaving the country and it would be refunded to me in South African rand. Consequently, I would be receiving a currency which would then be useless to me. The Immigration Officer was becoming rapidly more angry as I tried to reason with him, and kept disappearing to consult with his superior who was lurking in another office refusing to show his face. Eventually the officer emerged triumphantly with his ultimatum. I was to return to Rhodesia before my present entry permit expired at midnight. I looked at my watch. It was 2 pm. I had exactly ten hours in which to cycle the one thousand miles from Port Elizabeth to the Rhodesian border. Unable to believe that, after cycling nine and a half thousand miles, the Immigration Officer seriously expected me to turn back five hundred miles from my goal, I pointed out that travelling on a bicycle at one hundred miles an hour would not only be difficult but could also be dangerous. His blank expression did not waver as he stoically replied, 'Then you had better get started.' I had no alternative but to cycle on to Cape Town with an expired entry permit and hope that my passport was not checked by the police. I left the Immigration Office and pedalled out of Port Elizabeth. It would be at least three weeks before I left South Africa. Plenty of time in which to think of an excuse as to why I had not renewed my permit.

Though some of the Afrikaans officials seemed to go out of their way to be awkward, many South Africans were so overwhelmingly friendly that at times it seemed as if I was back in Egypt for, as I cycled along the main street of a town, figures would emerge from parked cars and leap into the road in front of me to inform me, as if making some shattering revelation, that they had passed me on the road some miles back. Motorists would stop to enquire about my journey. It had been reported in occasional local newspapers that an apparently masochistic English character had, more than a year previously, bought himself a bicycle and that he could now be seen on the last leg of his journey trundling along the road somewhere between Durban and Cape Town. Cars would overtake me, faces leering at me from the rear windows, glancing down at a newspaper on the back seat and then looking back at me, as if checking an Identikit picture of a wanted criminal. Often they would stop in front of me, usually half way up a steep hill, tumbling enthusiastically out of the cars and flagging me down, forgetting that they had a thousand or more cubic centimetres of engine to start them moving up the slope again. At times they almost queued up to ask questions about the journey and, as they always had been, the questions were invariably the same. I had been used to receiving questions that were the same, but in South Africa they even asked them in the same order. Usually they would end with, 'Do you want to put your bicycle in the boot of the car and take a lift for a few miles?' and when I replied in the negative they would say with satisfaction, 'No, I knew you wouldn't', leaving me wondering why they had asked in the first place.

As I entered the scenic area of the Indian Ocean coast known as the Garden Route, a westerly wind sprung up, blowing strongly into my face as if making a last stand against me. For a while I was partly sheltered by the pine trees of the Tsitsikama Forest and by the steep slopes of the Bloukranspas and the Grootrivierpas, both of which I had to pedal up, but for four days it seemed that the closer I got to Cape Town the stronger the wind became, and cycling was a demoralizing battle with so little distance to go yet so much effort needed. A little over a hundred miles before Cape Town I turned off on the road to Cape Agulhas and reached the most southerly point of the continent, an unspectacular projection of low rocky shore jutting out into a grey sea.

The final pass before Cape Town was the Sir Lowry Pass, just under one and a half thousand feet above sea-level. As I rode up the slopes the wind was blowing towards me; at the top a battle appeared to be in the process of being fought between the forces of nature as great gusts blasted in different directions making it difficult to even maintain my balance on the bicycle. As I crossed the top of the pass and began to descend, it was as if the wind that seemed to have blown against me for so much of the journey had finally conceded defeat. It howled down the pass, this time at my back, and I travelled for several miles, mainly freewheeling, at a greater speed than I had cycled at any time during the journey. The traffic increased and, though the road became motorway, I continued cycling along it because, in the distance, I could see the flat top of Table Mountain, Cape Town's unique physical feature, a fine layer of cloud drifting above it like a freshly laundered tablecloth. Only thirty miles of pedalling now remained from Cape Town through the Cape Nature Reserve, until I reached the Cape of Good Hope itself.

October 1979. Cape Nature Reserve. One year and two months out from England. Miles cycled, ten thousand and twenty-seven. Miles yet to cycle, two.

I remembered thinking, as I had come to the last miles of the Nubian Desert, that the poisonous gourds that had looked like tempting water melons had seemed to have been left there as a last desperate attempt to prevent me from crossing the desert. The memory returned to me now for, as I rounded a corner and saw the Cape of Good Hope jutting out into the Atlantic, rising up against a background sky of pure blue, to the west the ocean stretching away towards the Americas and with the promontory of the Cape grey topped with green, four feet of poisonous snake was stretched across the road in the path of my front wheel. Having cycled so far and for so long to reach the headland, it would have been natural to have been looking at it rather than at the road for those first few seconds after it came into view. It seemed, therefore, more good luck than good judgement that I saw the snake before I rode over it. It was a beautiful specimen, the thickest snake I had seen outside captivity, and from the markings and the way that it lazily wriggled across the tarmac it was clearly a puff-adder. Any self-respecting snake would have sensed the vibrations as I dropped the bicycle on to the road and would have quickly made itself scarce, but the puff-adder crawled nonchalantly on its way as I selected some sizeable pieces of rock from the roadside. In Africa it is not considered cruel to kill a poisonous snake. No indignant soul will step forward with arm upraised, because it is realized that snakes have a tendency to turn up in the most unlikely places and that an unexpected bite could be inflicted on anyone. When the snake was virtually dead I used a stick to tactfully manoeuvre it into a plastic bag and put it into a pannier to await skinning.

The Cape of Good Hope was first sighted almost five hundred years earlier by the Portuguese navigator, Bartholomew Diaz. It is a sheer cliff face protruding into the sea, the traditional meeting place of the waters of the Indian and Atlantic Oceans. Beside it is Cape Point, where a tower has been built and from where the tourists who flock there can peer hopefully through a mounted telescope towards the nearest sizeable landmass, Antarctica, two and a half thousand miles away. Close by the two promontories is a car park where the tourists can leave their vehicles and walk either a quarter of a mile to Cape Point or a mile to the Cape of Good Hope. There were scores of visitors and they all seemed to be more inclined to visit Cape Point, presumably because a tarmac roadway is provided to walk on, whereas a visit to the Cape of Good Hope requires a scramble across rocks and through thorn bushes. I considered leaving the bicycle at the car park while I walked to the cairn on the cliff-top of the Cape of Good Hope, but it did not seem quite right to cycle ten thousand miles and then leave the bike a mile short, so I set off to push it and soon wished I had left it at the car park after all. It took an hour to cover that last mile and, as I stumbled along, lifting the bicycle over rocks and dragging it through bushes, I realized that, apart from sections of the Sudan, this was the slowest mile of the journey.

When I reached the edge of the cliff I skinned the puff-adder, slitting it open with a razor blade, performing at the same time a similar dubious privilege on one of my fingers. The body of the snake I then threw over the edge of the Cape where it seemed to hang in the air, still writhing from nervous reaction, before it plunged, like a sacrificial offering as thanks for safe completion of the journey, into the surging breakers below. Behind me, Rover leaned against the cairn marking the cliff-top and I remembered that, on the numerous occasions when I had kicked it, thrown stones at it and cursed it, I had vowed that, when I reached the Cape of Good Hope, I would throw it over the edge. I removed the panniers, lifted the bicycle until it was raised above my head and stood on the edge of the cliff, facing out to sea. For a moment I held it there, then I put it down and rested it back against the cairn. I couldn't throw it off the Cape of Good Hope; – I still had to get back to Cape Town!

Excluding the four months of work in Rhodesia between May and August 1979 it took ten months to cycle the ten thousand mile distance. From the Cape of Good Hope I returned to Rhodesia where I worked for a further two months before flying back to England in time for New Year, 1980. On the journey from Cape Town to Rhodesia I adopted a method of travelling to which I decided I was far better adapted than cycling – taking lifts on goods trains. Stealthily approaching a train at a station, climbing unnoticed into a wagon, and lying on a bed of granite chips or steel girders beneath a cloudless sky while the countryside rolled by, made the world of handlebars and pedals seem distant and undesirable.

I had sent the bicycle back to Rhodesia on a lorry. I had considered selling it but, after what it had been through, it would have seemed like allowing a thoroughbred racehorse to be used to pull a milk-cart and when I returned to England I brought it back as part of my baggage allocation on the aeroplane. I still use it for occasional journeys to the local pub, have still been known to fall off it on my way home, and, one of these days, may even get round to cleaning it.